Dein Englischbuch enthält folgende Teile:

Hello/Welcome	Einstieg in das Buch
Units	die sechs Kapitel des Buches
Topics	besondere Themen – z.B. „Weihnachten in Großbritannien“
Skills File (SF)	Beschreibung wichtiger Lern- und Arbeitstechniken
Grammar File (GF)	Zusammenfassung der Grammatik jeder Unit
Vocabulary	Wörterverzeichnis zum Lernen der neuen Wörter jeder Unit
Dictionary	alphabetische Wörterverzeichnisse zum Nachschlagen

Die Units bestehen aus diesen Teilen:

Lead-in	Einstieg in das neue Thema
A-Section	neuer Lernstoff mit vielen Aktivitäten
Practice	Übungen
Text	eine spannende oder lustige Geschichte

In den Units findest du diese Überschriften und Symbole:

I can ...	Hier kannst du zeigen, was du auf Englisch schon sagen kannst.
Looking at language	Hier sammelst du Beispiele und entdeckst Regeln.
STUDY SKILLS	Einführung in Lern- und Arbeitstechniken
DOSSIER	Schöne und wichtige Arbeiten kannst du in einer Mappe sammeln.
ACTIVITY	Aufgaben, bei denen du etwas vorspielst, malst oder bastelst
GAME	Spiele für zwei oder für eine Gruppe – natürlich auf Englisch
GETTING BY IN ENGLISH	Alltagssituationen üben; Sprachmittlung
LISTENING	Aufgaben zu Hörtexten auf der CD
Now you	Hier sprichst und schreibst du über dich selbst.
POEM	Gedichte
PRONUNCIATION	Ausspracheübungen
REVISION	Übungen zur Wiederholung
SONG	Lieder zum Anhören und Singen
WORDS	Übungen zu Wortfamilien, Wortfeldern und Wortverbindungen
Checkpoint	Im Workbook kannst du dein Wissen überprüfen.
Extra	Zusätzliche Aktivitäten und Übungen
	Partnerarbeit/Gruppenarbeit
/	Nur auf CD / Auf CD und im Schülerbuch
>	Textaufgaben

Inhalt

Inhalt

Hello!

My name is Polly.
Pretty Polly! Pretty Polly!
What about you?

I'm from
What about you?

My mum
and dad are
from

I'm
What about you?
My favourite
colour is
My favourite song is
'If you're happy and
you know it,
clap your
And I like
and
What about you?
What about
you?

Welcome

I can ...

... talk to my partner in English.

Hi! My name is ... What's your name?
I'm ... years old. How old are you?
I'm from ... Where are you from?
...

Now meet Jack, Ananda, Sophie, Dan and Jo from England:

This is *Jack Hanson*.
Jack is 11 years old. He's from Bristol.

This is *Ananda Kapoor*.
She's 11 years old. She's from Bristol too.

This is *Sophie Carter-Brown*.
She's new in Bristol. She's 11 years old.

This is *Dan Shaw* – with his twin brother *Jo*.
They're 12 years old. They're from Bristol.

I can ...

... talk about my partner.

This is ...
He's/She's ... years old.
He's/She's from ...
...

▸ *WB 1–2 (pp. 3–4)*

1 Welcome to Bristol

Bristol is in England. It's a great place!

a) *What can you see in the photos?*
I can see ... in photo number 1.
I can see ... in photo number 3.

a band • a boat • boys •
a football • girls • a kite •
a skateboard • trees • water

b) *Now listen and act.*

▸ WB 3 (p. 5)

1

2

3

4

2 Welcome to Cotham Park Road

17 Cotham Park Road is a big, old house in Bristol.

a) *Who is in the house? Listen and find out.*

b) *Complete the sentences.*
When the house is empty, Prunella is ...
When the house is full, Prunella is ...

happy • not happy

3 SONG Prunella's song

Sing and act the song.

Prunella's song

I'm Prunella the poltergeist,
Hee, hee, hee!
I close things and I open things,
I push things and I pull things,
I drop things
And then I laugh:
Hee, hee, hee!

I'm Prunella the poltergeist,
Hee, hee, hee!
I can see you, you can't see me.
You look, but you can't find me,
I drop things
And then I laugh:
Hee, hee, hee!

Prunella the poltergeist,
That's me.
Prunella the poltergeist,
Hee, hee, hee!

4 Sophie and Prunella

a) *Match the letters and numbers.*

A: I think 1 is B.

B: Yes, I think that's right.
No, I think 1 is ...

Listen and check.

b) *Who is in the pictures?*

Picture 1: Sophie, Sophie's mum, ...

Picture 2: Sophie, Sheeba, ...

Listen and check.

▸ WB 4 (p. 5)

A This is very nice!

B You can take baby Hannah, Emily.

C Sophie, you can help me in here.

D Oh! Who are you?

E That's your room there.

F What? You can see me?!

baby Hannah • Emily • Prunella • Sheeba • Sophie • Sophie's dad • Sophie's mum • Toby

5 Welcome to Hamilton Street

The twins Dan and Jo Shaw live at 7 Hamilton Street, Bristol, with their father.
Today is the last day of the summer holidays.

Mr Shaw Sorry, I'm late, boys.
Jo OK, Dad.
Dan I've got the shopping list.
Mr Shaw Thank you, Dan. Let's look at the list ... school bag. Jo, you need a school bag, right?
Jo Yes, Dad.
Dan Me too, Dad.
Mr Shaw Pencil case. Dan, you need a pencil case, right?
Dan Yes, Dad.
Jo Me too, Dad.
Mr Shaw OK, OK. Two bags, two pencil cases, two ... rubbers, two pencil sharpeners, two pens – felt tips?
Jo Yes, Dad.
Mr Shaw Two exercise books, two rulers, two glue sticks, two MP3 players ... hey, what's this?!
Jo We need MP3 players, Dad.
Mr Shaw Not for school! This is a school shopping list. Let's go, you two!

▸ *WB 5 (p. 6)*

I can ...

... say what's in my classroom.

I can see a ...

Now draw a network with things in your classroom. Swap networks. Say what's in your partner's network.

I can see a ...

•••

I can …

… talk about colours in English.

A: What colour is your rubber/…?
B: It's white/pink/purple/…

Talk to different partners.

…

6 My favourite colour

Dan My favourite colour is blue: the blue school bag for me, please.
Jo And the red school bag for me.
Mr Shaw OK. What about pencil cases?
Jo Orange for me, please.
Dan The blue pencil case for me. And I need a rubber: the green rubber, please.
Jo Ugh! A green rubber! Yellow for me.
Mr Shaw Right … pencil sharpeners …
Dan A blue pencil sharpener, please.
Jo Black for me, please.
Dan And we need the glue sticks.
Jo And the MP3 players!

7 Now you

a) *Act out the dialogue in* ***6****.*

b) *Act out a new dialogue with your favourite colours.*

8 SONG Prunella's plates

Listen. Then sing and act.

I like red,
Red, red, red.
Here's my red plate.
Ooops!
Crash! Bang! Wallop!
Aaaaw. Oh well …

I like green,
Green, green, green.
Here's my green plate.
Ooops!
Crash! Bang! Wallop!
Aaaaw. Oh well …

I like brown,
…

▸ *WB 6–7 (pp. 6–7)*

9 Welcome to Paul Road

The Kapoors have got a shop at 13 Paul Road in Bristol. They live in a flat over the shop.

Ananda — Well, is my new school uniform OK?

Mrs Kapoor — Very nice, Ananda, very nice.

Dilip — Monday today, Tuesday tomorrow ... the big day for my baby sister ... first day at the new school ...

Mrs Kapoor — It's a nice school, Ananda.

Dilip — It's a big school, Ananda.

Mrs Kapoor — Stop that, Dilip! You can go to the shop and help your father.

Dilip — OK, OK, Mum. But why me? It's the last day of my holidays too.

10 POEM The days of the week

a) *Listen. Then write down the poem with the days.*

The days of the week

Day one of the week is ...,
Two ..., three ..., OK?
Then ... and ... and then: Hooray!
..., ... : we can play.

b) *Read the poem to a partner. Are the days right?*

► WB 8 (p. 7)

11 Two newspapers for number 19

Boy ______ Good morning, Mr Kapoor.
Mr Kapoor ___ Good morning, Mark.
You need the newspapers for ...?
Boy ______ Cotham Park Road, Mr Kapoor.
Mr Kapoor ___ Right ... Cotham Park Road:
one 'Times' for number 2,
one for number 3, one for
number 8, two for number 19 ...
Ah, Dilip! Very good.
You can help Mark now.
And I can have breakfast.

12 The numbers

1	one	11	eleven	21	twenty-one
2	two	12	twelve	22	twenty-two
3	three	13	thirteen	30	thirty
4	four	14	fourteen	40	forty
5	five	15	fifteen	50	fifty
6	six	16	sixteen	60	sixty
7	seven	17	seventeen	70	seventy
8	eight	18	eighteen	80	eighty
9	nine	19	nineteen	90	ninety
10	ten	20	twenty	100	a hundred

13 Telephone numbers

14 POEM Numbers

Say and act the poem.

Numbers

One, two, three,
I can see.

Four, five, six,
I can do tricks.

Seven, eight,
Oh, I'm late!

Nine, ten,
Goodbye, then.

▸ *WB 9–10 (p. 8)*

15 Welcome to the Pretty Polly Bed and Breakfast

Mary, Peter and Jack Hanson
(and Polly, the parrot)
welcome you to

The
PRETTY POLLY
Bed & Breakfast
28 Cooper Street Bristol BS6 6PA
(0117) 969 22 00

Wheelchairs Families Pets

It's Monday.
Mrs Hanson is at work.
Mr Hanson is at work too.
He's at work in the Pretty Polly Bed and Breakfast.

Jack	Morning, Dad.
Mr Hanson	Morning? It's 12.15, Jack!
Polly	12.15! 12.15!
Jack	Well, it is the last day of the holidays, Dad.
Mr Hanson	Yes, half past seven tomorrow, Jack!

I can …

… say what the time is.

It's eleven o'clock

It's quarter past …

It's half past …

It's quarter to …

It's eleven o'clock.

It's eleven fifteen.

It's eleven thirty.

It's eleven forty-five.

It's eleven o nine.

It's eleven twenty-five.

It's eleven thirty-seven.

It's eleven fifty-two.

16 Now you

a) *Say these times:*
6.05, 9.15, 4.25, 7.45, 3.40, 8.30, 12.18, 10.55, 2.36, 5.00

b) *Draw five clocks.*
Listen and fill in the correct times.

c) *Swap your clocks. Listen again and check.*

d) *Draw five clocks with five different times.*
Your partner asks you:
A: Excuse me, what's the time, please?
B: It's ...
A: Thank you.
B: You're welcome.
Then you ask your partner.

▸ *WB 11–13 (p. 9)*

DOSSIER ***About me***

Start your dossier.

My name is ...
I'm ... old.
I'm from ...
My favourite colour is ...
My telephone number is ...

17 Good luck!

Mrs Schmidt	Excuse me, can I say goodbye?
Mr Hanson	Oh, Mrs Schmidt ...
Mrs Schmidt	Your B&B is great. Thank you, Mr Hanson, and goodbye.
Polly	Goodbye. Goodbye.
Mrs Schmidt	Goodbye, Polly. And goodbye, Jack.
Jack	Goodbye ... and a nice trip back to Germany, Mrs Schmidt.
Mrs Schmidt	Thank you, Jack. And good luck with your new school.
Mr Hanson	Thank you, Mrs Schmidt.
Polly	Good luck! Good luck!

New school, new friends

I can ...

... say lots of things in English.

What can you see in the photos?
– I can see a comic in photo B.
– There's an apple in photo ...
– There are books in photo ...
...

D

A

B

C

1 In the morning

It's 8 o'clock in the morning in Bristol and day one of the new school year.

a) *Copy the chart.*

	Ananda	Dan + Jo	Jack	Sophie
Photo				
Words				

b) *Listen. Match the photos and the names.*

c) *Match the words from the box to each name.*

apple • bed • book • box • boy • breakfast • CD • chair • girl • milk • mobile phone • pen • pencil • pencil case • school bag • table

2 Extra GAME

*Draw one thing from the box in **1c**. Who can guess what it is?*

A: It's a chair!

B: Yes, it is. / No, it isn't.

► WB 1 (p. 10)

1 Before lessons

It's 8.30 and the new students are at school.

Dan Look, Jo. Room 14!
Jo OK. – You're nervous, right?
Dan Me? No! You're nervous.
Jo No, no.
Dan OK. Then you go first.
Jo No, you go first.
Dan No, you.
Jo No, you.
Dan Oh, OK.

Ananda Hi! Oh, you're twins!
Dan Hi. Yes, we're Dan and Jo. I'm Dan, the clever twin. He's Jo, the mad twin.
Jo Don't listen to Dan. *He's* the mad twin.

Ananda Come and sit with me and Jack. – Hey, Jack! Here are Dan and Jo. They're twins. This is ... er ...
Dan It's OK. I'm Dan and he's Jo.
Jack Well, *I'm* Jack. And *she's* Ananda.

2 ACTIVITY

Write your name on a piece of paper. Put the papers in a box. Take a piece of paper and make one or two sentences about the student.

Anton Max: He's 11 years old. ... from Bonn.
Max Yes, that's right. /
No, that's wrong. I'm ...
My turn. Eva: She's ...

Looking at language

Copy and complete.

I'... Dan, the clever twin.

Yes, we'... Dan and Jo.

You'... nervous, right?

Oh, you'... twins!

He'... Jo, the mad twin.
She'... Ananda.
It'... 8.30.

They'... twins.

► P 1–3 (pp. 25–26) • WB 2–3 (p. 11)

3 Ananda is a nice name

Dan Ananda is a nice name. Is it Indian?
Ananda Yes, it is.
Jo Are your mum and dad from India?
Ananda No, they aren't. My mum is from Bristol. My dad is from Uganda.
Jack And how old are you?
Ananda I'm 11. What about you, Jack? Are you 11 too?
Jack Yes, I am.
Jo We aren't 11. We're 12.
Jack And you're from Bristol, right?
Dan Yes, that's right.
Ananda Are your mum and dad from Bristol?
Dan Our dad, yes. But our mum ...
Jo Our mum isn't here. She's in New Zealand with her new partner. Our mum and dad aren't together.
Jack Oh, I'm sorry.
Dan I'm sorry too.
Ananda Oh look. Here's the teacher.

> *Who are they?*
– Her dad is from Uganda.
– Their mum is in New Zealand.

4 ACTIVITY

Make a mobile or a poster for your classroom.

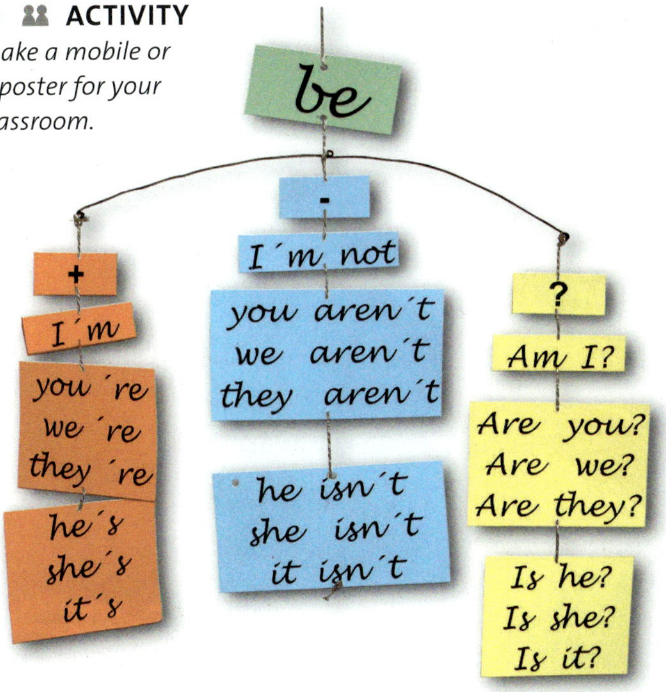

5 GAME

Mime things from the box. Can your group guess?
A: Are you nervous/...?
B: Yes, I am. / No, I'm not.

a baby • a dog • happy • a house • a kite • mad • nervous • a parrot • a poltergeist • a teacher • a tree • a twin

▸ *GF 1–2: Personal pronouns + be (pp. 127–128) • P 4–6 (p. 26) • WB 4–6 (pp. 11–13)*

6 Meet Mr Kingsley

Mr Kingsley — Good morning. Welcome to Cotham School. I'm your form teacher *and* your English teacher. My name is Paul Kingsley, K–I–N–G–S–L–E–Y. And you're Form 7PK: P for Paul, K for Kingsley. And now please tell me your names. Oh, and can you play football? I'm your PE teacher too! – Yes, you please.
Ananda — I'm Ananda Kapoor. I can't play football, but I can play hockey.
Mr Kingsley — Thank you, Ananda. Now you.
Sophie — My name is Sophie Carter-Brown.
Jo — Carter-Brown? One name isn't enough?
Form 7PK — Ha ha ha.
Mr Kingsley — Quiet, please. – And who are you?
Jo — I'm Jo. Jo Shaw.
Mr Kingsley — Can you play football, Jo?
Jo — Yes, I can, Mr Kingsley.
Mr Kingsley — Good. Football is good. Jokes about names are bad. Can you remember that, Jo?
Jo — Yes, Mr Kingsley.

> *Who can play football? Who can play hockey?*

► *GF 3: can (p. 129) • P 7 (p. 27)*

7 Now you

A: Can you play badminton?
B: Yes, I can. / No, I can't.
Can you play ...?

badminton • basketball • football • hockey • tennis

8 SONG Alphabet rap

A B C D E F G
Throw a ball, climb a tree.

H I J K L M N
Write your name, drop your pen.

O P Q R S T U
Yes, that's right. Do what I do.

V W X Y Z
Enough, enough, your face is red.

9 Now you

A: Can you spell your name, please?
B: It's Lilli Schröder. L–I–double L–I.
New word: S–C–H–R–O with two dots–D–E–R.

► *WB 7–9 (pp. 13–14)*

10 Timetable time

Mr Kingsley — OK, quiet please. Now, take out your exercise books. Listen and write down the timetable for today, Tuesday.
At 8.45 on Tuesday it's English with me, here in Room 14.
Then it's Geography in Room 16.

Jo — Mr Kingsley? I'm sorry. Can you spell 'Geography', please?

Mr Kingsley — That's OK, Jo. I can write it on the board:
G–E–O–G–R–A–P–H–Y.

Jo — Thank you, Mr Kingsley.

Mr Kingsley — You're welcome, Jo. After the morning break it's …

11 Form 7PK's timetable

a) *Look at these subjects:*

Drama • Maths • Music • PE • RE • Science

You don't understand the words? Look in the Vocabulary.

b) *Listen and complete a copy of the timetable.*

Timetable, Form 7PK
TUESDAY

Time	Subject	Room
8.45	English	14
9.40	Geography	16
10.35	Morning break	–
10.50	…	…
11.45	…	…
12.40	Lunch break	–
1.40	…	…
2.35	…	…

c) *Swap timetables. Listen again and check.*

► GF 4: Imperatives (p. 130) • P 9–12 (pp. 28–29) • WB 10–13 (pp. 14–16)

STUDY SKILLS Wörter lernen

Das „Vocabulary" (ab S. 146) gibt dir viele Informationen zu den neuen Wörtern einer Unit und hilft dir, diese Wörter zu lernen.

Schau dir Seite 154 an. Welche Schulfächer findest du dort?

Weitere Tipps zum Wörterlernen findest du im Skills File auf den Seiten 118–119.

► SF 1 (pp. 118–119) • P 8 (p. 27) • WB 14–15 (p. 17)

12 Extra SONG Wonderful World

Listen. Which school subjects from the board can you hear?

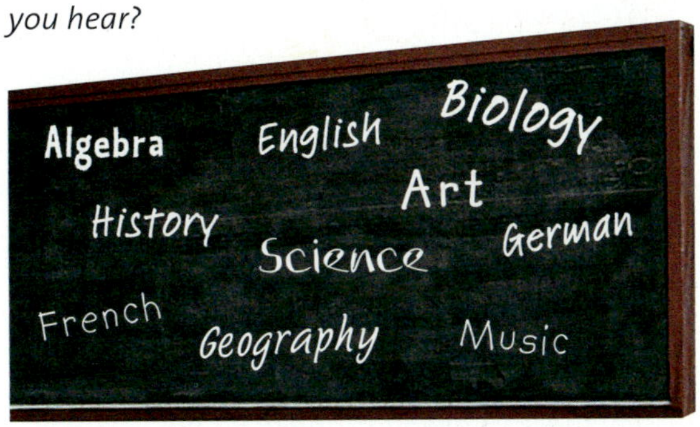

13 Lunch break

Ananda — Let's sit here.
Sophie — OK.
Jack — Hi! Can we sit with you?
Ananda — Yes, you can.
Jo — Is the food OK?
Sophie — Mmm, I've got the lasagne. It's OK.
Ananda — I've got the pizza. It's really good.
Dan — Oh, I haven't got a chair.
Ananda — Look, there's an empty chair at that table.
Sophie — Jack, do you like the Geography teacher?
Jack — The bank robber?
All — What?!
Ananda — Mr Barker isn't a bank robber!
Jack — Well, no, but he has got a face like a bank robber. I can see him on a poster: 'Wanted: bank robber'.
Sophie — Your ideas are really mad, Jack!
Jo — Hey, what have we got next?
Sophie — Music, and then Maths.
Ananda — Oh, I like Maths.
Dan + Jo — You're mad!

14 My lunch break

a) *Write a dialogue.*
A: Is the food OK?
B: Yes, I've got ... It's ...
A: I've ... It's ...
B: What have we got next?
A: We've ... next.
B: Oh, I like ...
A: You're mad. Then we've ... I like ...
B: Oh, I like ... too.

b) *Practise your dialogue and act it out.*

▸ *GF 5: have got (pp. 130–131) • P 13–16 (pp. 30–31) • WB 16–19 (pp. 18–19)*

DOSSIER ***My school***

My school
My school is ...
I'm in Class ...
My class teacher is ...
My friends are ...
My favourite subjects are ...
I like ...

Extra *Write your timetable. Put it in your dossier too.*

▸ *P 17 (p. 31) • WB 20–21 (p. 20)*

1 WORDS What's different?

Look at the pictures. Say what's different.

There's one apple in Picture A. There are two apples in Picture B.
There are three ... There are ...

2 Photos (Personal pronouns)

a) *Complete the sentences with **I**, **you**, **he**, **she**, **it**, **we** or **they**.*

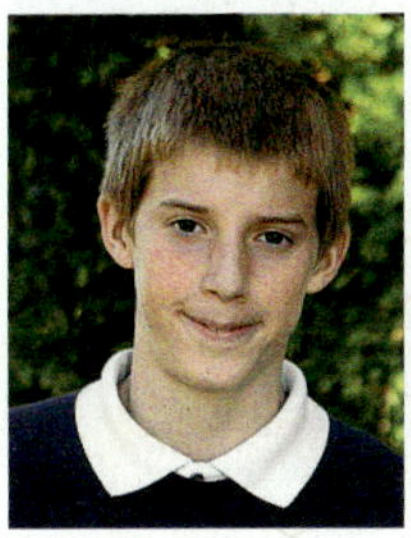

This is Dan. ...'s in my form.

This is Dan with Jo. ...'re twins.

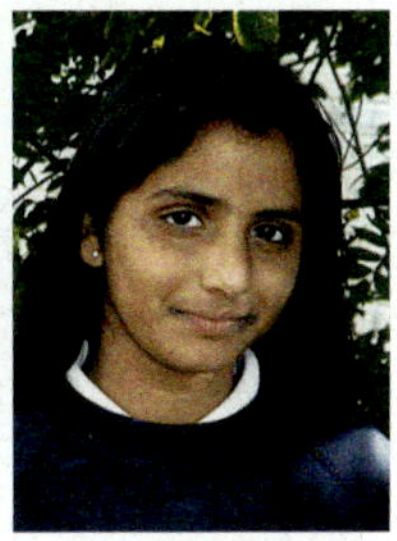

This is Ananda. ...'s very nice

This is my school. ...'s very big.

This is me. ...'m at school here.

This is me with Ananda. ...'re friends.

And this is you, Dad. ...'re with Polly!

b) **Extra** *Bring photos of your family and talk to your partner.*

A: This is Oskar. He's my brother. He's ... Now it's your turn.
B: This is me in the park/... I'm with ...

3 The new school (personal pronouns; be: positive statements)

Use I, you, he, she, it, we or they and the correct form of be.

1 Ananda: 'This is Jack. *He's* my new friend.'
2 Dan and Jo are at school. ... nervous.
3 Ananda is at school too. ... nice.
4 Jo: 'Hi, ... Jo. That's Dan. ... my brother. ... twins.'
5 Dan: 'Jo! ... mad!'
6 The school is an old school, but ... a good school.

4 Prunella isn't a parrot (be: negative statements)

a) *Use the lists and write negative statements.*

1 *Prunella*		from Bristol.
2 Polly		twins.
3 Dan and Jo Shaw		a boy.
4 I	'm not	a poltergeist.
5 My friend and I	*isn't*	sisters.
6 Dilip and Ananda	aren't	*a parrot.*
7 Dan and Jo's mum		in Bristol.
8 Sophie		teachers.

b) **Extra** *Now add positive statements.*

1 Prunella isn't a parrot. *She's a poltergeist.*
2 Polly ...

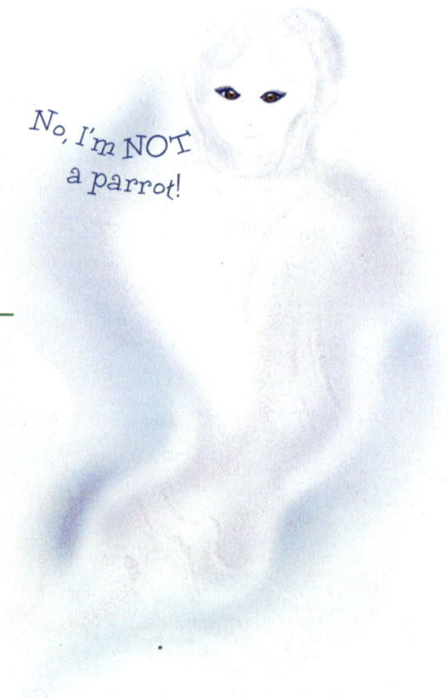

5 Yes, he is. No, he isn't (be: questions and short answers)

Match the questions and the answers.

a) 1 *Is Dilip Ananda's brother?*	Yes, they are.
2 Is the school a big school?	*Yes, he is.*
3 Are the Carter-Browns new in Bristol?	Yes, I am.
4 Are you a student?	Yes, it is.
b) 1 Is 17 Cotham Park Road empty now?	No, they aren't.
2 Is Mrs Hanson in a wheelchair?	No, she isn't.
3 Are the twins from London?	No, we aren't.
4 Are you and your family in Bristol now?	No, it isn't.

c) **Extra** *Now make five questions like in a) and b) for your partner. Answer his/her questions.*

6 About you (be: questions and short answers)

Answer the questions.

1 Is your mum 42? — Yes, she is. / No, she isn't.
2 Are you 12? — Yes, I am. / No, I'm not.
3 Are you and your mum friends? — Yes, we ... / No, we ...
4 Is your English teacher from England? — ...
5 Is your school big?
6 Is your father a teacher?
7 Are your mum and dad from Bristol?
8 Are you and your friends from Germany?

7 Can Ananda play hockey? (can/can't)

a) *Ask each other questions about the pictures. Use* **can/can't** *and words from the box. Swap after four questions.*

> do tricks • find their school things • open and close things • play football • play hockey • play tennis • sing • talk

Can Ananda ...?
– Yes, she ...

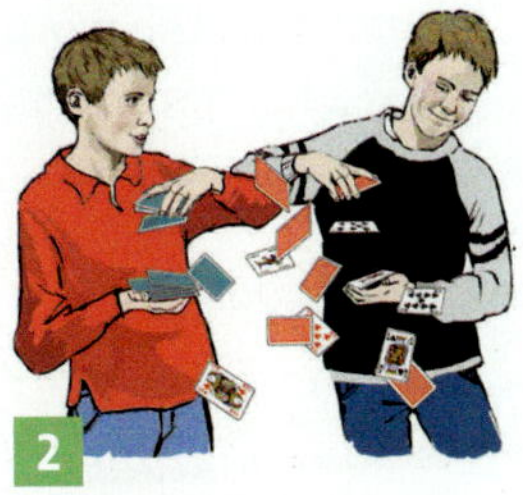

... the twins ...?
– No, ...

... Prunella ...?
– ...

... Dilip ...?
– ...

... the baby ...?
– No, she ...

... Mr Kingsley ...?
– Yes, ...

... Sophie and Emily...?
– ...

... Jack ...?
– ...

b) *Now ask your partner questions. You can use words from a).*

A: Can you ...?
B: Yes, I can. / No, I can't.

8 STUDY SKILLS Das Vocabulary

a) *Finde im Vocabulary folgende Informationen.*

1 Welches Wort benutzt man mit „welcome" (S. 8) für das deutsche „willkommen *in*"?
to ▸ S. 146: „Welcome (to Bristol). Willkommen (in Bristol)."
2 An welcher Stelle des Satzes steht „too" (S. 8)?
3 Wie sagt man auf Englisch „auf dem Foto" („photo", S. 9)?
4 Was ist das Gegenteil von „empty" (S. 10)?
5 Welches Lautschriftzeichen steht für die Aussprache von „th" im Wort „think" (S. 11)?
6 Was musst du bei der Aussprache von „very" (S. 11) beachten?
7 Wo liegt die Betonung bei „exercise book" (S. 12)?
8 Welches Wort benutzt man mit „work" (S. 16) für das deutsche „*bei* der Arbeit"?

b) **Extra** *Stellt euch gegenseitig je drei bis vier Fragen zu einigen Vocabulary-Einträgen: Partner A zu den Seiten 18–19, Partner B zur Seite 20.*

9 LISTENING Classroom English

a) *Read the phrases in the box. You can hear and use these phrases in the classroom.*

Quiet, please! • What's that in English? • Can I open/close the window, please? • Sorry, I haven't got my exercise book. • Can you help me, please? • Look at the picture. • What page are we on, please? • Sorry? • It's your turn. • Can I go to the toilet, please? • Write down the words on the worksheet. • Can we work with a partner? • What's for homework? • Write sentences in your exercise book. • Can we go now, please?

Listen to the CD. When a student says one of the phrases, put up your hand.

b) Who can say what? Make ticks (✓) in a copy of the chart.

	teachers can say	students can say	students or teachers can say
Quiet, please!	✓		
What's that in English?			✓
Can I open/close the window, please?			✓
Sorry, I haven't got my exercise book.		✓	
...			

c) *Listen again and check.*

d) *Prepare and act classroom scenes.*

Yes, I can help you.

What ...?

Can you help me, please?

Write ...

Can ...?

10 ACTIVITY Classroom ladders

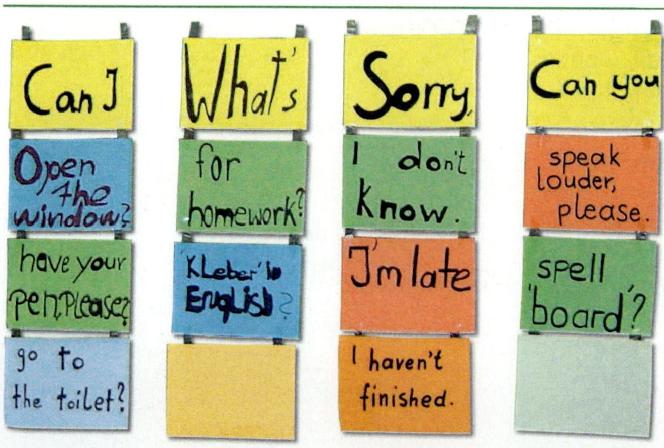

*Make English 'classroom ladders' with phrases from **9**.*

11 Do this! Don't do that! (Imperatives)

a) *Look at the picture and complete the sentences. Use words from the box.*

be • don't climb • eat • listen • don't open • don't play • don't push • sing

1 *Sing* the song for me, please.
2 No, ... to the CD.
3 ...

b) **Extra** *Draw a picture. Write three sentences like in a). Can your partner complete the sentences?*

12 WORDS The new timetable

a) *Partner B: Look at page 114.*
Partner A: What lessons aren't in your timetable? Ask your partner.
A: What's lesson 1 on Monday?
B: Lesson 1 on Monday is Maths.

b) *Now answer your partner's questions.*

	Monday	Tuesday	Wednesday	Thursday	Friday
1	...	German	...	...	...
2	Science	Geography	Maths	Maths	Drama
3	Science	RE	English	English	Science
4	Drama	...	...	PE	PE
5	...	PE	Geography	PE	Music
6	English	Music	...	German	Maths

13 Jo has got a twin brother (have got/has got)

a) *Make sentences with* **have got/has got**.

1 Jo
2 The twins
3 Sophie
4 Prunella
5 The Kapoors
6 Jack
7 Ananda
8 Mr and Mrs Hanson

a nice name.
a shop.
mad ideas.
a twin brother.
a B&B.
a great dad.
a nice room.
two sisters.

1 Jo *has got* a twin brother.
2 The twins *have got* a …
3 …

b) *Now say what you've got:* 'I've got …'

c) *Say what they've got (✓) and what they haven't got (✗).*

	brother	*sister*
Dan	✓	✗
Jack	✗	✗
Ananda	✓	✗

Dan *has got* a brother. He *hasn't got* a sister.

d) **Extra** *Add the names of three friends to the chart. Complete the chart. Make sentences.*

Lisa *has got* a sister. But she *hasn't got* a brother.

14 GAME What have you got?

Nils — I've got a blue pencil case.
– Laura, have you got a blue pencil case too?

Laura — Yes, I have.
– Malek, have you got a blue pencil case too?

Malek — No, I haven't. But I … a blue school bag.
– Maja, … you … a blue school bag too?

Maja — No, I … . But … a red school bag.
– Lukas, …?

15 PRONUNCIATION 'a' or 'an'?

a) *Listen and read.*
An apple, a green apple, an English apple, a red English apple, an old apple, a brown apple: Ugh!

b) *Now write these words with* **a** *or* **an**.

rubber • English teacher • blue ball • orange chair • pencil case • felt tip • happy mum • exercise book • old house • student • empty box

c) *Listen and check your answers.*

Looking at language

– ***a*** *vor b, c, d, f, g, … (Konsonanten)*
– ***an*** *vor a, e, i, o, u (Vokalen)*

Vorsicht! Es kommt darauf an, wie man ein Wort ausspricht, nicht, wie man es schreibt. Deshalb: ***an*** MP3 player *und* ***a*** uniform.

16 PRONUNCIATION 'the' with [ə] or [i]?

a) *Listen.*

For ***the*** *with* [ə]:

For ***the*** *with* [i]:

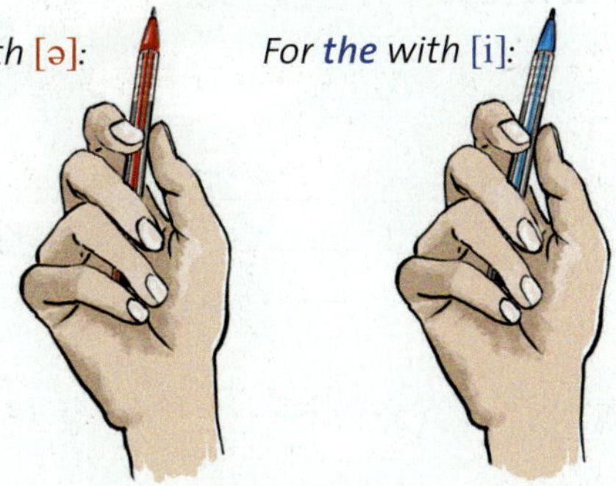

b) *Say this:*

The classroom, the empty classroom,
the students, the teacher, the English lesson,
the break, the apple, the chair, the art lesson,
the German lesson: 'Auf Wiedersehen!'

c) *Listen and check.*

17 GETTING BY IN ENGLISH New friends

a) *Can you say these things in English?*

1 Ich bin Dan. (p. 20)
2 Komm und setz dich zu mir. (p. 20)
3 Danke. – Gern geschehen. (p. 23)
4 Magst du den Erdkundelehrer? (p. 24)
5 Ich mag Mathe. (p. 24)
6 Du bist verrückt. (p. 24)

b) *Make a dialogue. Use the words from a).*

A: Grüße B. Sag, wer du bist.
B: Grüße A. Sag, wer du bist.
A: Schlag vor, dass B sich zu dir setzt.
B: Bedanke dich.
A: Frag B, wie alt er/sie ist.
B: Antworte und frag dasselbe.
A: Antworte. Frag B, ob er/sie Englisch mag.
B: Sag, dass du Englisch magst. Aber dein Lieblingsfach ist Mathe.
A: Sag B, dass er/sie verrückt ist.

c) *Act out your dialogue.*

STUDY SKILLS Stop – Check – Go

Es ist wichtig, dass du manchmal kurz anhältst (STOP) und dir Fragen darüber stellst, was du gelernt hast (CHECK). Dann überlege, wie es am besten weitergeht (GO). Also etwa so:

Stop *Einmal pro Unit, z.B. jetzt für Unit 1.*

Check *Kenne ich wirklich die Vokabeln aus Unit 1? (Lass dich zehn abfragen!)*
Kann ich die Grammatik von Unit 1?
Kann ich z.B. jemandem sagen, dass er etwas nicht tun soll?
Kann ich einen Mini-Dialog zum Thema „New friends" schreiben?

Damit du nicht vergisst, dich zu „checken", wirst du am Ende jeder Unit daran erinnert:
Checkpoint ► *im Workbook*

Go *Was kannst du besser machen?*
Tipps, was du tun kannst, wenn etwas noch nicht so „sitzt", findest du auf Seite 120.

► *SF 2 (p. 120)*

Checkpoint 1 ► *WB (p.23)*

How's the new school?

It's 3.30 and it's the end of school for today.

Ananda, how was the first day at your new school?
They're great! Jo and Dan are twins – they're very nice, and you really can't see who is Jo and ...
Hello, Mrs Smith. 'Computer World'?
Good, thank you, Mrs Smith.
I like the uniform! Thank you, Mrs Kapoor. See you.
Well, go on, go on. Jo and Dan and ...?
Then there's Jack. He's very nice and his mad ideas are great!
A packet of mints, please. Oh, your little girl is at Cotham now!
Yes, first day today.
Bye, then.
Bye, Mr Brown, and thank you. Now, Ananda, tell me more: Are there girls in your form too?
Little girl, tell Mum everything!
There's a very nice girl. Her name is Sophie. Her sister Emily isn't nice, but she's very pretty and Dilip likes her ... a lot!

Working with the text

1 Who is it?

Match the speech bubbles to the photos. Then put everything in the right order.

Mrs Kapoor

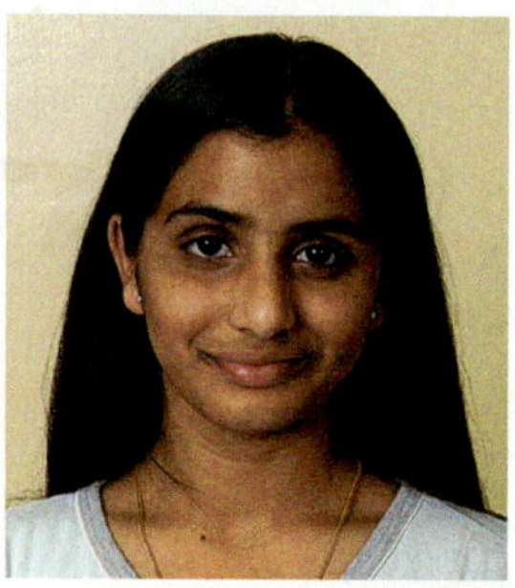

Ananda

- **A** He's very nice too.
- **B** Jo and Dan are twins.
- **C** Hi, Mum. I need my tea.
- **D** Are there girls in your form too?
- **E** Is the teacher nice?
- **F** First tell me about your classmates.
- **G** Dilip, who is this Emily?
- **H** There's a very nice girl.

2 After the first day at the new school

a) *Write a dialogue for Jack and his dad. You can use phrases from* **1**.

Mr Hanson __ Tell me about your new form.
Jack ________ The form is ...
Mr Hanson __ And who is your form t...?
Jack ________ His name ...

b) Extra *Write a dialogue for Sophie and Prunella.*

c) *Act out your dialogue(s) for the class.*

3 Extra Now you

Write about your school. You can look at p. 24 (DOSSIER) and the photo story for ideas.

▸ WB 22–23 (pp. 20–21)

Make a birthday calendar

I can ...

... say when my birthday is.

My birthday is in May.
When's your birthday?

...

1 Months of the year

a) Write the months in the right order. Listen and check. Say the months in English.

b) Mark where the words are different from the German words.

January, ...

c) Swap lists and check.

2 Dates

a) Listen. Then read out loud.

1st	first	12th	twelfth
2nd	second	13th	thirteenth
3rd	third	14th	fourteenth
4th	fourth	...	
5th	fifth	20th	twentieth
6th	sixth	21st	twenty-first
7th	seventh	22nd	twenty-second
8th	eighth	23rd	twenty-third
9th	ninth	...	
10th	tenth	30th	thirtieth
11th	eleventh	31st	thirty-first

You write	You say
9th April	the ninth of April
on 31st May	on the thirty-first of May
1998	nineteen ninety-eight
2005	two thousand and five

b) Say these dates.

18th July • 20th May • 3rd April • 19th August • 12th February • 31st December • 14th January • 22nd September, 2015 • 15th June, 1986

the eighteenth of July, ...

3 GAME When's your birthday?

Talk to different students:

A: When's your birthday?
B: My birthday is on 13th June.

Try to find one student for each month. Who can find twelve students first?

▸ WB 24–26 (p. 22) • Activity page 1

4 ACTIVITY The birthday calendar

Make a card about yourself for the class birthday calendar.

A weekend at home

I can ...

... talk to my partner about my home.

- I live in a flat/... What about you?
- There are ... rooms in my ... What about your home?
- In my room there's ... / there are ... And in your room?
- I share a room with my ...

...

Homes for people ...

My room – Ananda Kapoor

1 House or flat?

a) *Can you remember?*

The Carter-Browns live in a ...
The Hansons ...
The Kapoors ...
The Shaws ...

b) **Extra** *Listen and check.*

2 Now you

Bring a picture of your room to school. Tell different partners about it.

DOSSIER ***My room***

Label your picture.
Put it in your dossier.

▸ *WB 1–2 (p. 24)*

A a hutch in the garden

B a basket in the kitchen

... and homes for pets

C a cage in the living room

D a cage in the living room

E a basket in the bedroom

3 Where are the pets?

a) *Say where the pets are.*

The rabbits are in a hutch ...

The dog is in ...

b) *Listen. Make ticks (✓) in a copy of the chart. Then fill in the name of the owner.*

	cat	parrot	rabbit	dog	hamster	owner
Sheeba				✓		Sophie
Hip and Hop						
Harry						
Polly						
Bill and Ben						

4 Now you

Talk to a partner about pets.

budgie • cat • dog • fish • guinea pig • hamster • horse • mouse • parrot • rabbit • tortoise

A: We've got a/two ...
His/Her name is ... / Their names are ...
... two years old/black/...
What about you?

B: We haven't got a pet. But my friend has got a ... His/Her name is ...

► *P 1 (p. 42) • WB 3–4 (p. 25)*

I can ...

... sing and act the song 'This is the way I ...'

... clean my teeth ... ... wash my face ...

... eat my toast ... ... go to school ...

'... early in the morning.'

•••

1 Friday afternoon

► GF 6: Plural (p. 131) • P 2–3 (p. 42) • WB 5–6 (p. 26)

Ananda Have you got plans for the weekend?
Jack Well, we've got that essay for Mr Kingsley: 'A day in the life of ...'
Jo Oh, that's easy! Listen: 'A day in the life of Jo Shaw. I get up at 7.15 every morning. Then I clean my teeth.'
Dan No, no, no. I get up at 7.15, you sleep. I clean my teeth, you sleep. I wash my hands and face, you sleep. You get up at 7.45.
Jo OK, OK. 'We go to the kitchen and have breakfast. Then we go to school.' The end.
Jack You two write boring essays. – Oh, there's my bus! Bye!
All Bye, Jack.

STUDY SKILLS Mindmaps

Mit einer Mindmap kannst du gut Ideen sammeln und ordnen.

Gestalte eine eigene Mindmap. Verwende sie, um über deinen eigenen Tag zu sprechen.

► SF 3 (p. 121) • P 4 (p. 42) • WB 7 (p. 27)

2 On Saturday mornings

On Saturday mornings Sophie gets up at 9 o'clock. She gets dressed. Then she gives the pets their breakfast.
First she feeds Sheeba, the dog. Sheeba eats meat. Sophie gives her water too.
Then she goes to the living room and feeds Harry, the hamster. He likes toast and carrots and water. Toby watches. Then he tries to help Sophie. He cleans the cage and puts hay in it.
After that Sophie goes to the rabbit hutch. It's in the garden. Sophie feeds Hip and Hop. They like rabbit food, carrots and water.
Then Sophie has *her* breakfast.

Who has breakfast first: Harry? Sophie? Sheeba?

Looking at language

a) *Copy the chart and complete the sentences from* ***1*** *and* ***2****.*

Singular			Plural
1st person	I ... up at 7.15 every morning.	Then we ... to school.	*1st person*
2nd person	You ... up at 7.45.	You two ... boring essays.	*2nd person*
3rd person	Sophie ... up at 9 o'clock.	They ... rabbit food.	*3rd person*

b) *What's different in the 3rd person singular (he, she, it)?*

▸ GF 7a–b: Simple present (pp. 132–133) • P 5–7 (pp. 43–44) • WB 8–10 (pp. 27–28)

3 POEM My fish Wanda

My fish Wanda

My fish Wanda, she's OK.
She lives in a bowl and she plays all day.
She eats fish food and drinks and drinks.
I really wonder what she thinks.

Practise the poem with a partner. Then read it to the class.

4 Now you

a) *Write a poem about a pet.*

My	dog hamster ...	Hasso Flecki ...	he's she's	OK.

He She	lives in	our house a cage ...	and ...	he she	sleeps plays ...	all day.

He She	eats	meat carrots ...	and drinks and drinks.

I really wonder what	he she	thinks.

b) *You can put your poem in your DOSSIER.*

▸ P 8–9 (pp. 44–45)

5 Saturday afternoon

Prunella — Can I help you with your homework, Sophie?
Sophie — No thanks, Prunella. I don't need your help.
Prunella — You don't like me.
Sophie — Of course I like you, Prunella. But I really don't need your help.
Prunella — Well, can I see your essay?
Sophie — Yes, here you are.
Prunella — 'A day in the life of the Carter-Brown family.' Hmm ... This is all wrong, Sophie.
Sophie — Wrong? Why?
Prunella — Look here: 'My sister Emily and I sometimes argue.' Sometimes? You don't argue sometimes – you argue all the time.
Prunella — And here: 'My brother Toby does judo on Saturdays.' He doesn't do judo on Saturdays – he plays football on Saturdays.
And here: 'My mum and dad go to bed early.' They don't go to bed early. They watch TV till 11.30 every night! Sorry, Sophie. This isn't very good.
Sophie — No?
Prunella — No. Let's write a new essay. We don't need the old essay.
Sophie — No?
Prunella — No!

Looking at language

***a)** Complete these sentences from **5**:*
I *don't need* your help.
You ... me.
He ... judo on Saturdays.
We ... the old essay.
You ... sometimes.
They ... to bed early.

***b)** Which sentence is different?*

► GF 7c: Negative statements (p. 133) • P 10–12 (pp. 45–46) • WB 11–14 (pp. 28–30)

6 GAME My friend Nora

Play the game like this:
A: My friend Nora likes numbers. But she doesn't like letters. Your turn.
B: My friend Nora likes November. But she doesn't like December.
C: My friend Nora likes no. But she doesn't like yes.

Go on.
You can play the game with different names:
Heike, Patrick, ...

7 Sunday afternoon: Tea at the Shaws' house

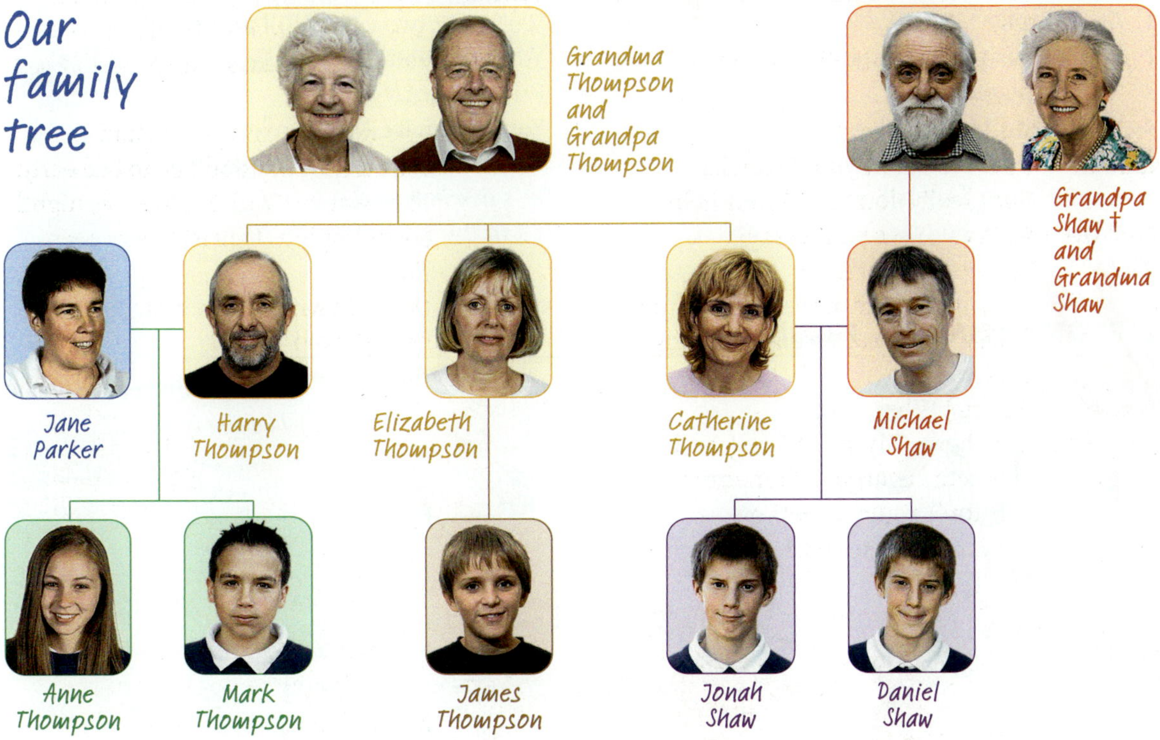

Grandma — Well boys, here's your family tree. Look. Your grandparents are at the top: Grandpa and me, and your Grandpa and Grandma Shaw.

Dan — And the cross is there because Grandpa Shaw is dead, right?

Grandpa — Right.

Grandma — And here are our children: one son, two daughters.

Jo — Oh yes, here's Uncle Harry, mum's brother. And here's Aunt Elizabeth, her sister. And here's our mum, Catherine.

Grandpa — Yes, Jonah.

Grandma — And Harry is married to your Aunt Jane, and here are your cousins, Anne and Mark.

Dan — And you're their grandparents too. So you've got five grandchildren.

Grandpa — Yes: all one big happy family.

Dan — One big happy family?

Grandpa — Yes, Daniel: children and parents – married, single or divorced – they're all family.

Dan — A family without a mum!

Jo — We've got a mum. She just isn't here.

Dan — Yeah, right.

▸ *GF 8–9: Possessive determiners, possessive form (p. 134) • P 13–16 (pp. 46–47) • WB 15–18 (pp. 30–32)*

8 Extra Now you

a) *Make your family tree. You can put it in your DOSSIER.*

b) *Talk about your family tree.*

That's …

Who's that boy/girl/…?

Is that your …?

This is my …

What's his/her name?

▸ *P 17 (p. 47)*

1 REVISION Bristol people and pets (Personal pronouns)

Match these sentences.

1 This is Sophie.	'We've got two cats – Bill and Ben.'
2 Sophie has got two rabbits.	'You're a good dog!'
3 'No, Dan and Jo!'	'I'm a parrot.'
4 'Dan and I like pets.'	'You can't have MP3 players.'
5 Sheeba has got a nice basket.	They're in a hutch in the garden.
6 'Come here, Sheeba!'	She's new in Bristol.
7 'My name is Polly.'	It's in the kitchen.

2 PRONUNCIATION Plurals

Is the '-s' like this?

Or is it like this?

Or is the end of the word like the word 'is'?

a) *Listen and say the words.*

b) *Listen. Put the words from the box in a copy of the chart.*

[-s]	[-z]	[-ɪz]
boats	beds	boxes

beds • boats • books • boxes • boys • budgies • cats • cages • colours • dogs • friends • hutches • months • pages • pencil cases • plans • raps • shops • streets • things

c) *Swap charts. Listen again and check.*

3 Weekends (Simple present: positive statements)

a) *Make sentences.*

We	play football in the park	every weekend.
My friends and I	have got music lessons	every Saturday.
My friends	write e-mails	every Sunday.
My mum and dad	get up late	
They	listen to CDs	
	go to basketball games	

b) *Write four sentences about your weekends.*

4 STUDY SKILLS Mindmaps

a) *Make a mind map about pets.*

b) **Extra** *Write about 'My perfect pet'. You can use ideas from your mind map.*

My perfect pet is ...
He/she is pink/happy/... He/she lives in ...
He/she can ...

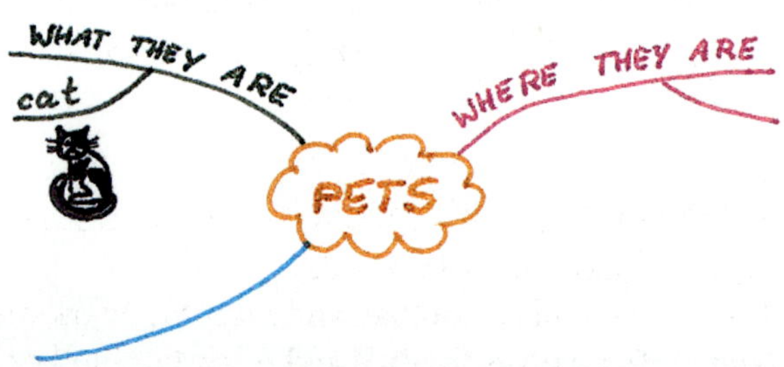

5 Extra PRONUNCIATION The '-s' in the simple present

a) *Read the poem.*

b) *Copy the poem. Use different colours for the different '-s' sounds:* [-s] [-z] [-ɪz]

c) *Listen and check.*

She comes and goes,
She sits and thinks,
She watches and listens,
She drops the books,
She drops the pens,
She opens and closes
a window, a bag, ...
Well, she's a poltergeist.

6 Every day after school (Simple present: positive statements)

a) *Say what they do every day.*

1 Jo plays (play) football every day after school.

2 Jack ... (feed) Polly ...

3 Ananda ... (eat) an apple ...

4 Dan ... (play) computer games ...

5 Sophie ... (read) books ...

6 Dilip ... (listen to) music ...

7 Jack ... (write) e-mails ...

8 Prunella ... (open) and ... (close) things every day.

b) Extra *What about you? Work in groups of six. Make a chain.*

Timo — I play football every day.
Anna — Timo plays football and I talk to my friends every day.
Lena — Timo plays football and Anna talks to her friends and I ... every day. ...

7 What they do every day (Simple present: positive statements)

a) *Partner B: Go to page 114.*
Partner A: Look at the chart below. Find out about Ananda.
A: Jack gets up at 7 o'clock. What about Ananda?
B: Ananda gets up at ... She gets dressed at ... What about Jack?

b) *What about you? Complete a copy of the chart. Then talk to your partner.*
A: I get up at ... What about you?
B: I get up at ... I get dressed at ... What about you?

c) **Extra** *Write about your partner's day.*

	Jack	Ananda	You	Your partner
get up	at 7.00	...	...	...
get dressed	at 7.15	...	...	...
have breakfast	at 7.20	...	...	
clean teeth	at 7.45	...		
come home from school	at 4.00	...		
listen to CDs	at 6.15			
go to bed	at 9.00			

8 LISTENING At the pet shop

a) *Look at the picture for two minutes. Then close your book. Say what's in the window.*
A: There are three rabbits in a hutch.
B: And a brown dog in ...

b) *Make a list of the pets in the window.*
3 rabbits, 2 ...

c) *The next day six pets aren't there. What are they? Listen to Dan and Jo.*

9 WORDS Clean a sandwich?

Which words can go with the verbs? Which can't?

1 clean | a cage / a sandwich / the board

2 write | an essay / a book / a picture

3 listen to | the teacher / a lamp / a CD

4 go to | the shops / homework / school

5 play | a book / a computer game / football

6 live | in a house / at 13 Paul Road / on a shelf

10 I don't, he doesn't (Simple present: negative statements)

a) *Complete the dialogue with* **don't** + *verb.*

Ananda I *don't like* (like) our Drama teacher.
Dilip You ... (like) him? But he's nice.
Ananda Well you ... (see) him every day.
Dilip That's right, we ... (see) him every day. We see him on Mondays for football.
Ananda Well, the girls at Cotham ... (play) football. They play hockey.
Dilip Of course you ... (play) football. You're girls.
Ananda Dilip! I really ... (like) big brothers!
Dilip Sorry, Ananda.

b) *Complete the dialogue with* **doesn't** + *verb*

Bill I like my twin, Dan.
Ben And I like my twin, Jo.
Bill But your Jo *doesn't clean* (clean) his teeth every morning.
Ben And your Dan ... (make) his bed every morning.
Bill Jo ... (read) books.
Ben Dan ... (write) e-mails.
Bill Jo ... (feed) you and me.
Ben No. But he ... (sing) in the bathroom.
Bill Dan sings nice songs! He ... (play) boring music, like Jo!

11 Can you remember? – A quiz (Simple present: positive and negative statements)

a) *Correct the sentences. Use* **doesn't** *or* **don't** + *verb.*

1 Mrs Hanson lives in New Zealand.
Mrs Hanson doesn't live in New Zealand. She lives in England.
2 The Kapoors live in a flat over a B&B.
The Kapoors don't ...
3 Jack lives in London.
4 Polly sleeps in a hutch in the garden.
5 Sophie gets up at 6 o'clock on Saturday mornings.
6 Toby helps Emily with the pets on Saturdays.
7 Jo gets up at 7.15.
8 Ananda plays football at school.

b) **Extra** *Make a quiz with a partner.*
Write five wrong sentences about people in the book or in your class.
Swap quizzes with different partners. Correct the sentences.

12 WORDS The right word

Complete the sentences with words from the box.

about • at • in • over • to • with

1 Please listen ... this CD. Then we can talk ... it.
Please listen to this CD. Then we ...
2 Can I talk ... you? I need help ... my homework.
3 Let's go ... the shops and look ... T-shirts.
4 Welcome ... Cotham. I play ... the school band.
5 The Kapoors live ... a flat ... their shop.

13 WORDS The fourth word

a) *Find the fourth word.*

1 father – mother
son – *daughter*
2 grandpa – grandma
uncle – ?
3 Mr and Mrs Hanson – married
Mr and Mrs Shaw – ?
4 mum – mother
dad – ?
5 play – hockey
? – judo
6 fish – bowl
rabbit – ?

b) *Put more words in groups of four like in a). Use words from the box.*

ball • carrots • climb • close • drink • eat • open • pull • push • throw • tree • water

1 open – close
push – p...
2 throw – ...
3 eat – ...

14 WORDS Family words

Find the missing words.

Grandpa and ... Thompson have got one son and two ... The twins' ... Elizabeth is single. James is Aunt Elizabeth's ..., and James is the twins' ... Their uncle Harry is ... to Jane. But Dan and Jo's mum and dad are ... Their dad's dad – Grandpa Shaw – is ...

Now check your answers on page 41.

15 My home, your home (Possessive determiners)

a) *Fill in* **my** *(3x),* **your, his** *(2x),* **her, its, our, their.**

1 The Hansons have got a B&B. ... name is the Pretty Polly Bed and Breakfast.
2 They've got five bedrooms in ... house.
3 Jack can see lots of houses from ... room.
4 Jack: 'I like ... room. It's little. But ... house is big. What about ... house, Sophie?'
5 Sophie: 'We live in a big house too. ... room is pink and very nice.'
6 Jack: 'Have you got pets? ... pet is a parrot.'
7 Sophie: 'Yes, we've got a hamster. ... name is Harry. And a dog – ... name is Sheeba.'

b) *Write sentences about your house, your room, your pet(s), your family. Use* **my, your, his, her, ...**

We live in a flat. Our flat is ...
My sister has got a dog. His name is ...

16 The Shaws' garden – Polly's cage (Possessive form)

Follow the lines.

the Shaws' garden, Polly's cage, Mr Kingsley's …

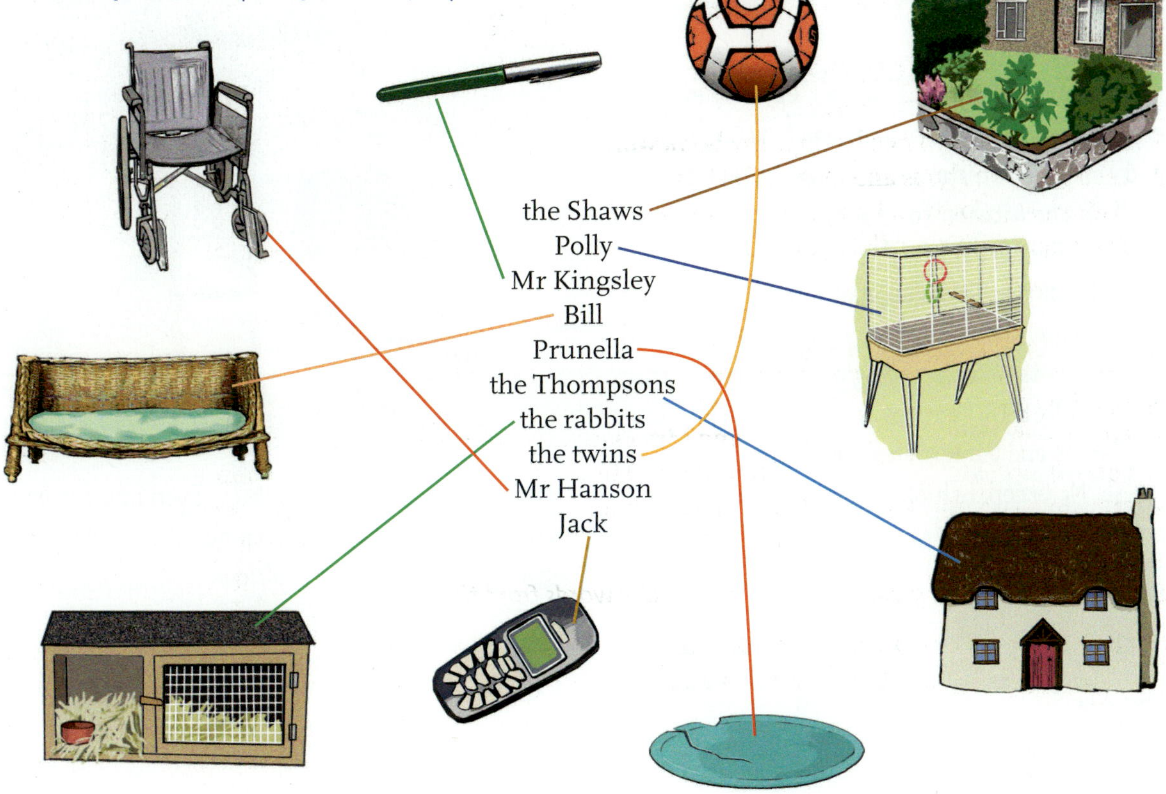

17 GETTING BY IN ENGLISH English guests

a) *Can you say these things in English?*

1 Hast du am Wochenende etwas vor? (p. 38)

2 frühstücken (p. 38)

3 Kann ich dir bei deinen Hausaufgaben helfen? (p. 40)

4 Nein danke. Ich brauche deine Hilfe nicht. (p. 40)

b) *Partner A: English guests come to your home.*
Partner B: You and your parents are the English guests.
Make a dialogue with words from a).

A: Heiße die Familie willkommen.
B: Sag danke.
A: Frag, ob du ihnen helfen kannst.
B: Sag danke, aber ihr braucht keine Hilfe.
A: Frag, ob sie am Wochenende etwas vorhaben.
B: Sag, dass ihr keine Pläne habt.
A: Sag, dass ihr samstags um halb neun frühstückt.
B: Sag, dass das eine gute Zeit ist.

c) *Practise your dialogue and act it out in class.*

A day in the life of ...

A day in the life of Jack Hanson

by Jack Hanson

My family has got a B&B. We get up early every morning. First I make my bed and have my shower. And then I get things ready for breakfast: the table in the kitchen for the family, the table in the living room for the guests.

After breakfast I go to school. I'm at home again at 4 o'clock. Then I do my homework, or I help my parents. Lots of interesting people come to the Pretty Polly B&B: families from other countries, film stars and bank robbers. We've got a new guest, Mr Green. I think he's a bank robber. Or a spy. He wears sunglasses all day! And he doesn't talk to us. It all fits.

After my homework I watch TV. Then I play games on my computer or listen to music or write stories. I go to bed at 9 o'clock.

Extra

A day in the 'life' of a poltergeist

by Prunella the poltergeist

I don't get up in the morning. I don't sleep. I'm a poltergeist!

At 1 o'clock in the morning I go to Mr and Mrs Carter-Brown's room. I open the window. At 2 o'clock, Mr Carter-Brown gets up and closes it. Then he and Mrs Carter-Brown argue. 'You open the window every night,' he says. 'You're mad,' she says. Hee, hee, hee!

At 3 o'clock I go to Emily's room. I don't like Emily. She isn't nice to her sister Sophie. Sophie is my friend. I open Emily's school bag. Then I drop it. After that, Emily can't sleep. Hee, hee, hee!

At 7.30 I go to Sophie's room. 'Sophie, get up! It's time for school!' But she can't hear me. She just sleeps and sleeps. Then I push and pull her bed. Or I drop her books. Or her alarm clock. She doesn't need an alarm clock. She has got me! Hee, hee, he

Extra

A day in the life of Bill and Ben

by Daniel Shaw

Bill and Ben are cats. Every morning after breakfast I open the door for them. Then Bill and Ben go out.

First the two cats go to the park. They play their favourite game, 'Chase the birds'. After the game, Bill and Ben are hungry and thirsty. They find lots of water in the park, but no food.

Then they go to the shops. Their favourite shop is Mr King's fish shop. Bill and Ben like fish a lot. They watch Mr King. They watch and watch. Then Ben gives the signal. He goes to Mr King and miaows. 'I'm hungry,' he miaows. But Mr King doesn't give Ben a fish. He chases him. Ben runs away. Bill runs too. But he runs to the shop. He takes a fish before Mr King sees him. And then he runs to the park again. Bill and Ben have a great lunch. Then they sleep. And after that they go home and wait for Jo and me.

Working with the text

1 Right or wrong?

Correct the wrong statements.

a) Jack's essay

1. Jack's family has got a little shop.
   Wrong. They've got a B&B.
2. Jack helps at the B&B before school.
3. The Hansons have got a new guest.
4. Jack thinks Mr Green is a film star.
5. Jack does his homework at 9 o'clock.

b) **Extra** Prunella's essay

1. Prunella gets up early every day.
2. Mr and Mrs Carter-Brown argue.
3. Sophie needs a new alarm clock.

c) **Extra** Dan's essay

1. Bill and Ben play 'Chase the dogs'.
2. Mr King likes cats in his shop.
3. After lunch Bill and Ben sleep in the park.

2 Now you

Talk about the essay(s). Use words from the box.

I think Jack's essay is/isn't very ...
I like/don't like it because it's ...

boring · clever · difficult · easy · good · interesting · nice

3 Your essay

Write an essay: 'A day in the life of ...'.
Use words and phrases like ***first, then, after that, at 9.15, in the morning/afternoon/evening, on Saturdays, ...***

DOSSIER ***A day in the life of ...***

Draw a picture for your essay. Put the essay and the picture in your dossier.

▸ WB 19 (p. 33)

Checkpoint 2 ▸ WB (p.35)

My dream house

1 The Carter-Browns' house

Look at the picture of the Carter-Browns' house. What can you see?

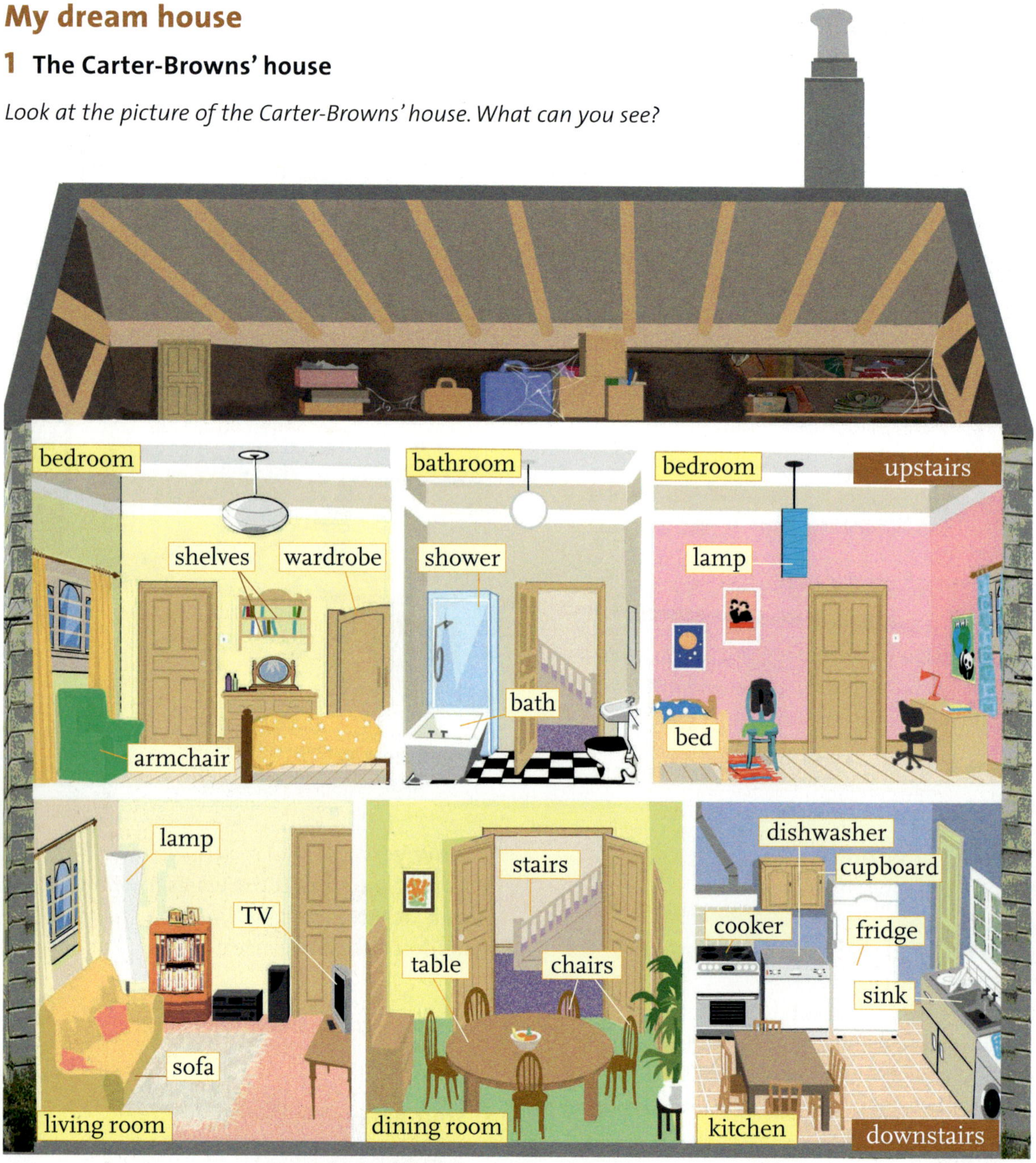

2 Can you remember?

Partner A: Close your book. Answer your partner's questions about the picture.
Then open your book. Ask your partner five questions.

Partner B: Ask your partner five questions about the picture. Close your book. Answer your partner's questions.

What colour is the fridge/...?

Where is the TV/...?

What's in the ... room?

3 Prunella's tour of the house

Prunella has got a visitor.

Listen to Prunella's tour. What is new to Uncle Henry?

4 A tour of your dream house

a) *Make a collage or model of your dream house.*

b) *Collect words for your tour in a mind map.*

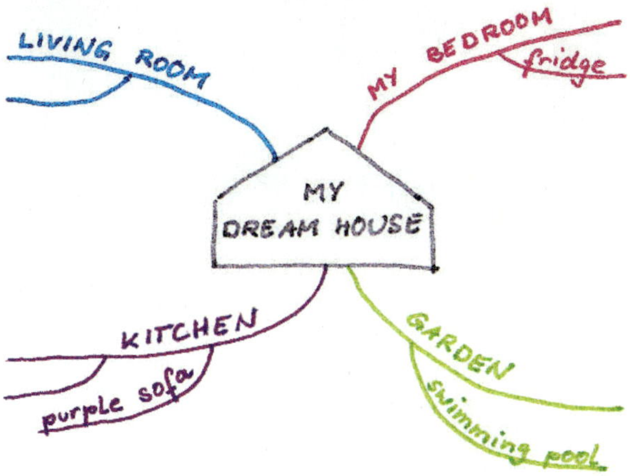

c) *Take your partner on a tour of your dream house. Use your collage or model and your mind map.*

This is my dream house.
It has got ... rooms.
I've got a ... in my room.
It's very nice/big/...
There's a ... upstairs/downstairs.
We play/... in ...
And this is ...

▸ WB 20 (p. 34)

Sports and hobbies

I can ...

... talk about my sports and hobbies.

A: After school I play football/...
I read ... / I listen to ... / I watch ...
What about you?
B: I play ... too.
On Mondays I go to ... lessons.
I like ...
...

Form 7PK

Our sports and hobbies

1

2

4

3

5

1 Form 7PK's hobbies

a) Look at pictures 1–8. Match the activities from the blue box to the pictures. Then add verbs from the green box.

dancing lessons • football • the guitar • hockey • models • riding • stamps/cards • swimming

collect • go (2 x) • go to • make • play (3 x)

1 – play football
2 – ...

b) Listen and check.

c) Listen again. Add the names to your list.

Ananda • Anne • Dan and Jo • Jack • Jo • Michelle • Simon • Sophie

d) Write a sentence for each picture.
1 – Jo plays football a lot.

2 ACTIVITY

a) Bring a picture of yourself and one of your hobbies to school. Tell your class about your picture.

In the photo I'm at my kickboxing lessons. I go to kickboxing lessons on Monday afternoons. I like kickboxing a lot. And I like swimming.

b) **Extra** *Make a classroom poster like 7PK's.*

► P 1–3 (p. 58) • WB 1–2 (p. 36)

DOSSIER *My sports and hobbies*

Glue pictures of your hobbies on a page and write about them.

MY HOBBIES
I play basketball at the weekend.
I'm in a team.
I like swimming too.

1 The Kapoors at the sports shop

Shop assistant Good afternoon. Can I help you?
Mrs Kapoor Yes, please. We need hockey shoes for my daughter: Size four, please.
Shop assistant Here you are, a size four hockey shoe.
Mrs Kapoor Thank you. Try it on, Ananda. Does it fit?
Ananda Yes, it does.
Shop assistant Does she like the colour?
Mrs Kapoor Do you like the colour, Ananda?
Ananda No, I don't.
Mrs Kapoor No, she doesn't.
Shop assistant What about these red and white shoes? Does she ... ?
Ananda I can talk too, you know.
Mrs Kapoor Ananda!
Ananda Can I try them on, please?
Shop assistant Yes, of course. Well?
Ananda Do they look nice, Mum?
Mrs Kapoor Yes, they do. Do you want them?
Ananda Do I want them? Oh yes, I do!
Mrs Kapoor OK, let's buy them then.

> *Right or wrong? Ananda likes the red and white shoes.*

2 Now you

a) *Prepare a shopping dialogue.*

a dress • football boots • shoes • shorts • socks • a top • a T-shirt

A: Good ... Can I help you?
B: Yes, please. I need ..., size ...
A: Here you are. Do they fit? / Does it fit?
B: Yes, they do. / Yes, it does.
A: Do you like ...?
B: Yes, I do. / No, I don't.

b) *Practise your dialogues. Act them out.*

Looking at language

Complete the questions from 1.

Singular

1st person	... I ... them?
2nd person	... you ... the colour, Ananda?
3rd person	... she ... the colour?

Plural

1st person	Do we need an assistant?
2nd person	Do you two need help?
3rd person	... they ... nice, Mum?

► *GF 10a–b: Simple present: questions (p. 135) • P 4–7 (pp. 59–60) • WB 3–7 (pp. 37–38)*

3 Prunella plays tennis

Prunella — Sophie, come and play with me!
Sophie — I can't. I've got homework. It's an English project: 'What do people do in their free time?'
Prunella — Great, you can ask me!
Sophie — You? Oh ... OK. What do you do in your free time, Prunella?
Prunella — I sing, and I play the piano, and I collect plates and I play tennis.
Sophie — You play tennis? Alone?
Prunella — No. I play with Uncle Henry. He hasn't got a head, so I always win.
Sophie — How do you play tennis?
Prunella — With your racket, of course!
Sophie — Oh! And when do you play tennis?
Prunella — At night, when you're all in bed.
Sophie — And where do you play?
Prunella — We play in the garden.
Sophie — But the neighbours ...?
Prunella — Oh, they think your family is mad anyway.

> *What hobbies has Prunella got?*

4 Now you

*Talk to your partner. Use ideas from **3**.*

A: What do you do in your free time?
B: I ... and I ...
A: When ... you ...?
B: Every ...

Looking at language

*Look at **3** again. Find all the questions with question words, for example:*
What do people do in their free time?

▸ GF 10c: wh-questions (p. 136) • P 8–9 (pp. 60–61) • WB 8 (p. 39)

5 Extra Lazy Larry

Listen and act.

STUDY SKILLS Wörter nachschlagen

Was ist es?
Falls du ein Wort vergessen hast, kannst du es im Dictionary (S. 176–188) nachschlagen. Dort findest du alle Wörter dieses Buches.

Probier's mal
Schlag diese Wörter im Dictionary nach: **plate, know**. *Auf welchen Seiten findest du sie? Dann finde heraus:*
- *In welcher Reihenfolge stehen die Wörter?*
- *Welche Informationen gibt es zu ihnen?*

Schreib drei Wörter aus dem Dictionary auf. Dein/e Partner/in hat eine Minute Zeit herauszufinden, was sie bedeuten.

▸ SF 4 (p. 122) • P 10 (p. 61) • WB 9 (p. 39)

6 An e-mail to Jay

Ananda has got a cousin in New York. She often writes to him.

Send | Save | Attach | Tools

To: jay.gupta@newyork-ny.com

Subject: Your hobbies

Dear Jay

Just a quick e-mail today …
Here are some questions. Can you answer them for me?
It's for an English project.
- What are your hobbies?
- How often do you do them?
- Do you go to school matches?
- Have you got a bike? How often do you ride it?

Thanks a lot!

Love
Ananda

The next morning Ananda finds an answer from her cousin.

Hi, Ananda

Here's a quick answer to your e-mail.
- My hobbies are basketball, basketball and basketball.
- I play every day (I play for the school basketball team).
- I sometimes go to school baseball games. But I NEVER go to football games – they're boring! (American football of course!)
- Yes, I've got a bike. But I don't often ride it …
  I usually walk.

Say hi to Dilip for me.

Jay

► *GF 11: Adverbs: word order (p. 136) • P 11–13 (pp. 62–63) • WB 10–12 (pp. 40–41)*

7 Extra Now you

a) *Work in groups of five. Think of five questions for a survey on hobbies.*
Do you do/like …?
Where/When do you …?
How often do you …?

b) *Ask another group your questions. Write down the answers.*

c) *Report to the class.*
Four people in the group do sport, but one person doesn't. One person plays computer games every day …

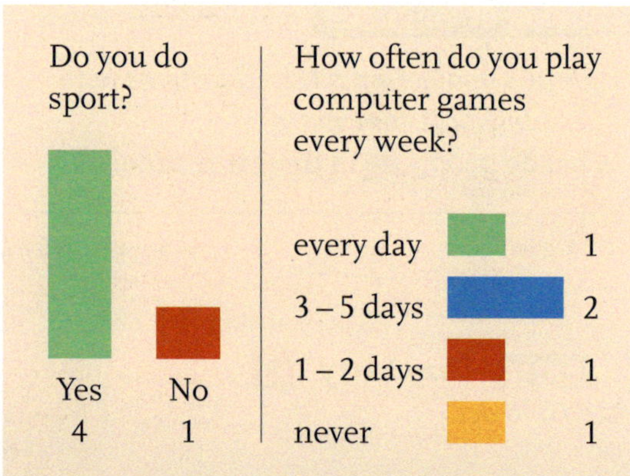

8 I hate sport

On Wednesdays Jack's mum does yoga after work, and his dad plays basketball. Jack has to do his homework.
'At least I don't have to do yoga or play basketball,' Jack says. 'I hate sport!'
'Hate sport, hate sport,' Polly says.
'And now we have to do our English project about free time. And what do most people do in their free time? Sport!'
'Hate sport, hate sport.'
'At least you understand me, Polly. Oh no, it's 5.30: I have to lay the table for dinner. Why do I have to do everything in this house? Does mum have to do yoga? And why does dad have to play basketball?'
'Basketball, basketball!' Polly says. 'Go team! Go team!'
'Oh no, Polly. Not you too!'

> *Why is Jack alone on Wednesday evenings?*

9 SONG I have to get up

a) *Listen. Make two groups (boys and girls). Sing and act.*

b) **Extra** *Write your own song. Just change the words.*

players ... play ball

... shout at us

... do sport

trainer ... train us

... go and play

I have to get up

I have to get up, I have to get up,
I have to get up in the morning.

(S)he has to get up, (s)he has to get up,
(s)he has to get up right now.

I have to get dressed, I have to get dressed,
I have to get dressed in the morning.

(S)he has to get dressed, (s)he has to get dressed, (s)he has to get dressed right now.

The teacher has to teach things.

The students have to learn things.

The teacher has to shout a lot.

And then we can all go home.

► *GF 12: have to (p. 137) • P 14–18 (pp. 63–64) • WB 13–15 (pp. 42–43)*

1 REVISION Jo plays football, he doesn't ... (Simple present statements)

a) *Complete the sentences.*

1. Jo ... (play) football every day after school. He .. ~~(go)~~ riding.
   Jo plays football every day after school. He doesn't go riding.
2. Dan ... (read) in the evenings, but he .... ~~(like)~~ big books.
3. Jack sometimes ... (make) model boats, but he ... ~~(collect)~~ stamps.
4. The girls in Form 7PK .... ~~(play)~~ football. They ... (play) hockey.
5. Sophie: 'I ... (go) to dancing lessons every Thursday, but I ... ~~(sing)~~.'
6. Sophie: 'Sheeba ... (play) ball, but she ... ~~(dance)~~.'
7. After school Ananda ... ~~(watch)~~ TV. She ... (do) her homework first.
8. Prunella ... (like) tennis, but she ... ~~(like)~~ computers.

b) *Write sentences about yourself, people in your family, or your pets.*
I ... My mum/brother plays ... She/He doesn't ...

2 WORDS A word snake

a) *Find ten words about sports and hobbies.*

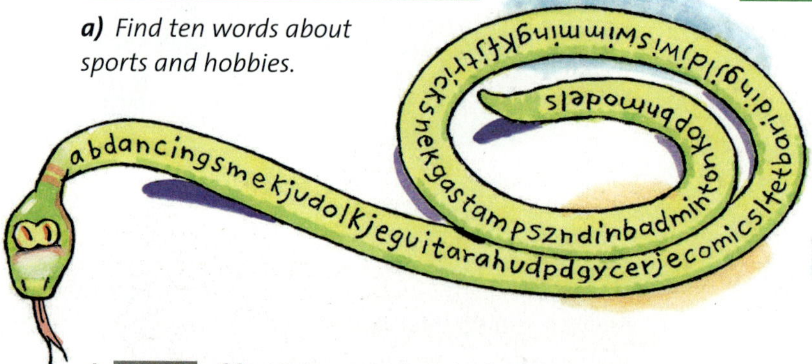

b) *Find five verbs. Match them to the words in a).*

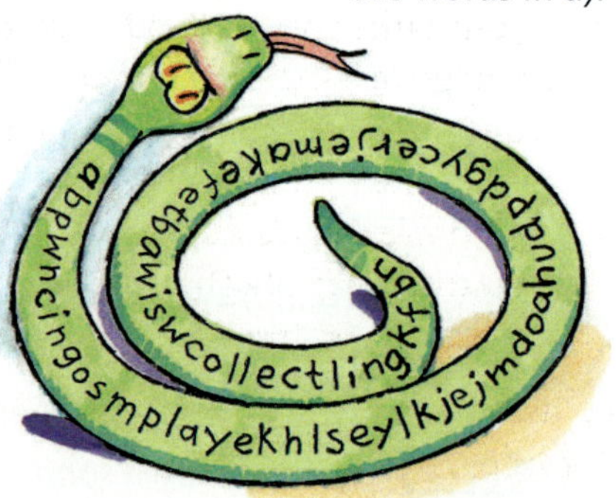

c) **Extra** *Make a word snake for your partner.*

3 WORDS A sports and hobbies mind map

Copy the mind map. Add to it. Add more words later.

4 Do you play hockey too? (Simple present: questions)

a) *Complete the questions.*

1 Jo plays football. *Do* you play football too?
2 ... I think football is easy? No, I don't!
3 ... the boys at your school play football?
4 And ... they play basketball?
5 ... we like basketball? Yes, we do!

b) *Complete the questions.*

1 *Does* Mr Kapoor come from Uganda?
2 ... Mrs Kapoor come from Uganda too?
3 ... Dilip work in the family shop?
4 And ... Ananda work there too?
5 ... the shop close at night or at weekends?

c) *Complete the questions with* ***do*** *or* ***does****.*

1 *Do* the twins live in a flat or a house?
2 And Ananda? ... she live in a flat or a house?
3 And you? ... you and your family live in a flat or a house?
4 ... you share a room with your brother or sister?
5 Have you got a favourite aunt? ... she live in Germany?
6 Mr Hanson plays basketball. ... your dad play basketball too?
7 ... you do sport?

5 Do your parents like sport? (Simple present: questions)

a) *Copy and complete the questions with* ***do*** *or* ***does****.*

1 ... your parents like sport?
2 ... your father play computer games?
3 ... you go to dancing lessons?
4 ... our teacher wear hockey shoes in class?
5 ... you collect stamps?
6 ... your friend go swimming?
7 ... your mother play tennis?
8 ... your grandparents watch sport on TV?

b) *Ask other students the questions in a).*
The answer is 'Yes'? Then write 'Y'.
Who has got the most 'Yes' answers?

6 Does it fit? (Simple present: questions)

Make Mrs Kapoor's questions.

1 *Ananda:* 'The T-shirt fits.'
< sweatshirt? >
Mrs Kapoor: 'Does the sweatshirt fit too?'
2 'I need white T-shirts for tennis.'
< shorts? >
'Do you need ...?'
3 'I like the boots.' < jeans? >
4 'Dilip likes blue.' < yellow? >
5 'The green top looks nice.'
< black top? >
6 'Sophie looks good in black tops.'
< red tops? >

7 Do you know your classmates? (Simple present: questions and short answers)

a) *Make appointments with three classmates.*
'Can we meet at 1/2/3 o'clock?'
Write their names in a list.

My appointments	
1 o'clock	Marco
2 o'clock	Sandra
3 o'clock	...

b) *Are the sentences below true for you? Write 'Y' (for Yes) in a copy of the chart. Not true? Write 'N' (for No).*

1 I play football in a team.
2 I make models.
3 I watch sport on TV.
4 I collect stamps.
5 I know lots of sports stars.
6 I go to the shops every Saturday.
7 I play the guitar.
8 I like books: I read a lot.

	me	Marco	Sandra	...
1				
2				
3				
4				
5				
6				
...				

c) *When the teacher says it's 1 o'clock, go to your first appointment. Find out about your classmate. Add 'Y' or 'N' to your chart.*
A: Marco, do you play football in a team?
B: Yes, I do. / No, I don't.

d) *Tell your class about your partners. Don't say their names. Can the class guess who they are?*
This boy doesn't play football in a team, but he makes models.

8 Sport in different countries (Simple present: wh-questions)

a) *Partner B: Go to p. 114. Partner A: Look at the chart below.*

Name	Where ... come from?	What sport ... do?	When ... do sport?
Sophie	Bristol	*goes riding*	on Saturdays and Sundays
Yoko		does judo	
Sanjay	Delhi		every Monday
Dan and Jo		go swimming	on Fridays
Britta and Lars		play basketball	

Ask your partner questions. Write the missing information in a copy of the chart.
A: What sport does Sophie do?
B: She goes riding.
A: Where does Yoko ...?
Then answer your partner's questions.

b) **Extra** *Write about the people:*
Sophie comes from Bristol. She goes riding on Saturdays and Sundays.
Yoko ...

9 Extra An interview (Simple present: questions)

a) *Write questions for the answers. Sometimes you need a question word.*

1 *Do you like sport?*
Yes, I like sport a lot.

2 *What sports ...?*
Well, I like all sports, but I really like basketball.

3 ...?
Yes, I play in a team – the team at my school.

4 ...?
We play at our school or at other schools.

5 ...?
We play after school or at weekends.

6 ...?
Yes, I do other things in my free time. I collect things.

7 ...?
Well, I collect football cards and stamps.

8 ...?
Yes, I listen to music. I like music a lot.

b) *Think of three questions for your partner. Interview him or her.*

10 STUDY SKILLS Wörter nachschlagen

a) *Write the words in alphabetical order.*

1 dead, divorced, difficult, different
2 classmate, clever, climb, class
3 plan, place, plate, play
4 weekend, well, wear, Wednesday
5 think, third, thing, this

b) *Copy the chart.*

a – answer	anyway – bag	ball – break
act ...	at	bowl

Where can you find these words?
Are they between ***a*** *and* ***answer, anyway*** *and* ***bag,*** *or* ***ball*** *and* ***break****?*
bowl, at, act, band, activity, because, aunt, all, again, baby, ask, back, bedroom

c) *Find the words in the Dictionary (pp. 176–188). Answer the questions.*

1 wardrobe: What word comes before it, what word comes after it?
2 grandpa: What letter don't you say in the word?
3 aunt, August: How do you say 'au' in the two words?
4 get dressed: Can you find this under 'get', under 'dressed' or under 'get' and 'dressed'?
5 lesson: What word comes before it, what word comes after it?
6 sunglasses: Where can you find this word first in the book? Check the page and find the sentence.

11 PRONUNCIATION [æ] and [eɪ]

a) *Listen to the poem. Then read it out loud.*

b) *Say the words for the things in the pictures.*

c) *Now say these words. What is the odd one out?*

1	bank	baby	band
2	date	day	dad
3	take	thank	that
4	make	May	mad
5	play	plan	page
6	mad	make	match
7	packet	great	name
8	eight	happen	hey

d) *Listen and check.*

e) *Put the words from c) in the chart.*

'cat' words [æ]	'skate' words [eɪ]
bank	*baby*
band	...
...	

12 LISTENING Sport on the radio

a) *Listen. Write down what sports you can hear. The pictures can help you – four are right.*

b) *English and German sports words are often the same. Listen again and find some.*

c) **Extra** *Find pictures of different sports. Label them with German-English sports words.*

13 A computer virus (Adverbs: word order)

a) *Sophie's computer has got a virus. It mixes up her sentences. Correct them.*

1 often – go dancing. – I
I often go dancing.
2 sometimes – tennis. – plays – My brother
3 Sports TV. – My dad – watches – always
4 never – sport. – My cousin – does
5 usually – goes swimming – Our class – on Friday.
6 riding. – goes – never – My mum
7 She – always – in the morning. – walks
8 watch – school matches. – always – Tom and I
9 doesn't usually – play – My sister – hockey.
10 don't – We – often – play – football at school.

b) *Write an e-mail or a letter to a friend about your family. Use three of these words:*
always – usually – often – sometimes – never

Dear ...
Love, ...
Just a quick e-mail today ...
Can you answer ...?
Hi ...
Say hi to ... for me.

14 WORDS Link the words

a) *Which words from the yellow box go with the verbs from the orange box?*
clean – CDs, shoes, teeth

clean • come • do • listen to • make • play • write

bed • CDs • computer games • e-mails • home • homework • judo • models • music • shoes • stories • teacher • teeth • tennis

b) *Now complete these sentences.*

1 Jack *cleans* his teeth every morning.
2 When he comes ... from school, he does his ...
3 Jack sometimes writes ... after school.
4 In the evening he often sits in his room and ... computer games.
5 He sometimes ... CDs in the evening.

15 Who has to wash the car? (have to/has to)

a) *Look at the Carter-Browns' job timetable. What do they have to do this week?*

Week of 4th December

wash the car	Dad
clean the living room	Emily and Toby
feed the pets	Sophie and Toby
go shopping	Mum and Emily
help Dad in the garden	Toby

Mr Carter-Brown has to wash the car.
Emily and Toby have to ...

b) *What's different in this timetable?*

Week of 11th December

wash the car	Sophie and Emily
clean the living room	Mum
feed the pets	Sophie and Toby
go shopping	Dad and Sophie
help Dad in the garden	Sophie

Mr Carter-Brown doesn't have to wash the car this week. Sophie and Emily have to do it.

16 GAME Do you know your partner?

a) *Look at the things on the right. Do you think your partner has to do them at home? Copy them and write 'Y' or 'N' in the boxes.*

b) *Now ask your partner questions and check your answers – one point for each correct answer.*

A: Do you have to clean your room?
B: No, I don't.
A: I've got that right/wrong. Do you ...
Who has got more points?

- clean his/her room ☐
- feed the pet(s) ☐
- help in the kitchen ☐
- do his/her homework right after lunch ☐
- go to bed at 9 o'clock ☐
- make his/her bed ☐

17 WORDS Opposites

Find ten pairs of opposites.

			answer	black
right	go to bed	white	never	empty
question	late	I understand		early
answer	play	get up	work	always
I don't understand	full	wrong		ask

18 GETTING BY IN ENGLISH In a sports shop

a) *Can you say these things in English?*

1 Kann ich sie bitte anprobieren? (p. 54)
2 Ja, natürlich. (p. 54)
3 Sehen sie gut aus? (p. 54)
4 Willst du sie haben? (p. 54)
5 Vielen Dank! (p. 56)
6 Warum muss ich in diesem Haus alles machen? (p. 57)

b) *Work in groups of three. Student A: You're the shop assistant. Student B: You need new football boots. Student C: You're Student B's friend. Prepare and act out the dialogue.*

A: Begrüße die beiden anderen. Frag, ob du ihnen helfen kannst.
B: Sag höflich, dass du neue Fußballschuhe brauchst, Größe 36.
A: Gib B Schuhe in Größe 36.
B: Bedanke dich und frag, ob du sie anprobieren kannst.
A: Sag ja, natürlich.
B: Frag C, ob die Schuhe gut aussehen.
C: Sag ja. Frag, ob sie passen.
B: Sag ja.
A: Frag B, ob er/sie die Schuhe haben will.
B: Sag ja, bitte.
C: Frag B, ob er dich braucht. Du musst nach Hause gehen.
B: Sag OK und vielen Dank für die Hilfe.
C: Verabschiede dich.
B: Verabschiede dich.

The SHoCK Team

Before you read the story about the SHoCK Team, look at the pictures. What do you think?

- Is the man at the Pretty Polly B&B Mr Green/a spy/a bank robber/...?
- Who's in the SHoCK Team – the man or Jack and his friends?

It's 7.45 on Wednesday night. Mr and Mrs Hanson aren't at home. Mr Green is the only guest at the Pretty Polly B&B. And he isn't there. Jack is alone in his room. Suddenly there's a noise downstairs. He listens. Yes, there it is again. He goes to the stairs and looks. Downstairs, outside Mr Green's room, there's a man in black jeans and a black sweatshirt. Jack can't see his face, but he looks very scary.

Jack — Er, excuse me! Can I help you?

The man sees Jack and runs.

Polly — Hurry up! Hurry up!

Jack runs downstairs and out of the house. He looks, but the street is empty.

Jack — Where is the man in black? I have to call the police.

Jack runs back into the house. He goes to Mr Green's room.

Jack — It's locked! Maybe I don't have to call the police.

The next day Jack tells his friends about the scary visitor.

Ananda — You have to tell your parents.

Dan — You have to call the police.

Jo — You have to tell Mr Green.

Jack — But I think this is about Mr Green.

Sophie — About Mr Green?

Jack — I think maybe he's a spy ... or a bank robber ... or ... I know: This is what we have to do. We have to find out about Mr Green. We have to be detectives.

Sophie — Great idea, Jack.

Jo — Yes! 'Detective Jo Shaw' – I like it.

Sophie I need a piece of paper.
Ananda I've got a piece of paper.
Sophie Good. And a pencil?
Jo I've got a pencil. Why do you need it?
Sophie Well, we need a name for our team of detectives.

Sophie writes and writes. The others watch. Suddenly ...

Sophie I've got it. We're the SHoCK Team.
Jack We're what?!
Sophie Look: S for Shaw, H for Hanson, C for Carter-Brown and K for Kapoor. Add one little 'o' and you've got SHoCK: The SHoCK Team.
Jack Great, Sophie! The SHoCK Team: I like it. Right, team, when we aren't at school, we watch Mr Green. We start today at five o'clock. Synchronize watches!

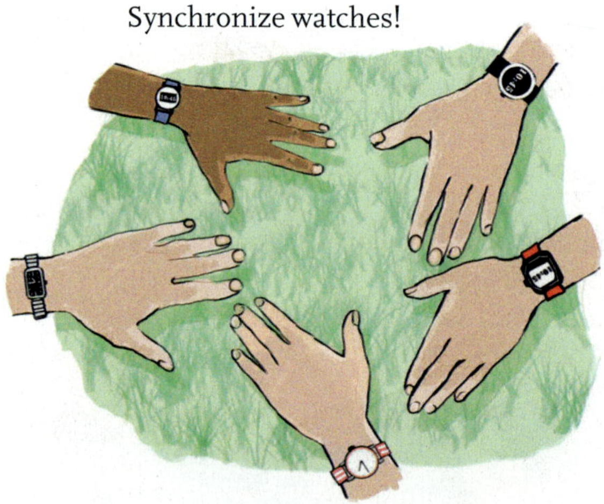

Working with the text

1 Extra What's right?

Which statement matches the story?

a Jack and his friends start a team at school. They plan to play bank robbers and police at the Pretty Polly B&B.

b Jack sees a bank robber at the Pretty Polly B&B. He and his friends watch him and then tell the police.

c Jack and his friends think Mr Green is a spy or a bank robber. They start a team of detectives. They plan to watch him.

2 Right or wrong?

a) *Correct the wrong sentences.*

1 On Wednesday night Mr and Mrs Hanson are alone in the house.
2 A scary man in black jeans and a black sweatshirt is outside Mr Green's room.
3 The next day Jack sees the scary visitor at school.

b) *Write two more wrong sentences. Swap and correct your partner's sentences.*

▸ WB 16 (p. 44)

3 Jack's e-mail to the SHoCK Team

Complete the sentences and put them in the right order.

- A man in a black sweatshirt is trying to ...
- Jack
- I think Mr Green is a ...
- Please come to ...
- Hi, SHoCK Team!
- He looks ...
- Let's meet at ...

Checkpoint 3 ▸ WB (pp. 46–47)

An English jumble sale

At a jumble sale in England people sell things – old, used things. They give the money to a charity like Oxfam or a local hospital or youth group.

1 The money

▸ *WB Activity page 2*

Pounds and pence

	You say:
1 p	one p [piː]
45 p	forty-five p
£ 1	one pound
£ 1.25	one (pound) twenty-five (p)
£ 2	two pounds
£ 3.69	three (pounds) sixty-nine (p)

Euros and cents

	You say:
1 c	one cent
20 c/€ 0.20	twenty cents
€ 1	one euro
€ 50	fifty euros
€ 9.55	nine (euros) fifty-five (cents)

2 The jumble

a) *Bring jumble (old clothes, games, books etc.) to school. Or make a cake, a model, ...*

b) *Decide on prices for your jumble.*
What about ... for this?
– Good idea!
– No, that's too much/not enough.

Write a price list on a piece of paper.

red T-shirt	€ 1
*NSYNC CD	€ 2.25
Hitchcock book	50 c

3 Your jumble sale

One person from each group sells the group's things. The others can buy things from the other groups.

A: Excuse me, how much is the .../this?
B: It's ...
A: Oh, no, that's too much. / I've only got ...
B: Well, I can take 10 c off.
A: Good, I'll take it. Here's 1 euro.
B: Thank you. Here's your change.

▸ *WB 17 (p. 45)*

Unit 4

Party, party!

I can ...

... talk to my partner about food and drink.

My favourite food/drink is ... What's your favourite food/drink?
I have ... for breakfast/lunch/dinner. What do you have?
I like ..., but I don't like ... What about you?
...

1 Food and drink

a) *Write down the numbers 1–14. Match the words from the box to the numbers in the photo.*

birthday cake • cheese • chicken • chips • chocolate biscuits • cola • crisps • fruit salad • lemonade • orange juice • salad • sandwiches • sausages • sweets

b) *Describe the food in the picture. Use words from the box. Can your partner guess what the food is?*

bottle • bowl • glass • jug • plate

A: It's green and it's in a brown bowl. It's next to ...
B: It's ...
A: That's right. Now it's your turn. / That's wrong, try again.

c) *Prepare a dialogue. Use words from a).*

A: Are you hungry? Would you like something to eat?
B: Yes, please. I'd like some sausages.
A: Are you thirsty too? Would you like some cola?
B: No thank you. But I'd like some ...

Then act out your dialogue.

► *P 1–2 (p. 75) • WB 1–3 (pp. 48–49)*

1 A party invitation

Sophie — Now, where's the invitation list for my birthday party? Let's look at it.
Prunella — It's a very long list! Why do you want to invite Ananda?
Sophie — Because I like her, of course.
Prunella — And Jack?
Sophie — Because I like him too.
Prunella — And Jo and Dan?
Sophie — Prunella, I like them too. They're my friends.
Prunella — And I'm your friend, so I want an invitation too.
Sophie — Well, no Prunella. I can't invite you – you're a poltergeist.
Prunella — What about Uncle Henry?
Sophie — No!
Prunella — You don't like us! Just because we're different ...
Sophie — I like you both, Prunella, but my party is for real people. I'm sorry.

> *Who is on Sophie's list? Who isn't? Why?*

2 ACTIVITY

Make an invitation to ...

a barbecue • a disco • a fancy-dress party • a sleepover • a Halloween party

You can put your invitation in your DOSSIER.

Looking at language

Look at these sentences from 1.

1 'Let's look at **it**.'
2 'Because I like **her**, of course.'
3 'Prunella, I like **them** too.'

*What is **it**? Who are **her** and **them**?*
*Translate **it**, **her** and **them** into German.*

► *GF 13: Personal pronouns (p. 137)* • *P 3–5 (pp. 75–76)* • *WB 4–6 (pp. 49–50)*

3 SONG The invitation rap

Listen. Then do the rap!

I invite you, you invite him,
he invites her, she invites us,
we invite you,
you invite them, they invite me

TO A PARTY!

4 A present for Sophie

Sophie's birthday party is today. Ananda and Jack still need a present.

Jack — Let's buy her some soap.
Ananda — No, soap is boring.
Jack — What about socks? Let's buy her some funny socks.
Ananda — No, too expensive.
Jack — OK, OK. Have you got any ideas?
Ananda — Yes, let's buy her some earrings. She hasn't got any earrings.
Jack — But they're expensive too.
Ananda — Well, then what about ...
Jack — Hey, look. There's Mr Green. And he's in a hurry! Can you follow him, Ananda? He knows me.
Ananda — OK. Good luck with the present. Bye!

> *What are Jack's ideas for a present? And Ananda's?*

Looking at language

Find sentences with **some** *and* **any** *in* **4**.

Positive	Negative	Questions
Let's buy her some soap.	She hasn't got ...	...
...		

How do you say these things in German?

► GF 14: some/any (p. 138) • P 6–7 (p. 76–77)

5 Now you

a) *What presents can you buy for a friend? Make a list.*

b) *Prepare and act out a dialogue.*
A: Let's buy Tim/Eva/... some ...
B: No, he's/she's got lots of ...
A: Let's buy him/her some ...

STUDY SKILLS Notizen machen

Wenn du etwas hörst oder liest und dich an etwas erinnern willst, schreibst du dir Stichworte (key words) *auf. Zum Beispiel:*

Let's buy her some funny socks. – No, too expensive. *-> funny socks – too expensive*

Probier das mal bei **6** *aus.*

► SF 5 (p. 123)

6 Another present for Sophie

a) *Copy the chart. Listen and write down Dan's ideas.*

b) *Listen again. Why doesn't Jo like Dan's ideas? Write down key words.*

Dan's ideas	Jo's reasons
DVD	not enough money
...	

c) *Swap your charts. Listen again and check.*

► P 8 (p. 77) • WB 7–10 (pp. 51–52)

7 The Carter-Browns are getting ready for the party

It's 12 o'clock on Saturday. Sophie's dad is cleaning the bathroom. Her mum is in the kitchen. She's making the birthday cake. Sophie is tidying her room.

Prunella — I'm helping too!
Sophie — No, Prunella! You aren't helping, you're making a mess. Please go away!

It's 2.30 now. Sophie's mum is making the sandwiches.

Mum — Where's baby Hannah?
Toby — She's with me, Mum! We're taking the hamster up to my room.
Emily — Mum, I'm going to Jenny's now, OK?
Mum — No, Emily, it isn't OK. The others are helping.
Emily — Dad is watching sport on TV. He isn't helping!
Mum — And you aren't going to Jenny's! You can go later. Now please put the sandwiches on the table. Dennis! Are you ...?
Dad — I'm not watching TV, dear! I'm ... cleaning the living room.

> *Find a sentence in **7** for each picture. Say what the people are doing.*

Looking at language

Complete a copy of the chart.
*Use sentences from **7**.*

Subject	*form of 'be'*	*-ing form*
The Carter-Browns	are	getting ...
Sophie's dad	is	cleaning ...
Her mum	is	making ...
Sophie	...	...
I	...	...

► *GF 15a–b: Present progressive (pp. 138–139)* • *P 9–11 (pp. 78–79)* • *WB 11–14 (pp. 53–54)*

8 Extra Now you

Imagine what your mother is doing now. And your father/brother/sister/grandma/pet?

is dancing • is drawing • is eating • is listening to • is playing • is reading • is shopping • is sleeping • is teaching • is working • is writing

Tell the class.

– I think my grandpa is playing with my little brother now, and my mum is teaching her class.
– I think my rabbit is sleeping now.

9 What's he doing now?

Ananda — Jack, is that you?
Jack — Yes, Ananda. Are you still following Mr Green?
Ananda — Yes, of course I am.
Jack — I can hear trains. Are you calling from the station?
Ananda — Yes, I am. Mr Green is waiting for the train from London ... here it is now ...
Jack — And?
Ananda — I think he's meeting somebody. A woman is getting off the train.
Jack — Sorry, I can't hear you, Ananda. Ananda?
Ananda — A woman is getting off the train! Now he's talking to her ... she's giving Mr Green a little parcel. Now he's looking round ... oops ...
Jack — Ananda! What's happening?
Ananda — I'm hiding! Now they're running.
Jack — Where are they running?
Ananda — They're running to another train ... she's getting on the train back to London! But he isn't getting on.
Jack — So what's he doing?
Ananda — He's walking out of the station ... see you at the party, Jack.
Jack — Ananda, about our present ... I've got this idea and Mrs Carter-Brown says it's OK. Sophie would like a ... Ananda? Ananda!

> *Where is Ananda? What's she doing there? What's Mr Green doing? Where is Jack?*

10 Which picture?

a) *Which pictures are right for text **9** on p.73 – a or b?*

b) *Put the pictures in the right order. Write a caption for each. Use words and phrases from **9**.*
The first picture is 4b: 'Ananda is following Mr Green.'

▸ GF 15c: Present progressive: questions (p. 139) • P 12 (p. 79) • WB 15 (p. 55)

11 Extra What's Mr Green doing?

a) *Mr Green is leaving the station. What can you hear next? Write the numbers 1–7. Listen and take notes.*

b) *Compare your notes.*

A: What's Mr Green doing in number 1?
B: He's running.
A: I've got that too. / No, I think he's ...

12 GAME Musical statues

Write an activity on a card. Put the cards in a box. Make two groups.
Group 1: take a card.
Group 2: close your eyes. The teacher starts the music.

Group 1: mime to the music. When the music stops, freeze.
Group 2: open your eyes and guess the activity.
Swap after three mimes.

I'm swimming.

I'm singing.

I'm riding my bike.

▸ P 13–15 (p. 80) • WB 16–17 (p. 55)

1 WORDS Food and drink

a) *Match these phrases to words in the box.*

a basket of *apples, oranges, ...*

a bowl of ... a bottle of ... a jug of ...
a glass of ... a packet of ... a plate of ...
a piece of ...

apples • bananas • biscuits • cake • carrots • cheese • chicken • chips • chocolate • cola • crisps • fish • juice • lemonade • meat • milk • mints • oranges • pizza • salad • sandwiches • sausages • sweets • toast • water

b) *Combine words from the box.*

apple cake, cheese sandwich, ...

DOSSIER ***My favourite party food***

Make a list of your favourite food and drink for your party.

Food
Carrot salad
Chicken
Chocolate cake

2 REVISION A quiz (Subject pronouns and 'be')

a) *Answer these questions about the book.*

1 Is Dilip Ananda's brother?
– Yes, he is.
2 Are Ananda's parents from Germany?
– No, they aren't. Mr Kapoor is from ..., and Mrs ...
3 Is Mr Kingsley's name John?
4 Is Polly a dog?
5 Is Mr Hanson in a wheelchair?
6 Are Bill and Ben Sophie's pets?
7 Is Emily Sophie's sister?
8 Are Dan and Jo twins?
9 Is Toby Jack's brother?
10 Are Prunella and Sophie friends?

b) *Make five new quiz questions like in a). Can your partner answer them?*

A: Is Mrs Shaw in Uganda?
B: No, she isn't. She's in New Zealand.

3 I can see him (Object pronouns)

Complete what Sophie and Ananda say.

Sophie:
Look, I can see ...

- Jack
- Dan and Jo
- my garden
- Emily and me
- two rabbits
- you and me
- our school
- your mum
- you
- me

Ananda:
I can see ... too!

- me
- you
- him
- her
- it
- us
- you
- them

Sophie: Look, I can see Jack. *Ananda: I can see him too.*

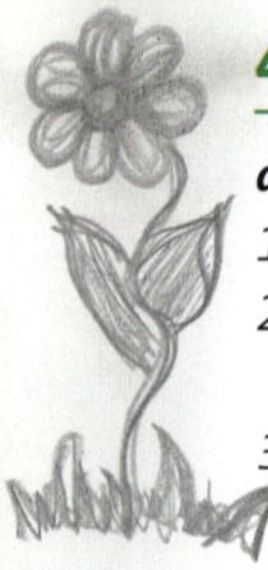

4 Can you help me? (Object pronouns)

a) *Complete the sentences with **me**, **her**, **him**, **it**, **them**.*

1 I need help. Can you help *me*?
2 Please take the juice and put ... on the table in the living room.
3 These glasses really look bad. Can you wash ..., please?
4 I want Nicole at the party! I like ...
5 These are my mum's good plates. Don't drop ...!
6 The cake is very good. Try ...
7 I like chicken salad. Can you give ... to me, please?
8 Where's John? Can you call ..., please?

b) **Extra** *Complete the sentences with **me**, **you**, **her**, **him**, **it**, **them**.*

Kim — Do you like parties, Jim?
Jim — Yes, I really like ...
Kim — Well, my party is on Friday.
Jim — Invite ..., please!
Kim — OK. You can help me to plan ...
Jim — Yes, OK. What about my cousin Laura? Can I bring ... too?
Kim — Of course.
Jim — Who are the others?
Kim — Well, there's Tim –
Jim — Oh, I like ...
Kim — The party is in the park.
Jim — Great.
Kim — Do you like pizza?
Jim — Only with bananas on ... And banana sandwiches, please make lots of ... And banana juice. I need ...!
Kim — I don't know why I invite ... to my parties!

5 WORDS Fourth word

1 evening – dinner
morning – ...
2 orange juice – drink
sandwich – ...
3 push – pull
open – ...
4 black – white
big – ...

5 sing – a song
... – a story
6 collect – stamps
... – models
7 play – tennis
... – judo
8 married – divorced
... – sell

6 Shopping day at the Carter-Brown house (some and any)

a) *Complete the dialogue with **some** or **any**.*

1 *Mrs Carter-Brown:* Is there *any* milk in the fridge, Sophie?
Sophie: No, there isn't *any* milk, but there's *some* lemonade.
2 Is there ... apple juice?
– No, there isn't ... apple juice, but there's ... orange juice.
3 Are there ... sausages?
– No, there aren't ... sausages, but there's ... chicken.
4 Are there ... apples in the basket?
– No, there aren't ... apples, but there are ... oranges .
5 Are there ... crisps?
– No, there aren't ... crisps, but there are ... biscuits.
6 Are there ... sweets?
– No, there aren't ..., but there's ... cake.

b) **Extra** *Act out the dialogue.*

7 Happy birthday! (some and any)

Partner B: Go to p. 115.
Partner A: Tell your partner what you've got in your picture. Ask about his/her picture.

I've got I haven't got	some any	bananas • biscuits • books • cakes • CDs • chicken • crisps • fruit salad • lemonade • orange juice • presents • sausages • soap • socks • sweets	in my picture.

A: I've got some crisps in my picture. What about you?
B: Yes, I've got some crisps too. And I've got some books. What about you?
A: No, I haven't got any books. I've got some ...

8 STUDY SKILLS Notizen machen

a) *Partner B: Go to p. 115.*
Partner A: Read what Jack does when Ananda follows Mr Green.
Take notes. Where does Jack go? Why doesn't he buy a present for Sophie?

First Jack goes to 'Belle', a shop for girls. But everything there is boring.
So he goes to 'Bristol Sports'. But Jack doesn't like sports things.
Then he goes to 'Ann's Second Hand'. But the things there aren't very nice.
After that Jack goes to 'M&S'. But everything there is too expensive.
Then he goes to a café. He can't find a present for Sophie there – but the cake is very good!

b) *Use your notes. Tell your partner where Jack goes and why he doesn't buy a present.*

c) *Listen to your partner's story. Where does Mr Green go? What does he do?*

9 It's 10 o'clock on Saturday (Present progressive: positive statements)

a) *Complete the sentences with the correct form of* be*.*

1 It's 10 o'clock on Saturday and the twins *are* buying a present for Sophie.
2 Their dad is at home. He ... cleaning the house.
3 Now it's 1 o'clock. Mr Shaw ... making sandwiches and Jo ... feeding the cats.
4 'Dan, lunch is ready!' Mr Shaw calls. – 'I'm on the phone, Dad! I ... talking to Ananda.'
5 Now the twins and their dad ... eating the sandwiches.
6 It's 3.20. Mr Shaw ... reading a book, the twins ... walking to Sophie's house.

b) *Complete the sentences with the correct form of* be *and the* -ing *form of the verb.*

1 It's 3.45. Mr Shaw ... (call) a friend.
2 'Hi, Indira. I ... (make) tea. Have you got time to come?'
3 'Thank you Mike, but I ... (write) e-mails now.'
4 It's 3.55. Mr Shaw is calling again. 'I've got a nice cake too. I ... (put) it on the table now.'
5 'Sorry, Mike, but now I ... (get) things ready for our jumble sale.'
6 It's 4.15 and Mr Shaw is on the phone again. 'Indira? I ... (put) some nice music in the CD player.'
7 'Oh, OK. I ... (come)!'

10 Bill and Ben are playing (Present progressive: positive and negative statements)

It's 11 o'clock on Saturday, 26th March. Say what the pets and people are and aren't doing.

Bill and Ben are playing in the park. They aren't eating fish. Jack is talking on ...

1 play in the park/ eat fish

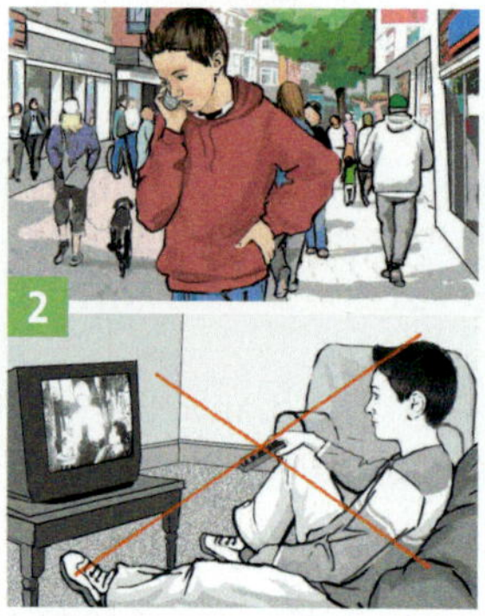

2 talk on his mobile/ watch TV

3 watch Mr Green/ play hockey

4 play football/ play the piano

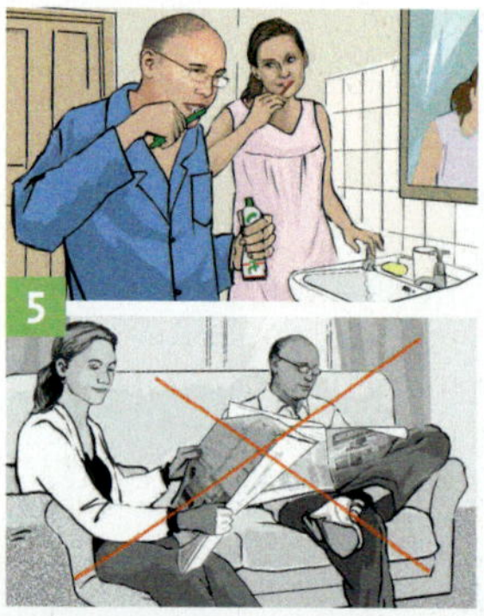

5 clean their teeth/ read the newspaper

6 feed the rabbits/ play tennis

7 work in the shop/ clean the kitchen

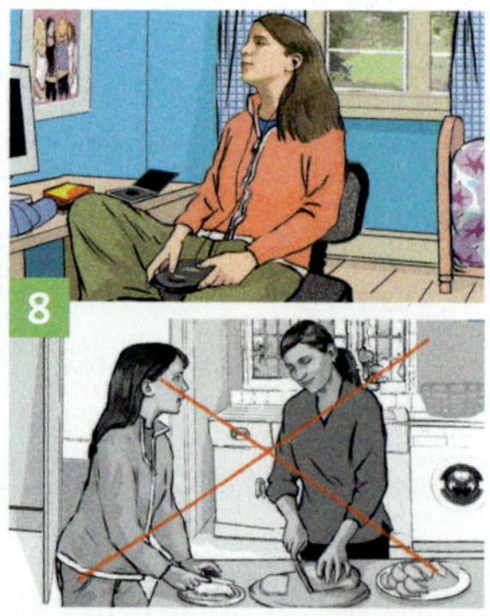

8 listen to music/ make sandwiches

11 I think Sophie is ... (Present progressive)

Make groups of three. Which group can find more right answers?

a) *Decide what the people are doing. Write down your answers.*

A: I think Sophie is eating in picture 1.
B: No, I don't think she's eating. I think she's ...
C: I think that's right. Let's write 'Sophie is ...'

b) *Tell your class what you think.*

Group A: We think Sophie is ...
Group B: We think that's right. / No, we think she's ...

c) *Who's right? Check on p.117.*

1

2

3

4

5

6

7

8

12 Questions and answers (Present progressive: questions)

a) *Jack and Jo are talking on the phone. Complete their dialogue.*

1 'Hi, Jack. ... you ... (write) your essay?'
'No, ...'
'Hi Jack. Are you writing your essay?'
'No, I'm not.'
2 'Oh, ... you ... (read) a book?'
'Yes, ...'
3 'And ... your dad ... (play) basketball?'
'No, ...'
4 'So, ... your mum and dad ... (watch) TV?'
'No, ...'
5 'Well, ... your mum ... (make) dinner?'
'Yes, ...'
6 'Hmm, you're very quiet. ... I ... (talk) too much?'
'Yes, ...!'

b) *Dilip is listening to CDs. He can't hear Ananda. Write his questions.*

1 Ananda: Mum is calling.
Dilip: *Sorry, what is Mum doing?*
2 Ananda: She's calling. She's working in the shop.
Dilip: *Sorry, ... is she working?*
3 Ananda: In the shop. Dad is cleaning the windows.
Dilip: *... is Dad cleaning?*
4 Ananda: He's cleaning the shop windows. And I'm reading a magazine.
Dilip: *Sorry, ... are you reading?*
5 Ananda: A magazine. But it's difficult with your music. I'm going out.
Dilip: *Sorry, ... are you going?*
Ananda: OUT! Goodbye!

13 LISTENING The Hokey Cokey

Do you know the Hokey Cokey?
Children often dance it at English parties.

a) *Do you know these words? If not, look them up in the Dictionary on pp. 176–188.*

circle • arm • shake • leg • jump • turn around • hold hands • bend • knee • stretch

b) *Listen and dance.*

14 PRONUNCIATION [əʊ] or [ɒ]

a) *Listen to some yellow [əʊ] words and some orange [ɒ] words on the CD.*
Hold up a yellow pencil for yellow words. Hold up an orange pencil for orange words.

b) *Say the words. Which is the odd one out?*

1 got – joke – lots
2 sock – most – close
3 shop – box – phone
4 bowl – drop – throw
5 not – toast – boat
6 photo – road – top

Listen and check.

c) *Listen to Sophie and Ananda. Then learn the dialogue. Act it out with a partner.*

15 GETTING BY IN ENGLISH Would you like ...?

John, a student from Bristol, is staying with Marcel Schmidt and his family in Münster. Tonight he's having dinner with Marcel's grandmother.

a) *Match the words to the pictures.*

sausages • potato salad • roll

1

2

3

b) *Grandma can't speak English. Marcel has to help her and John. Complete his sentences.*

Oma ___ Frag John, ob er etwas essen möchte.
Marcel ___ John, would you like something ...?
John ___ Yes, please!
Marcel ___ Ja, möchte er.
Oma ___ Frag ihn, ob er ein Brötchen oder etwas Kartoffelsalat möchte.
Marcel ___ Would you like a ... or some ...?
John ___ I'd like some potato salad, please.
Marcel ___ Er möchte ...
Oma ___ Mag er Würstchen zum Salat?
Marcel ___ Would you like ... with your ...?
John ___ Yes, please.
Marcel ___ Ja bitte.
Oma ___ Hat er Durst?
Marcel ___ Are you ...?
John ___ Yes, I am.
Oma ___ Möchte John Orangensaft oder Wasser?
Marcel ___ Would you like ... or ...?
John ___ I'd like some orange juice, please.
Marcel ___ Oma, er möchte ...

Sophie's party – a play

> *Look at the pictures of Sophie's party. Who are the guests? What are they doing?*

Scene 1:
Saturday, 26th March, 3.34 pm. Sophie and her mum are waiting for the party guests in the living room. Prunella is there too.

Sophie — They aren't coming, Mum.
Mum — Don't worry, Sophie. Good guests always come five minutes late!
Sophie — Really?
Mum — Really!
Prunella — To audience The doorbell!
Mum — See? There's somebody now.

At the front door

Sophie — Hello, Dan. Hello, Jo. Come in.
Dan — Hi, Sophie!
Jo — And happy birthday! We've got a present for you – here!
Sophie — Thank you. Thanks a lot.
Dan — You're welcome.
Prunella — What's the present? What is it? Oh, the doorbell again.
Sophie — Oh, sorry, there's the doorbell again.

Back at the front door

Sophie — Hello, Jack. Come in.
Jack — Hi, Sophie. Happy birthday! This present is from Ananda and me.
Sophie — Thank you. But where *is* Ananda?
Jack — She's following Mr Green.
Sophie — Wow! Tell me everything later.

Scene 2:
Now all the guests are there. Sophie is opening Dan and Jo's present.

Sophie — A necklace! Wow, it's great. Thanks, Dan, thanks, Jo.
Jo — Now open Jack and Ananda's present.
Dan — Look, there's a box inside.
Jo — With holes.
Dan — Maybe it's a pet. A hamster?
Jo — Or a snake?
Dan — Or a tortoise?

Sophie — It's a mouse! Fantastic!
Jack — And your mum says it's OK, you can have a mouse.
Sophie — Oh, it's so sweet! Thank you, Jack!
Prunella — To audience And Emily is afraid of mice, so that's great too! – Oh good, here's the birthday cake! Let's sing ...
All — Happy birthday to you, happy birthday to you, happy birthday, dear Sophie, happy birthday to you!

Scene 3:
After tea it's time for some party games.

Prunella — Look, they're playing 'Pass the parcel' now. The music is playing and they're passing a parcel round ... Oops! No more music. Jack has got the parcel.
Jo — Open it, Jack! Hurry up!
Jack — OK, OK. Ah, here's a piece of paper.
Ananda — What's on it?
Jack — 'Sing a song.'

Prunella — Ouch: Jack can't sing! Ah, good, now the music is playing again … Oh, no more music! And who has got the parcel?

Dan — Hurry up, Jo!

Jo — I *am* hurrying! It's another note: 'Choose a partner and walk arm in arm.' … Sophie?

Prunella — How sweet! Jo and Sophie are walking arm in arm. Oh, now the parcel is going round again … and … no more music!

Dan — Is it another note, Ananda?

Jo — Hurry up Ananda, we're all waiting!

Ananda — It's the prize! A really cool pen!

Scene 4:
The party games are over – but now Prunella is playing games.

Prunella — Mmm, Dan's crisps are good!

Dan — Hey, Jo, don't eat from my plate!

Jo — What are you talking about?!

Prunella — Hee, hee, hee! Now let's pull Ananda's hair.

Ananda — Ouch! Who was that?

Jack — Who was what?

Sophie — Stop that, Prunella! Go away! This party is for real people.

Prunella — Hee, hee, hee!

Dan — Are you talking to me, Sophie?

Sophie — To you? No, I'm talking to … oh, here's my sister.

Emily — Hi, Baby Soph! How's the party? Any orange juice for me?

Jo — Baby Soph! Is that your nickname, Sophie? I like it! Baby Soph, Baby Soph … uuurrrgghh …

Suddenly there's a piece of cake in Jo's mouth.

Emily — Ha, ha, ha! That's a big piece of cake! Aaaah!

And now there's a mouse on Emily's head.

Emily — Take it away! Take it away!

Ananda — What's happening here? How can a little mouse get from a box to …?

Sophie — Ananda, come and tell me all about Mr Green.

▸ *WB 18 (p. 56) • Activity page 3*

Working with the text

1 Extra Right or wrong?

Are these sentences from the play right or wrong? Correct the wrong sentences.

1 'Hee, hee, hee! Now let's pull Emily's hair.'
2 'Choose a partner and dance the Hokey Cokey.'
3 'Oh, sorry, there's my mobile again.'
4 'It's a mouse! Fantastic!'
5 'This party is for poltergeists.'
6 'It's the prize! A really nice book!'

2 Scenes

a) *Read 'Sophie's party' in groups. Give each scene a title. Compare titles with other groups.*
A: Scene 1 – our title is 'Where are the guests?'
B: Our title is 'The …'

b) *Write another scene for 'Sophie's party'. Think of a title, for example* 'Outside the house', 'Ananda the detective', …
Read out your new scene to the class. Choose the best scene.

c) *Act out the play.*

Checkpoint 4 ▸ *WB (p. 57)*

Extra Party doorstoppers

You need ...

brown or white bread, butter, chutney

a board, knives, salt and pepper, cocktail sticks

lettuce, tomatoes, cucumber, avocados

ham, chicken, salami

cheese

How to do it

1 Put butter on three pieces of bread.

2 Put ingredients on one piece of bread. Put a second piece of bread on top. Add more ingredients and the third piece of bread.

3 Cut your doorstopper like this.

You can make ...

an Italian doorstopper – with tomato, mozzarella cheese and lettuce.

an Indian doorstopper – with cucumber, chicken and chutney.

ACTIVITY

Think of two new doorstoppers. Give them a name. Now you can make them.

Unit 5

School: not just lessons

I can …

… remember lots of words and phrases about school.

a) *Collect your ideas in a mind map.*

b) *Say what you like about school – and what you don't like!*

• • •

1 The Spring Show

Find Ananda, Jack, Sophie, Dan and Jo. What are they doing in the photos? What clubs or groups are they in?

dance • make the programmes
paint a ship • play the clarinet • sing

Dan is painting a ship. He's in the Art Club.
Sophie …

2 School activities

a) *What activities are there at Cotham School? And at your school?*

Cotham School	My school
Camera Club	…

b) *Compare your charts.*

3 Ananda and Dilip

a) *Read the notices.*

b) *Listen and answer the questions:*

- *Which notices do Dilip and Ananda talk about?*
- *Is Ananda in the Spring Show?*

► *P 1 (p. 90) • WB 1–2 (p. 58)*

Rehearsals for the Spring Show

Photos by the Camera Club

Remember! Spring Show: 6th May

The Junior Choir is getting ready for the Spring Show.

The Dance Club is rehearsing with the Drama Club!

The Art Club is painting a pirate ship for Wednesday's show.

The Computer Club is making the programme. It has to be ready on 6th May!

The Junior Band is practising for the big day.

1 After the rehearsal: Sophie

Prunella — You're late, Sophie. Where were you?
Sophie — I was at the dress rehearsal.
Prunella — How was it?
Sophie — It was OK. We were all very nervous because the show is tomorrow.
Prunella — And was the Music teacher happy?
Sophie — Miss White? Yes, I think she was.
Prunella — And were you good?
Sophie — Well, I wasn't bad. My group was in the big pirate scene at the end.
Prunella — Pirates? Wow! Oh, the show sounds so good, and I can't go.
Sophie — I'm sorry. Poor Prunella.

\> *Right or wrong? Correct the wrong statements.*
- Sophie was home from school early.
- The kids in the rehearsal weren't nervous.
- Sophie's group was in the pirate scene at the end.

\> - *How old are the kids in the show?*
- *When does the show start?*
- *How much are tickets for a family with two parents and two children?*

2 Now you

Say a time yesterday/on Sunday/... Your partner has to find out where you were.

A: 4 o'clock yesterday.
B: Were you at home/...?
A: No, I wasn't.
B: Were you at judo lessons/...?
A: No, I wasn't. / Yes, I was.

Swap after two questions.

Looking at language

*In **1** Prunella and Sophie are talking about the past. What pronouns do they use with **was** and **were**? Copy and complete the chart.*

was	were
...	...
...	they

▸ GF 16–17: Simple past: was/were (p. 140) • P 2–4 (pp. 90–91) • WB 3–5 (pp. 59–60)

3 After the rehearsal: Jack

Jack was home at 6 o'clock.
'Hi, Mum. Hi, Dad – I'm home!' he shouted.
'I'm in here, Jack,' his dad answered from the kitchen. 'How was your rehearsal?'
'We were fantastic, Dad! Yesterday we were terrible! But today the band played two songs without a mistake.'
'That's great. Mum and I can't wait to see this show. We talked about it last night.'
'Where *is* Mum?' Jack asked.
'Upstairs, I think. She was here a minute ago.'

Jack stopped at Mr Green's room. There were people in there. Jack listened.
'Look at this!' It was Mr Green.
Then there was another voice. It was very quiet. It was a woman's voice, but who was it?
The woman talked again. 'I see you're using plastic explosives now.'
Suddenly it was clear: the woman in Mr Green's room was Jack's mother.
Jack walked to the stairs. 'Plastic explosives! I have to tell the SHoCK Team. But ... my mother – a part of this?!'

4 Who was it?

Complete the sentences.

1 ... shouted.
   Jack shouted.
2 ... asked about the rehearsal.
3 ... asked about his mum.
4 ... listened at Mr Green's door.
5 ... talked about plastic explosives.
6 ... wanted to talk to the SHoCK Team.

5 Now you

Tell a partner what you did.

I	called ... helped ... listened to ... played ... talked to ... walked ... watched ...	yesterday evening. at the weekend. last Wednesday. two weeks ago. on my last birthday.

Looking at language

a) *When was it?*
*Find the words and phrases in the first part of **3**.*

at 6 o'clock
yesterday
...

b) *Make a chart with these verbs and their simple past forms from **3**.*

shout • answer • play • talk • ask

What letters do you add to make the simple past?

► *GF 18a: Regular verbs (p. 141) • P 5–8 (pp. 91–92) • WB 6–9 (pp. 61–62)*

6 Pirate King

***a)** Listen. Put the pirates' jobs in the order on the CD.*

***b)** Listen again. Do the pirates' jobs. Sing the chorus with the Cotham students.*

All — For I am a Pirate King!
And it is, it is a glorious thing
To be a Pirate King!
For I am a Pirate King!

Girls — You are!

Boys — Hurrah for the Pirate King!

A

B

C

D

7 Dan's diary

Tuesday, 5th May
After school we had our dress rehearsal for the Spring Show. I came home late, had dinner and did my homework. Now it's time for bed. I'm really tired!
SHoCK Team: no news

Wednesday, 6th May
The Spring Show was this evening, so we came home very late. The show was great. Dad went, and he liked it a lot. The pirate scene was fantastic – our ship looked really good.
SHoCK Team: Jack said Mr Green is doing something with plastic explosives! Is Jack's mum helping him!?

Thursday, 7th May
We went swimming after school. At least Jo can't sing when he's under water! He sings the pirate song all the time! He thinks he's got a great voice. He hasn't – I know!!!
SHoCK Team: Jo and I got up very early. We went to school at 7.30 to meet the SHoCK Team. Ananda and Sophie don't think Mrs Hanson is a spy, but Jack, Jo and I aren't so sure.

\> *– Why was Dan home late on Tuesday?*
– What does Dan say about the Spring Show?
– Who thinks Jack's mum is a spy?

Looking at language

*Find these simple past forms in **7**. What are the infinitives?*

had • came • did • went • said • got up

Now make a chart with the infinitives and the simple past forms.

Infinitive	Simple past
have	had
…	came
…	…

▸ GF 18b: Irregular verbs (p. 141) • P 9–11 (p. 92–93) • WB 10–11 (p. 62–63)

8 Extra After the Spring Show

Listen to the CD.
What was the highlight of the Spring Show for Ananda? And for Mr Shaw?

9 An article for the school magazine

The Computer Club · by Ananda Kapoor (7PK)

It was a good year for the Computer Club. We were a part of the Spring Show. We didn't go up on stage, of course: we made the programmes. The teachers and the students liked them. They liked our CD cover too. There it is, on the right.
But the highlight of the year was our internet project. We linked up with a school in Hanover, Bristol's twin town in Germany. They mailed us lots of interesting information. For example: German schools haven't got uniforms. And they start at 8 o'clock. Did you know that? I didn't. Now we know a lot about Hanover and we often write to our German e-friends.

> – *Who made the CD cover?*
> – *What is Bristol's twin town in Germany?*

10 Extra GAME

Make teams of four. Two teams play together.
Team A: call a number from the box.
Team B: make a sentence with the verb.
Team B: call a number from the box ...

1 didn't call	5 didn't talk
2 didn't come	6 didn't walk
3 didn't have	7 didn't want
4 didn't hear	8 didn't write

Team A: Number 5!
Team B: We didn't talk in class today. / The man in black didn't talk to Jack.

The team with the most correct sentences wins.

Extra

▸ GF 19: Negative statements (p. 142) • P 12–14 (pp. 93–94) • WB 12–13 (pp. 63–64)

▸ GF 20: Questions (p. 142) • P 15 (p. 95) • WB 14 (p. 64)

11 German schools, English schools

a) *Compare your school with Cotham School. What's different? Make a chart like this:*

My school	Cotham School
School starts at ...	School starts at ...
...	...

Find four more different things. You can use your mind map from p. 84.

b) *Compare your charts. Can you add to them?*

▸ P 16–18 (p. 95) • WB 15 (p. 64)

DOSSIER *My diary*

Write your diary for a day last week.
It can be a real day, a funny day, a ...

1 REVISION The SHoCK Team – a flow chart

a) Copy the flow chart into your exercise book. Complete it with verbs from the box.

be (2x) • follow (2x) • give • have got • run • see • start • talk • think • walk • watch

Jack's family *has got* a B&B, the Pretty Polly B&B. There ... a new guest there, Mr Green. ▶

Jack ... Mr Green ... a spy or a bank robber. ▶

One day Jack ... a scary man in black at Mr Green's door. ▶

Jack ... to the man in black. The man ... away. ▼

Jack and his friends ... a team of detectives, the SHoCK Team. ◀

In their free time they ... Mr Green. One Saturday Ananda ... Mr Green to the station. ◀

A woman from London ... Mr Green a little parcel. ◀

Mr Green ... out of the station and Ananda ... him.

b) Swap flow charts. Check your partner's work.

2 Mr Kingsley's phone call (was/were: positive and negative statements)

*Fill in **was** (4x), **were** (6x), **wasn't** (2x) and **weren't** (1x).*

Mr Kingsley — Today is over. I'm so happy!
Friend — Oh, why?
Mr Kingsley — Well, there ... too much work at school. First there ... seven lessons, then there ... the dress rehearsal for the Spring Show. We ... all very nervous, but the rehearsal ... OK. The students in my drama group ... good. First they ... in a sketch. They ... bad in that. At the end they ... pirates and they ... really scary.
Friend — What about the music?
Mr Kingsley — Well, the band ... OK, but the choir ... so good. Poor Isabel, she ... very happy.
Friend — Isabel? Oh, the new music teacher, Miss White? She's very pretty.
Mr Kingsley — Yes. That's Isabel.

3 Were you at home yesterday? (was/were: questions and short answers)

Partner A: Ask questions. Partner B: Use short answers. Swap after six questions.

Was Were	your mother your father your pet you your friends your grandparents ...	at home at school at work in the garden at the shops at the football match ...	yesterday? at the weekend? ...?

A: *Were your friends at the football match yesterday?*
B: *Yes, they were. / No, they weren't. / I don't know.*

4 Mr Kingsley's old school (was/were: wh-questions)

a) *Form 7PK is asking about Mr Kingsley's school days. Write down their questions with* **what, when, where, who** *or* **how + was/were**. *Match the questions to the answers.*

1 *Where was* your old school?
2 ... ... your favourite subject?
3 ... ... your friends?
4 ... old ... you on your first day at Cotham?
5 ... ... you here?

a) It was English, of course!
b) I was eleven.
c) It was in Bristol. I was here at Cotham too.
d) They were two boys – Mike and Winston.
e) I was here from ... – No, I don't want to tell you that!

b) *Ask your teachers the questions.*

5 WORDS The Cotham club-finder

a) *Students often ask: 'What club can I go to?' Make a 'Cotham club-finder'. Use these ideas:*

Can you ...?		Then go to the ...
act	with a computer	Art Club
do	football	Junior Band
paint	hockey	Junior Choir
play	jazz dance	Computer Club
sing	pictures	Dance Club
work	the clarinet	Drama Club
	songs	football team
	in plays	hockey team

Can you act in plays? Then go to the Drama Club.

b) **Extra** *Make a club-finder for your school.*

c) *GAME*
Make groups of four.
Write each activity from the club-finder on a card.
Put the cards in a box.
Take a card and mime the activity.
Can the group guess your club?

A: You're shouting.
B: No, I'm not.
C: You're singing songs!
A: You're in the choir!
B: Right. Your turn.

6 School a hundred years ago (Simple past: regular verbs in positive statements)

a) *Fill in the simple past forms of the verbs.*
A hundred years ago children usually ... (start) school early in the morning. They ... (walk) to school, and after school they often ... (help) their parents in the house or garden.
Lessons ... (look) very different. The teachers ... (talk) all the time and the children ... (listen) to them. They never ... (work) in groups, ... (talk) to their partners or ... (play) games in the lessons.

b) *Write about your first year at school. Use words and phrases from a) or from the chart.*

My teacher	(always)	answer • ask • help • listen to • play • shout • start • talk • work	questions.
I	(usually)		stories.
We	(often)		games.
My school	(sometimes)		partner.
...	(never)		music.

My teacher always answered my questions. I ...

7 After school (Simple past: regular verbs in positive statements)

Partner B: Look at p. 116.
Partner A: Tell your partner what Jo did after school last week. Ask him/her about Dan.

A: On Monday Jo played football.
What about Dan?
B: He ... On Tuesday Dan ...
What about Jo?

On one day the twins did the same thing. When?

	Jo	Dan
Monday	play football	?
Tuesday	start his Maths project	?
Wednesday	work on his Maths project	?
Thursday	call his mum	?
Friday	listen to sport on the radio	?

8 PRONUNCIATION Past forms

blue verbs (*-ed* = no extra syllable)	red verbs (*-ed* = extra syllable)
Liz liked lists. Pat played the piano.	Harry hated homework. Sheila shouted at Shirley.

a) *Listen. Hold up a blue pen for the blue verbs and a red pen for the red verbs.*

b) **Extra** *How many verbs can you remember from a)? Make lists, then compare your lists with a partner. Listen again and check.*

blue verbs	red verbs
watched	started
...	

c) *Listen to the poem. Read it out loud to your partner.*

I climbed a tree and looked for Lee.
I wanted to play, I waited all day.
I lived in that tree till January.
I waited and waited for my good friend Lee.

9 Dan's report (Simple past in positive statements)

Dan watched Mr Green yesterday. Write down his report.
Put the verbs in the simple past.

19.35 Green (go) out. He (have got) a little parcel.
19.38 Outside the house he (look) round.
19.39 Then he (start) to walk to the end of the street.
19.42 Suddenly the man in black (come) out of a shop.
19.46 Green (start) to run.
19.47 I (follow) Green.
19.52 Green (go) back to the B&B. He (be) very nervous.

19.35: Green went out. He ...

10 WORDS An e-mail to Ananda's cousin

Complete Ananda's e-mail to her cousin Jay in New York.

Subject: Spring Show

Dear Jay
Our Spring Show was *on* (at/on) Wednesday. It was great. I wasn't ... (in/on) the show. I'm ... (at/in) the computer club – it was our job to make the programmes.
The week ... (before/for) the show, the kids practised every day ... (after/on) school. And ... (at/on) Tuesday, 5th May, we had our dress rehearsal ... (at/on) 4 o'clock. Then we were ready ... (at/for) the big day! The show was ... (at/in) the evening. Lots of people came and watched the scenes ... (of/from) different musicals. Jo was one ... (of/from) the pirates. ... (At/On) the end ... (for/of) the show we were all very happy.
What about your school? Are there shows there too? Tell me ... (from/about) them.
Love
Ananda

11 REVISION My 'don't' alphabet (Simple present: negative statements)

a) *Make a 'don't' alphabet.*

I don't ...

A	*... like*	*apple cake*
B	*... read*	*books about spies*
C	*... eat*	*chocolate*
D	*...*	*d ...*

b) *Read your partner's 'don't' alphabet. Tell the class five interesting things about it.*

Lisa doesn't listen to CDs, she doesn't eat hamburgers, she doesn't ...

12 Extra What's wrong here? (Simple past: negative statements)

Look at the picture from 1850. Say what's wrong. Use verbs from the box.

1 *Dads didn't watch TV in 1850.*
2 *People ...*
3 *...*

drink • have got • listen to • play • use • watch

13 Extra Mr Shaw's list (simple past: negative statements)

Look at Mr Shaw's list for last weekend. Say what he didn't do.

Last weekend Mr Shaw didn't clean his bike. He didn't ...

14 Extra The Dance Club (Simple past: mixed forms)

Complete Sophie's article for the school magazine. Use the simple past forms of the verbs in brackets.

'The Dance Club' by Sophie Carter Brown (7 PK)

It ... (be) a very good year for us. Last month we ... (dance) in the Spring Show. Lots of parents ... (go) to the show and they all ... (like) it. It ... (not be) just good, it ... (be) great!

And the Spring Show ... (not be) the only highlight of the year. Three months ago, in March, Cotham's dancers ... (be) on stage at the Hippodrome Theatre. We ... (not be) the only dancers, of course. There ... (be) dance clubs from eight schools in Bristol, and we ... (wait) for a long time before it ... (be) our turn. We ... (be) very nervous, but we ... (not look) nervous on stage and we ... (not make) any mistakes. It ... (be) a fantastic day. Our parents and teachers ... (come) to see us. And there ... (be) lots of people from Bristol and other places too. They all ... (look) very happy after the show.

15 Extra Did Prunella go to the rehearsal? (Simple past: questions)

Match the questions and answers.

1. Did Prunella go to the rehearsal?
2. Did Dan listen at Mr Green's door?
3. Did Sophie sing in the show?
4. Did Dan and Jo play football on Thursday?
5. Did the kids in the band play in the show?
6. Did Ananda write an article?

a) No, they didn't. They went swimming.
b) Yes, she did. The article was for the school magazine.
c) Yes, they did. They were very good.
d) No, she didn't. She stayed at home.
e) No, he didn't. Jack listened at Mr Green's door.
f) No, she didn't. But she danced.

16 LISTENING The elephant sketch

Here's a sketch from the Spring Show. There are six people on a train: three kids, a man, a woman and the ticket inspector. Look up new words in the Dictionary (pp. 176–188).
Listen. Then put these sentences in the right order.

1 The ticket inspector tells the man to stop.
2 The kids find a place to sit.
3 The kids ask the man why. He says he's scaring away the elephants.
4 A woman comes in. She's got an elephant in the luggage van.
5 The man starts to throw pieces of paper out of the window.
6 The woman says her elephant is afraid.

17 ACTIVITY The elephant sketch

Act out the elephant sketch. Your teacher can give you the text. First think: What do you need for the sketch? How can you make the train in your classroom?

18 GETTING BY IN ENGLISH Last weekend

a) *Can you say these things in English?*

1 Wie war's? (p. 86)
2 Ich war nicht schlecht. (p. 86)
3 Gestern waren wir schrecklich. (p. 87)
4 Deine Mutter und ich können es kaum erwarten, die Show zu sehen. (p. 87)
5 Wir sind nach der Schule schwimmen gegangen. (p. 88)
6 Jo und ich sind früh aufgestanden. (p. 88)

b) *Prepare the dialogue with a partner. Then act it out.*

A: Frag B, wie sein/ihr Wochenende war.
B: Sag, dass es nicht schlecht war. Sag, dass du bei einer Show in der Schule warst und zwei Bands gesehen hast.
A: Frag, ob die Bands gut waren.
B: Sag, dass die erste Band schrecklich war.
A: Frag, ob die zweite Band auch schrecklich war.
B: Sag, dass sie toll waren. Du kannst es kaum erwarten, ihre nächste Show zu sehen.
A: Frag, ob du dann mit B mitgehen kannst.
B: Sag ja, natürlich. Frag A, wie sein/ihr Wochenende war.
A: Sag, dass du am Samstag spät aufgestanden bist. Am Nachmittag bist du schwimmen gegangen.
B: Frag, wo A am Sonntag war.
A: Sag, dass du zu einem Basketballspiel gegangen bist.
B: Frag, ob es gut war.
A: Sag, dass es toll war.

STUDY SKILLS Unbekannte Wörter verstehen

Nachschlagen oder nicht?
Du kannst beim Lesen viel Zeit sparen, wenn du nicht jedes unbekannte Wort nachschlägst. Manchmal brauchst du das Wort zum Verständnis des Textes nicht. Und häufig kannst du die Bedeutung erschließen.

Wie?
Schau dir die Bilder an. Oft zeigen sie Dinge, die du im Text nicht verstehst. Manchmal kennst du ein ähnliches Wort – auf Deutsch oder auf Englisch. Und oft hilft der Zusammenhang, die Bedeutung zu erraten.

► *SF 6 (p. 124)* • *WB 16 (p. 65)*

A pirate story

The tavern

It was in the Caribbean in the year 1719. The night was dark and windy. The ships were in the harbour, the sailors were in the tavern. They sat with their drinks and talked and laughed.

'And what ship are you from, friend?' said one young man to a sailor at his table.
'The *Silver Swordfish*,' answered the sailor.
'A great ship. Do many men sail on her?' asked the young man.
'Yes, 40 men.'
'Ah! 39 poor sailors on the ship and you here in the tavern!'
'No, no, boy, only two sailors are still on the ship,' said the sailor. 'The others are all here.'
'That's good, that's good,' said the young man.
'It is! Tell me, boy, what's your name?' asked the sailor.
'Bonny.'
'Well then, cheers, Mr Bonny!'
'Cheers!' said the young man. 'And goodbye.'

The ship

It was 2 o'clock in the morning. The harbour was dark. Two men ran to the *Silver Swordfish*: Mr Bonny and his captain, Jack Rackham. They had swords and pistols. In the shadows their men watched and waited.

Without a sound Captain Rackham and Mr Bonny climbed onto the ship.

'Who goes there?' called one of the sailors.
'A friend!' said Mr Bonny. 'But not *your* friend!' He took out his sword and killed the sailor.
'Who goes ... aaaaagh!' The second sailor was dead on the deck.
Captain Rackham called his men. They came out of the shadows and ran to the ship.
'We sail tonight, men!'

The gold

Captain Rackham and his men sailed for three days and three nights. On the fourth day the look-out saw a ship.
'Ship ahoy!' he shouted.
The pirates saw that it was a Spanish galleon.
'There's gold on that galleon,' said one of the pirates. 'And we want it!'

The *Silver Swordfish* rammed the galleon.

Mr Bonny started to take the gold back to the *Silver Swordfish*. Suddenly he saw a cabin boy.
'You!' he shouted. 'Help me with this gold!'
'Yes, Sir,' said the boy. He was very scared.

At last all the gold was on the *Silver Swordfish*.
'You, boy!' said Mr Bonny to the cabin boy.
'What's your name?'
'Jonah,' said the boy.
'Jonah!' shouted Mr Bonny.
'Go and clean the captain's cabin. Now!'

Jonah in danger

The cabin boy did his work. Then he sat down in a dark corner. 'Just for a minute,' he said. But he was very tired and soon he was asleep.
When the captain and Mr Bonny came into the cabin, they didn't see the boy in the corner.
Later Jonah opened his eyes. At the table sat Captain Rackham and ... a beautiful woman.
But who was the woman?
'Ah, my pretty Ann Bonny!' the captain said.
'*Ann* Bonny!' shouted Jonah. Suddenly all was clear. 'But, but ... a woman on a ship is bad luck!'
Then the captain and Ann Bonny saw Jonah.
'Bad luck for you, boy!' Ann Bonny said. 'Our secret goes to the bottom of the sea ... with you!'

The end

Boom ... boom ... boom. The sound of a drum mixed with the sound of the sea and the wind. All the men were on deck. The boy was on the plank. The captain pushed him with his sword. 'Walk, boy, walk!'
'Yeah. Walk the plank!' shouted the pirates. The boy took a step. The captain pushed. He took another step, and another ... and then: down, down, down ...

THUD!

Jo opened his eyes. He was cold ... and on the floor of his room. Dan was asleep in the other bed.
'Hurrah for the Pirate King?' Jo said. 'I don't think so!'

Working with the text

1 English words – German words

a) *Can you find pictures for some of the new words in the story? Example:* tavern, sailor, ...

b) *Can you think of German words like some of the new English words? Example:* windy – windig, silver – ...

2 The story

a) *Put these things in the right order.*

The tavern: *a)* The sailor said there were only two men on the *Silver Swordfish*.
b) The night was dark and windy.
c) Bonny talked to a sailor in the tavern.

The ship: *a)* Their men came out of the shadows and climbed onto the ship.
b) They killed two sailors.
c) Captain Rackham and Bonny climbed up onto the *Silver Swordfish*.

The gold: *a)* Bonny started to take the gold onto the *Silver Swordfish*.
b) Bonny told Jonah to help with the gold.
c) The *Silver Swordfish* rammed a Spanish galleon.

Jonah in danger: *a)* Jonah saw a beautiful woman.
b) Jonah was asleep in the captain's cabin.
c) 'Bad luck for you, boy!'

b) **Extra** *Make a comic: choose one section from a). Draw a picture for each sentence. Write speech bubbles for your pictures.*

► *WB 17 (p. 66)*

Checkpoint 5 ► *WB (p. 67)*

Extra Poems

1 Poems to read

a) Read the poems out loud.
b) Listen and check.
c) Make groups of four. Each group learns one of the poems and acts it.

The Cabbage is a funny veg

The cabbage is a funny veg.
All crisp and green and brainy.
I sometimes wear one on my head
When it's cold and rainy.

Roger McGough

Ode to a goldfish

O
Wet
Pet!

Gyles Brandreth

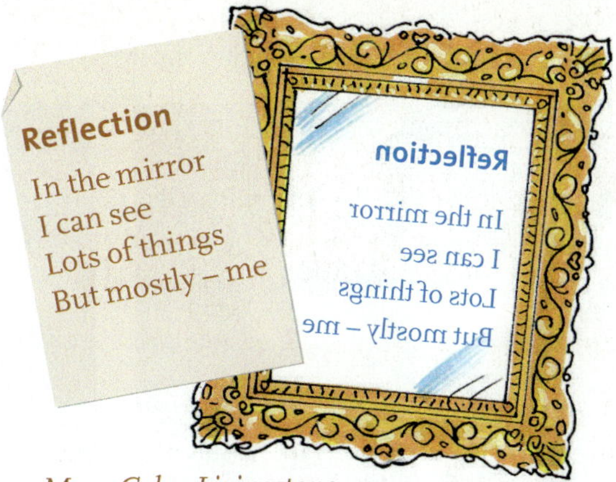

Reflection

In the mirror
I can see
Lots of things
But mostly – me

Myra Cohn Livingstone

2 Action poem

a) Listen and read the poem.
b) Do the chant with your class.

THE POETRY UNITED CHANT

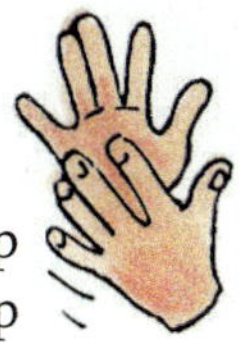

WHAT DO WE WANT clap clap clap
WHAT DO WE LIKE clap clap clap
WHAT DO WE LOVE clap clap clap

GIVE US A P clap clap clap
GIVE US AN O clap clap clap
GIVE US AN E clap clap clap
GIVE US A T clap clap clap
GIVE US AN R clap clap clap
GIVE US A Y clap clap clap

GIVE US THE RHYTHM ... POETRY
WHAT WE WANT IS POETRY

clap clap clap
clap clap clap
clap clap clap
YES!

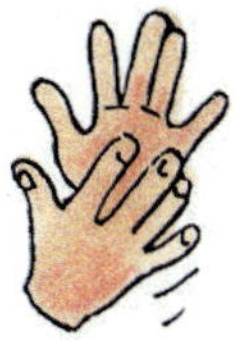

Les Baynton

3 Writing poems

Write a poem like Ode to a goldfish or THE POETRY UNITED CHANT. Act it for the class.

Here are some ideas:
Ode to Jo
Ode to Mum
...

The Basketball United Chant
The Geography United Chant
...

Great places for kids

I can ...

... talk about where I live.
Collect ideas on the board.

...

I live in a flat/house. I like it.
My bedroom/the garden/... is ...

I live in ...
It's a city/town/village.

There's
a park/church/... near my home.
It's great/...

... is a great place for kids.
You can ...

1

Cabot Tower: climb it and see Bristol!

2

Clifton Suspension Bridge: walk or ride your bike over it

3

The Downs: sit, walk or play – it's all free

4

The SS Great Britain: see a great old ship

5

Explore-at-Bristol: see tornados and lots more

6

Park Street: go shopping and meet friends

1 Mr Kingsley's photos

Look at photos 1–6. Which places would you like to visit? Why?

I'd like to go to the Downs.
You can take your dog/play ... there.

Yes, I'd like to go there too.

No, I wouldn't like to go there.
I don't like parks/museums/...

2 Form 7PK's project

Listen. Which photo does Mr Kingsley talk about? Which three questions do the students have to ask?

Is it easy to get there?

Is it old?

Is the price OK?

Is it good to look at?

Is it interesting or fun for kids?

How many places do the groups have to choose?

▸ P 1 (p. 106) • WB 1 (p. 68)

1 The project starts

Form 7PK project:

Great places for kids

Placemat activity

1. Make a placemat like this on a big piece of paper:

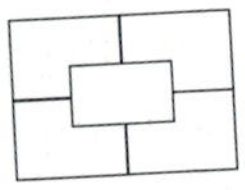

2. Each student must write three (or more) great places in one corner of the placemat. Use different colours! (3 minutes)
3. Talk about all the ideas in your group. Agree on the best three places. Write them in the middle of the placemat. (5 minutes)

Ananda, Jack, Jo and Sophie are in a group together. They've got their ideas in each corner of their placemat.

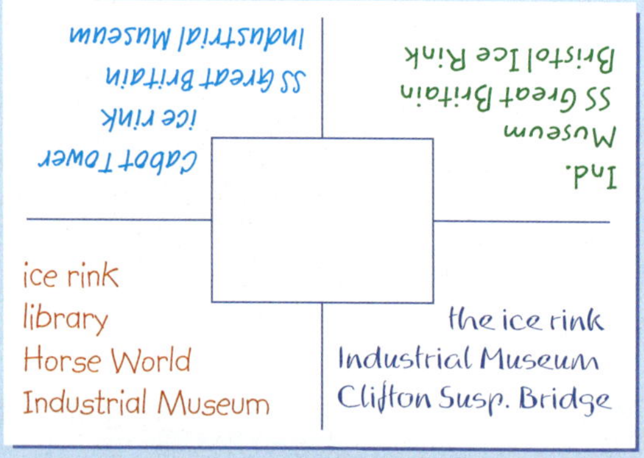

Now they have to agree on the best three ideas.

▶ *What two ideas have all the kids got?*

2 The third place

Sophie	We've all got the Industrial Museum and the ice rink.
Jo	So what's our third place?
Sophie	What about Horse World?
Ananda	I don't think Horse World is a good idea. It's too far away. You need a car.
Jack	I think Ananda is right.
Jo	I think so too.
Sophie	OK. Then it's Cabot Tower, the *SS Great Britain* or the library.
Jo	Not the Tower! It's so boring. I think the *SS Great Britain* is a good idea.
Ananda	I'm against the Industrial Museum *and* the ship. They're the same.
Sophie	You're right. So let's take the library.
Jo	The library?
Jack	Yes, why not? It's a great place.
Ananda	And it's free. OK, Jo?
Jo	OK.
Sophie	Good. Now let's write our three places in the middle of the placemat.

▶ *Which three places do they agree on?*

► *P 2–3 (p. 106) • WB 2 (p. 69)*

PROJECT Great places for kids (Part 1)

You can do a project like 7PK's.

Step 1 *Use a placemat like in **1**.*
Agree on three great places in your city/town/village.
You can use these phrases.

What about ... ?

I think ... is a good idea.

I think so too.

I'm for ... because ...

I don't think ... is a good idea.

I'm against ... because ...

Let's take the ...

Step 2 *Find out more about your places.*

3 At the library

'It's really quiet,' Ananda whispered.
'That's why I like it,' Sophie whispered back.
'I come here because it's always so loud at home.'
'Hey, Jack,' Jo said. 'Isn't that Mr Green?'
'Where?' Jack asked. He looked round and saw Mr Green. There was a big book on his desk.
'We have to find out what he's reading!'
Ananda went and looked. Then she came back to her friends. 'He's looking at plans,' she said. 'Plans of Clifton Suspension Bridge.'
'Oh no!' Jack said. 'He wants to blow up ...'

► P4 (p. 107) • WB 3–4 (p. 69)

4 Extra A library tongue-twister

5 At the Industrial Museum

'Let's take our photo over there, in front of that old car,' Jo said.
'No, here,' Jack said. 'This car is better.'
'All these cars look the same,' Sophie said.
'Let's take our photo with those buses over there. Look, that last bus is from Bristol.'
'Everything here is from Bristol, Sophie,' Jo said. 'You girls are ...'
'We girls are what, Jo?' Sophie asked. 'I hate it when people don't finish their sentences.'
'Yeah Sophie, and I hate it when ...'
'And I hate it when people argue,' Ananda said.
'Let's take the photo over there. Look, it's the world's first holiday caravan. Ready? OK, smile please!'

► GF 21: Word order (p. 143) • P 5–7 (pp. 107–108) • WB 5–8 (pp. 70–71)

6 Now you

a) *Find sentences in* **5** *with* ***I hate it when*** *...*
What do you hate? Write down two things:

I hate it when ...
... my bus is too early.
... it's cold in the mornings.

b) *Make appointments for 1, 2 and 3 o'clock. Ask your partners what they hate. Take notes.*

c) *Report to the class:*
Lennart hates it when ... I hate it when ...

7 You boys always make a mess!

Sophie — You boys always make a mess!
Jo — I'm not making a mess!
Sophie — Yes, you are. There's glue everywhere.
Jo — Oh. Well then, why don't *you* do it?
Ananda — Here, I can do it. Give me the next photo, please.
Sophie — Oh no, Ananda! *You're* using too much glue now. I never use so much glue.
Ananda — You know what, Sophie? You grumble all the time.
Sophie — I'm not grumbling. But our poster has to look nice.
Ananda — And it has to be ready. So hurry up. We still have to practise our presentation!

Looking at language

Copy and complete the sentence pairs from **7**.

You boys ... ... a mess!	I'm not ... a mess.
I ... ... so much glue.	You're ... too much glue ...
You ... all the ...	... not grumbling.

There are two different verb forms in the sentences. What are they?
Which form do you use with **all the time**, **always**, **never**? *Which form do you use to talk about* **now**?

► GF 22: Simple present and present progressive (pp. 143–144) • P 8–11 (pp. 108–109) • WB 9–12 (pp. 72–73)

8 The poster

Great places for kids in Bristol

Sophie Carter-Brown, Jack Hanson, Ananda Kapoor, Jo Shaw

Bristol Ice Rink

- Lots of fun
  - Meet friends
  - Junior disco on Saturdays
- In city centre: Frogmore Street
- Not too expensive: £3.50 for students

Bristol Industrial Museum

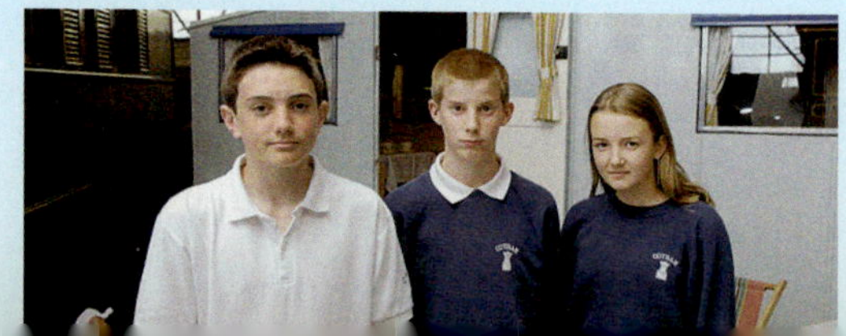

9 Presentation time

'Well, we've got time for one more presentation,' Mr Kingsley said. 'Let's take Jo, Sophie, Jack and Ananda.'
The group went to the front of the classroom.
Jack started.
'Our three places are the ice rink, the Industrial Museum and the library. Ananda is first.'
'Thanks, Jack,' Ananda said. 'I'd like to talk about the ice rink. We like it for lots of reasons ... '

10 The group's presentation

a) *Look at the phrases. Try and write them down in the right order.*

1 Our three places are ...
2 Ananda is first.

b) *Listen and check.*

c) *Listen again. Who used the yellow phrases? Who used the green phrases?*

First, ...
That's the end of our presentation.
Ananda is first.
Second, ...
We like ... for lots of reasons.
And third, ...
Our three places are ...
Have you got any questions?
Jo is next.
I'd like to talk about ...

PROJECT Great places for kids (Part 2)

Finish your project.
Step 3 *Make a poster for your presentation. Use pictures and key words like in* ***8****.*

Step 4 *Present your poster to the class. Use ideas from* ***9*** *and* ***10****.*

▸ P 12 (p. 109) • WB 13–15 (p. 74)

STUDY SKILLS Präsentation

Vorbereitung *Notiert euch in Stichworten, was ihr sagen wollt. Spielt die Präsentation auf jeden Fall einmal ganz durch.*
Arbeitsteilung *Teilt euch beim Vortrag so auf, dass jede/r etwas sagt. Zum Beispiel so: Eine/r führt durch die Präsentation und die anderen präsentieren je einen der Orte.*

▸ SF 7 (p. 125)

1 WORDS Are you a words champion?

a) *Put the words and phrases in the right baskets. (Some can go in two baskets.)*

b) *Add more words and phrases to the baskets.*

c) *How many words and phrases have you got?*

1–25: You aren't a words fan.
26–44: Good. You know lots of English words.
45–60: Great! You're a words champion!

badminton • basketball • birthday cake • bridge • church • clean your room • dance to music • do homework • do yoga • downstairs • drama lesson • flat • Geography • go swimming • go to bed • have a shower • have breakfast • hutch • invitation • kitchen • learn • lunch break • Maths • museum • open a present • party game • player • teacher • team • village • win • wardrobe

2 WORDS Word partners I

a) *Find word partners from the two boxes.* bank robber, baseball ...

bank • baseball • chocolate • drama • exercise • glass • ice • lunch • mobile • orange • pet • shop

assistant • book • bowl • break • cake • club • juice • phone • rink • robber • shop • team

b) *Write a story with five word partners from a).*

3 WORDS Word partners II

a) *Which words go with these verbs?*

take
have

away • breakfast • fun • lunch • notes • a train

get
do
make

dressed • home • homework • judo • a mess • a mistake • models • ready • up late

b) *Tell your partner four word partners from a). He or she has to make sentences with them.*

c) *What nouns go with these verbs?*
watch – read – play – write – ride – listen to watch TV/a show/...

d) **Extra** *Write one sentence with each verb from c).* After dinner I watch TV.

4 REVISION Ananda walked over the bridge (Simple past)

a) *Write sentences about what they did.*

1 Ananda ... (walk) over Clifton Suspension Bridge.

2 At the Bristol IMAX, Dan ... (watch) a film about animals.

3 At the Industrial Museum, Jo ... (look) at an old bus.

4 At Horse World, Sophie ... (go) riding.

5 Jack and Jo ... (climb) Cabot Tower.

b) **Extra** *Now write sentences about what they didn't do.*

Ananda *didn't ride* (ride) her bike over Clifton Suspension Bridge.
Dan ... (watch) a film about pirates. At the Industrial Museum, Jo ... (look) at old boats. At Horse World, Sophie ... (go) dancing. And Jack and Jo ... (play) football on the Downs.

5 What time is it when ...? (Word order in subordinate clauses)

1 What time is it when *an elephant sits* (sit) on your bike? – Time for a new bike!

2 What time is it when ... (sleep) in your bed? –Time for a new bed!

3 What time is it when ... (play) with your plates? – Time for new plates!

4 What time is it when ... (clean) the hamster's cage? – Time for ...!

5 What time is it when ... (like) you too much? – Time for you to go!

6 Remember? (Word order in subordinate clauses)

a) *Do you remember the stories in the book? Make sentences and write them in your exercise book.*

1 In Unit 1: The twins were nervous because ... (it / the first day at the new school / was).
The twins were nervous because it was the first day at the new school.
2 In Unit 1: The twins' mum isn't in Bristol because ... (she / to New Zealand / went).
3 In Unit 1: Mr Kingsley wasn't happy when ... (Jo / about Sophie's name / made a joke).
4 In Unit 2: Prunella helped Sophie when ... (she / an essay for homework / had to write).
5 In Unit 3: The SHoCK team started when ... (Jack / about the man in black / told his friends).
6 In Unit 4: Ananda followed Mr Green when ... (went / to the station / he).
7 In Unit 4: Sophie saw a mouse when ... (opened / Jack and Ananda's present / she).
8 In Unit 5: Dan was happy because ... (the Spring Show a lot / liked / his dad).

b) *Write sentences about yourself – remember the right word order.*

1 I always have lunch *when I get home from school.*
2 I'm happy when ...
3 I like ... because ...
4 I'd like to go to London/... because ...

7 Ananda and Dilip (this, that, these, those)

a) Write sentences with this is/these are.

1 … my room.
2 … my wardrobe.
3 … my stamps.
4 … my new hockey shoes.
5 … my sports T-shirts.
6 … my school bag.
7 … my new CD player.

b) Write sentences with that is/those are.

1 … my brother Dilip's room.
2 … his comics.
3 … his mobile phone.
4 … his skateboard.
5 … his favourite CDs.
6 … his MP3 player.
7 … Dilip's books about India.

8 REVISION Prunella's project (Simple present)

Prunella is working on a project. Finish her sentences. Use the simple present.

I … (not/know) lots of places because I'm a poltergeist. I … (live) in the Carter-Browns' house. My uncle Henry … (always/tell) me about fantastic places in different parts of the world. … (you/know) Paris? Well, my uncle Henry … (often/go) there. He … (say) it's beautiful, but I … (not/know) how he … (know). He … (not/have got) a head, so he can't see! My favourite place … (be) my room. I … (share) it with my friend Sophie. She … (always/say) it … (be) her room, but it … (be) really our room.

9 REVISION Ananda is reading a book (Present progressive)

Partner B: Look at p. 116.
Partner A: Look at the pictures. Tell your partner what the people are doing. Then ask your partner what they're doing in his/her pictures. Two pictures are the same – find out which.

A: In my picture 1, Ananda is reading a book. What's she doing in your picture 1?
B: In my picture 1, she's …

1 read

2 make

3 listen

4 write

5 work

6 follow

7 look at

8 go to

10 Today is different (Simple present and present progressive)

Today Prunella is trying to be nice.
Say what she usually/often/sometimes does and what she's doing today.

1 Prunella *often drops* (often/drop) cakes, but today she's *making* (make) a cake.
2 She (usually/hide) Sophie's T-shirts, but today she (wash) them.
3 She (often/play) football in the kitchen, but today she (clean) it.
4 She (often/make) a mess in Sophie's room, but today she (tidy) it.
5 She (usually/throw) plates, but today she (wash) them.
6 She (sometimes/eat) Emily's sandwiches, but today she (hide) them. – Oh! Maybe today isn't so different!

11 Who's who? (Simple present and present progressive)

Complete the sentences. Use the simple present or the present progressive.
Who are the men in the picture?

1 Mr Wiggle usually (wear) a white shirt, but today he (not wear) a white shirt.
2 Mr Woggle never (wear) red shoes, but he (like) red jeans.
3 Mr Waggle (like) red jeans, but he (not wear) them today.
4 Mr Waggle (wear) Mr Wiggle's white shirt today.
5 Mr Wiggle (think) green shoes are terrible. He never (wear) them.
6 Mr Woggle (not like) blue, but he (wear) blue today.

12 PRONUNCIATION th: [θ] and [ð]

*The **th** in the word **teeth** [θ]:*

*The **th** in the word **brother** [ð]:*

a) *Here are some words with **th**. Have they got the **th** from **teeth** or the **th** from **brother**? Listen. Then make lists.*

that • mother • thing • thanks • think • they • both • together • then • Maths • those • teeth • father • other • bathroom • Thursday • three • this

b) *Listen again and check.*

c) *Say one of the words in these pairs. Your partner then points to the word.*

1 ten – then
2 they – day
3 teeth – teas
4 things – sings
5 first day – Thursday
6 both – boat
7 say – they
8 three – free

d) *Just for fun. Try and learn this tongue-twister.*
My other brother thinks my mother's Maths is bad.

The Mr Green mystery

THE STORY SO FAR

Look at your flow chart from Unit 5 (p. 90). Update it. Compare your flow chart with the rest of your class. Now read the text.

Jack opened the front door.
'Oh, hi Sophie! You're early!' he said.
'Hi, Jack! I'm sorry, I know the SHoCK Team meets at 6 o'clock, but ...'
'Oh, that's OK. Come in. It's nice to see you.'
'Hello, hello, hello!' Polly called from her cage in the kitchen.
'Hello, Polly,' Sophie called.
'Let's go up to my room,' Jack said.
'Doorbell, doorbell!' Polly called.
'Sorry, Sophie.' Jack went and opened the door.
'Parcel for Mr Green.'
'Thank you.' Jack took the parcel in.
'I must put this parcel in Mr Green's room, Sophie,' he said. He took the key from the kitchen.
'Are you sure he's out, Jack?' Sophie asked.
Jack knocked on Mr Green's door. No answer.
'OK, you go in,' said Sophie.
Jack opened the door. He went in and took the parcel to the table. And then he saw a piece of paper on the table. There was a number on it.
'Hmm,' Jack said, 'I know that number.' Then he remembered: 'It's Mum's phone number at work. Why has Mr Green got her number?' Jack started to look at other things on the table.

What do you see on Mr Green's table?
Why do you think he has got these things?
Mr Green has got ...
Maybe he wants to blow up/go to/call ...

Now read on. Were your ideas right?

Suddenly Sophie called: 'Jack! Somebody's coming!'

'Oh, no – it must be Mr Green!' Jack said.

'I'm upstairs, OK?' Sophie whispered.

Then there was a voice in the hall. It wasn't Mr Green's voice. 'Hello, Michael!'

'How do you know my name? Who are you?' Mr Green sounded scared.

'I know everything about you, Michael. We have to talk, you and me. Let's go into your room.'

'Yes, but ...'

'No 'buts', Michael!'

The door opened. Jack saw the man in black push Mr Green into the room.

'Turn on the computer.'

'Do you work for Howard?' Mr Green asked.

'Yes. And you know what he wants.'

'When I worked for him he took all my ideas,' Mr Green said. 'But he can't have this idea!'

'Can't? Howard hates it when people say can't!' the man said. 'I don't want to hurt you, but ...' He pulled Mr Green's arm. Mr Green looked very scared.

'No!' Jack shouted. He took the lamp, ran to the man and hit him with it. The man dropped to the floor.

Working with the text

1 Right or wrong?

Correct the wrong sentences.

1 Mr Green is scared.
2 The man in black's name is Howard.
3 Jack calls the police.
4 Sophie hits the man in black.

2 What happens next?

Talk to a partner about these questions.

1 Does the man get up and hit Jack?
2 Is the man dead?
3 Does the SHoCK Team come and help?

3 The end of the story

a) *Check these words in the dictionary:*
invent • build • river • mountain • ground • save

b) *Now listen to the CD. Were your answers to 2 right or wrong?*

c) *Which of these sentences go with the story?*
1 The police take away the man in black.
2 Mr Green is writing a book about plastic explosives.
3 Jack's mum helped Mr Green.
4 Jack and Sophie saved Mr Green.

► WB 16 (p. 75)

Checkpoint 6 ► WB (pp. 76–77)

Extra Merry Christmas

1 Christmas in Britain

a) *What do you know about Christmas in Britain?*
– Christmas songs
– Christmas food
– …

b) *Look at the Christmas cards.*
Where can you see Father Christmas, presents, Christmas food, Christmas decorations, snow?

3 Christmas songs

a) *Look at the songs. Match them to a Christmas card.*

b) *Learn the songs and sing them to the music. Which song is the class favourite?*

O Christmas Tree

O Christmas tree, O Christmas tree,
Your leaves are so unchanging.
O Christmas tree, O Christmas tree,
Your leaves are so unchanging.

Not only green in summer's heat,
But also winter's snow and sleet.
O Christmas tree, O Christmas tree,
Your leaves are so unchanging.

Deck the Halls

Deck the halls with boughs of holly,
Tra la la la la, fa la la la la.
'Tis the season to be jolly,
Tra la la la la, fa la la la la.

Fast away the old year passes,
Tra la la, tra la la, fa la la.
Hail the new year, lads and lasses.
Tra la la la la, fa la la la la.

2 Now you

Talk about your family:

We don't write Christmas cards.

We don't have Christmas. But we have ... We eat ... And we ...

We have ... for Christmas dinner.

4 ACTIVITY Make a Christmas cracker

You need:

1 Make a hat.

2 Write a joke.

3 Cut the paper.

4 Put the hat, the joke and a small toy inside, roll up the cracker. Tie it.

► *WB Activity page 4*

Unit 1

12 WORDS The new timetable

a) *Answer your partner's questions.*

b) *What lessons aren't in your timetable? Ask your partner.*

B: What's lesson number 4 on Monday?

A: Lesson number 4 on Monday is Drama.

	Monday	Tuesday	Wednesday	Thursday	Friday
1	Maths	...	German	Geography	RE
2	Science	Geography	...	Maths	Drama
3	Science	...	English	English	Science
4	...	English	PE	...	PE
5	Music	PE	...	PE	...
6	...	Music	Drama	German	Maths

Unit 2

7 What they do every day (Simple present – positive statements)

a) *Look at the chart. Answer your partner's questions. Find out about Jack.*

A: Jack gets up at 7 o'clock. What about Ananda?

B: Ananda gets up at ... She gets dressed at ... What about Jack?

b) *What about you? Complete a copy of the chart. Then talk to your partner like this:*

A: I get up at ... What about you?

B: I get up at ... I get dressed at ... What about you?

	Ananda	*Jack*	*You*	*Your partner*
get up	*at 7.30*	...	...	...
get dressed	*at 7.40*	...	...	...
have breakfast	*at 7.45*	...	...	...
clean teeth	*at 8.00*	...	...	...
come home from school	*at 4.10*	...	...	...
listen to CDs	*at 7.30*	...	...	...
go to bed	*at 8.45*	...	...	...

c) **Extra** *Write about your partner's day.*

Unit 3

8 Sport in different countries (Simple present: wh-questions)

a) *Look at the chart below.*

Name	Where ... come from?	What sport ... do?	When ... do sport?
Sophie	Bristol	goes riding	
Yoko	Tokyo		at the weekend
Sanjay		plays table tennis	
Dan and Jo	Bristol		
Britta and Lars	Stockholm		on Mondays and Fridays
Your partner			

First answer your partner's questions. Then ask him/her questions. Write the missing information in a copy of the chart.

B: Where does Sophie come from?

A: From Bristol.

B: When does she ...?

A: On ...

b) **Extra** *Write about the people:*

Sophie comes from Bristol. She goes riding on Saturdays and Sundays.

Yoko ...

Unit 4

7 Happy birthday! (some and any)

Look at the picture. Tell your partner what you've got in your picture.
Ask questions about his/her picture.

I've got I haven't got	some any	apples • bananas • biscuits • books • cakes • CDs • chicken • crisps • fruit salad • lemonade • orange juice • presents • sausages • soap • socks • sweets	in my picture.

A: I've got some crisps in my picture. What about you?
B: Yes, I've got some crisps too. And I've got some books. What about you?
A: No, I haven't got any books. I've got some ...

8 STUDY SKILLS Notizen machen

a) *Read what Ananda sees when she follows Mr Green.*
Take notes. Where does Mr Green go? What does he do in each place?

First Mr Green goes to a little shop. He buys a newspaper and a cola.
Then Mr Green goes to the park. He sits and drinks his cola.

After that he goes to a shoe shop. He tries on lots of shoes, but he doesn't buy any.
Then Mr Green goes to a café. He sits and reads his newspaper.
And then he eats chicken and chips there.

b) *Listen to your partner's story. Where does Jack go? Why doesn't he buy a present?*

c) *Use your notes. Tell your partner what Ananda sees. Where does Mr Green go? What does he do?*

Unit 5

7 After school (Simple past: regular verbs in positive statements)

Tell your partner what Dan did after school last week. Ask him/her about Jo.

A: On Monday Jo … . What about Dan?
B: He watched TV. On Tuesday Dan … . What about Jo?

On one day the twins did the same thing. When?

	Jo	Dan
Monday	?	watch TV
Tuesday	?	clean his dad's car
Wednesday	?	listen to music
Thursday	?	call his mum
Friday	?	play cards with Jack

Unit 6

9 REVISION Ananda is reading a book (Present progressive)

Look at the pictures. Tell your partner what the people are doing. Then ask your partner what they're doing in his/her pictures. Two pictures are the same – find out which.

A: In my picture 1, Ananda is reading a book. What's she doing in your picture 1?
B: In my picture 1, she's …

1 follow

2 sit

3 listen to

4 feed

5 work

6 take notes

7 ride

8 go to

Unit 4 (Lösung)

11 I think Sophie is ...

Were you right? Here are the correct pictures.

SF 1 **Wörter lernen** (Units 1–6)

Hier sind ein paar Tipps, wie du Vokabeln lernen kannst. Natürlich kannst du nicht sofort alle Möglichkeiten ausprobieren, die hier beschrieben werden. Aber probiere jede Möglichkeit in den nächsten Monaten einmal aus. Dann weißt du, welche für dich am besten ist.

Gewusst wie – Vokabeln lernen mit dem Vocabulary

Wörter lernen fängt mit dem Vocabulary (S. 146–175) an. Dort sind die neuen englischen Wörter und Wendungen aufgelistet, die du lernen musst.
Das Vocabulary enthält viele Informationen. Auf S. 146 wird erklärt, wie es aufgebaut ist.

(to) **watch TV** [tiːˈviː]	fernsehen	TV = television [ˈtelɪvɪʒn] ! <u>im</u> Fernsehen = **<u>on</u>** TV: a good film **on TV**
after that	danach	First I feed the pets. **After that** I have my breakfast.

Schritt 1:
- Lies das englische Wort laut.
- Lies dann die deutsche Übersetzung in der mittleren Spalte.
- In der rechten Spalte findest du Tipps und Hilfen, z.B. einen Beispielsatz.
- Mach dies zunächst mit etwa 7–10 Wörtern.

Schritt 2:
Teste dich, ob du die Wörter weißt. Geh Zeile für Zeile durch.
- Deck die mittlere Spalte ab und sag die deutsche Übersetzung.
- Nun deck die linke und die rechte Spalte ab. Sag die englischen Wörter.
- Versuch auch den Beispielsatz zu nennen.

So kannst du dir eine Lernhilfe zum Abdecken der Spalten basteln:

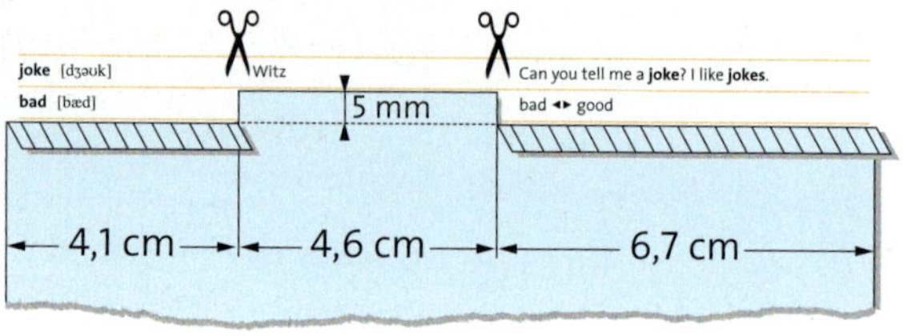

Englisch – Deutsch

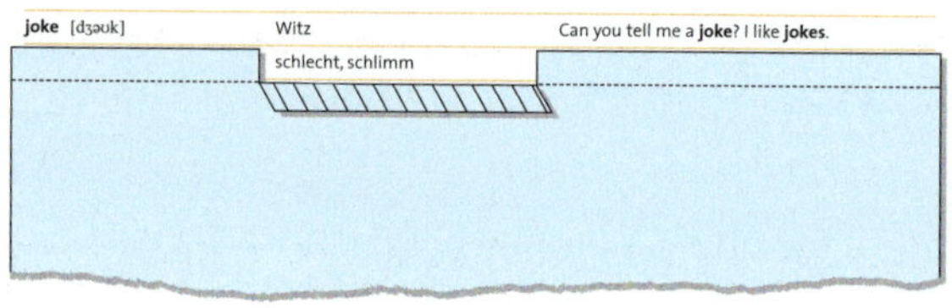

Deutsch – Englisch

Tipp
- Lerne immer 7–10 Wörter zusammen.
- Lerne Vokabeln regelmäßig. Lieber jeden Tag 5–10 Minuten als einmal pro Woche 2 Stunden.
- Wiederhole die gelernten Vokabeln einmal die Woche.
- Es macht mehr Spaß, wenn du die Vokabeln mit jemandem zusammen lernst. Fragt euch z.B. gegenseitig ab.

- Probier doch mal Aufgabe 8 auf S. 27.

Abschreiben erwünscht!

Besonders gut lernt man Vokabeln, wenn man sie aufschreibt.

- **Dreispaltiges Vokabelverzeichnis**

Leg ein Vokabelheft (mindestens DIN A5) mit drei Spalten an:
- Links das englische Wort, daneben die deutsche Übersetzung. Achte darauf, dass du die Wörter richtig abschreibst.
- In die dritte Spalte schreibst du einen Beispielsatz. Oft steht im Vocabulary ein Beispielsatz, den du abschreiben kannst. Du kannst auch ein Bild malen.
- Lies die geschriebenen Wörter noch einmal laut.

- **Elektronisches Vokabelverzeichnis**

Es gibt Computerprogramme, die dich beim Üben und Wiederholen wie ein „Vokabeltrainer" unterstützen. Du kannst dazu dein *e-Workbook* und den *English Coach* benutzen.

- **Networks**

Ordne neue Wörter in Gruppen – zum Beispiel mit einem Wörternetz (*network*).

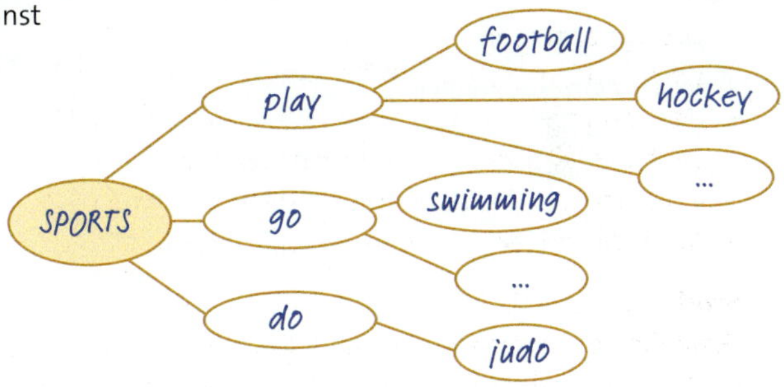

- **Persönliches „Bilderbuch"**

Zeichne eine kleine Skizze für ein neues Wort.

- **Karteikarten**

Auf die Vorderseite schreibst du das englische Wort mit einem Beispielsatz, auf die Rückseite die deutsche Übersetzung. Diese Karteikarten kannst du in einem Kasten sammeln (siehe unten).

Vorderseite Rückseite

Alles im Kasten – Vokabeln lernen mit einem Karteikasten

Mit einem Karteikasten kann man prima Vokabeln lernen. Nimm dazu eine Pappschachtel und unterteile sie in fünf unterschiedlich große Fächer.

Schritt 1: Du beschriftest die Karteikarten wie oben erklärt. Die Karteikarten kommen dann in das erste Fach. Nach kurzer Zeit ist dieses Fach voll. Nimm dann den Packen heraus und wiederhole ihn.

Schritt 2: Die Vokabeln, die du beherrschst, kommen in das nächste Fach. Die Vokabeln, die du nicht kannst, wiederholst du noch einmal. Steck sie dann ins erste Fach zurück.

Schritt 3: Nach einiger Zeit wird auch das zweite Fach zu voll. Vokabeln, die „sitzen", wandern ein Fach weiter. Steck Vokabeln, die du vergessen hast, wieder zurück ins erste Fach.

Schritt 4: So wandern die Karten Schritt für Schritt bis ins 5. Fach. Wenn du sie nach einiger Zeit wiederholst und immer noch beherrschst, kannst du sie herausnehmen, denn fünfmal gekonnt ist wirklich gekonnt!

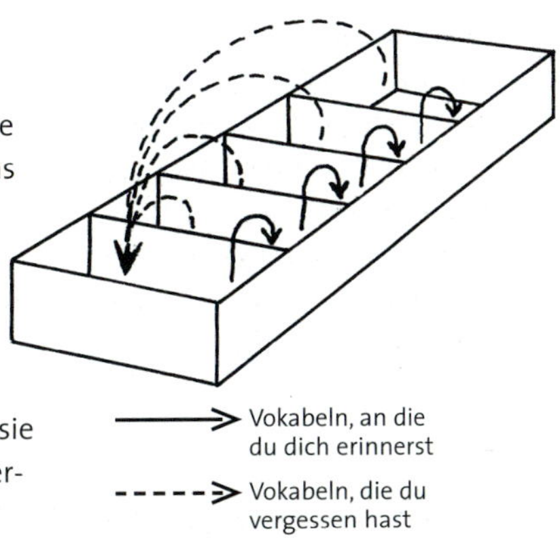

SF 2 **Stop – Check – Go** (Unit 1)

Hast du bei den Hausaufgaben viele Fehler gemacht? Hast du eine neue Grammatikstruktur nicht verstanden? Schreibt ihr in nächster Zeit eine Englischarbeit? Dann solltest du STOP – CHECK – GO anwenden.

Stop

Mindestens einmal pro Unit, besser häufiger.

Check

Überprüfe, ob du den Stoff einer Unit verstanden hast. Wenn du nicht sicher bist, was zum Stoff einer Unit gehört, kannst du im Inhaltsverzeichnis nachschauen oder deine/n Lehrer/in fragen.

Für Unit 1 könntest du dich z.B. fragen:

Kenne ich die Formen von *be* und die Personalpronomen?

Kann ich alle neuen Wörter schreiben und aussprechen? Weiß ich, was sie bedeuten?

Kann ich sagen, was ich und andere (nicht) tun können?

Kann ich Namen buchstabieren?

Kann ich sagen, dass jemand etwas besitzt?

Kann ich mich über Schulfächer unterhalten?

Der Checkpoint im Workbook hilft dir am Ende jeder Unit bei der Überprüfung. Dort findest du Testaufgaben.

Go

Was kannst du besser machen? Frag deine/n Lehrer/in um Rat oder probier die Vorschläge unten aus.

Tipp

Probleme mit den Vokabeln?
- Wenn du dir Wörter nicht merken kannst, schreib sie auf Karteikarten oder mal ein Bild dazu.
- Lass dich von jemandem abhören.
- Mach die WORDS-Übungen noch einmal. Du hast z.B. gemerkt, dass du dich nicht mehr an alle Schulfächer erinnerst? Dann mach die Übung 12 auf S. 29 noch einmal.

Probleme mit der Grammatik?
- Du hast z.B. gemerkt, dass du unsicher bist, wie die Formen von *be* sind? Schau dir das Grammar File dazu an (S.128).
- Dann mach die Übungen zu *be* nochmal (S. 26).
- Lass dir Dinge, die du nicht verstanden hast, von deinem Partner/deiner Partnerin erklären.

Probleme mit dem Inhalt?
- Übe kurze Dialoge zu den A-Sections der Unit mit deinem Partner/deiner Partnerin.
- Mach die *Getting by in English*-Übung im Practice-Teil mit deinem Partner/deiner Partnerin.
- Benutze Hilfsmittel, z.B. die Listening-CD zum Schülerbuch oder das Workbook.

SF 3 **Mindmaps** (Unit 2)

Wozu sind Mindmaps gut?

Mindmaps kannst du benutzen, wenn du deine Ideen sammeln und ordnen willst. Das kann z.B. sehr hilfreich sein, wenn du etwas vortragen sollst oder einen Text vorbereiten willst.

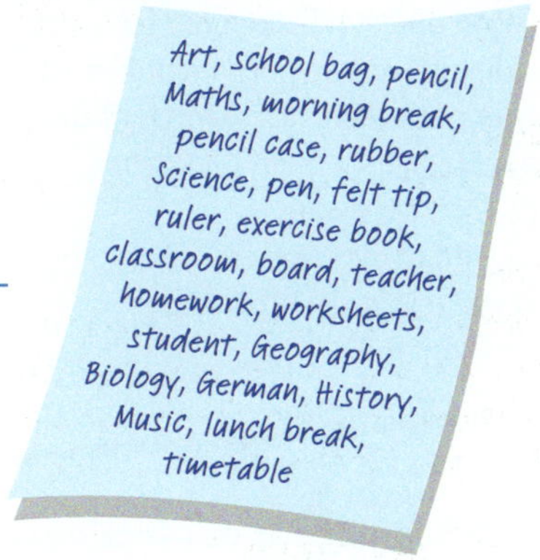

Wie mache ich eine Mindmap?

Stell dir vor, du möchtest alles ordnen, was du auf Englisch zum Thema Schule sagen kannst. Wie in diesem Beispiel zum Thema Schule kannst du zuerst einfach ungeordnet alle Begriffe aufschreiben, die dir zum Thema einfallen. Du kannst sie auch gleich in einer Mindmap sammeln und ordnen.

Was brauche ich?

- ein leeres, unliniertes Blatt Papier im Querformat
- Stifte in verschiedenen Farben

Wie gehe ich am besten vor?

1. Schreib in die Mitte des Blattes das Thema und umrahme es mit einem Kreis oder einer Zeichnung.

2. Überleg dir, welche Oberbegriffe zu deiner Sammlung von Ideen passen. Verwende unterschiedliche Farben.

3. Ergänze jede Idee, die zu einem Oberbegriff passt, auf einem Nebenast. Nimm dafür nur Schlüsselwörter – möglichst Nomen oder Verben.

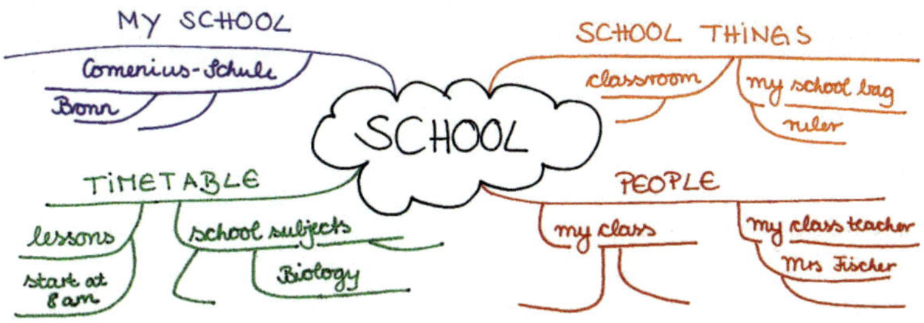

Du kannst statt Wörtern auch Zahlen oder Symbole verwenden und Bilder ergänzen.

Es gibt auch Computerprogramme, mit denen man Mindmaps erstellen kann.

- Alles verstanden? Dann probier doch mal Aufgabe 4 auf S. 42.

SF 4 Wörter nachschlagen (Unit 3)

Wozu ist das Dictionary gut?

Wenn du beim Lesen über ein Wort stolperst, das du noch nicht kennst oder vergessen hast, dann hilft dir das English-German Dictionary (S. 176–188) weiter.
Es enthält alle Wörter und Wendungen, die im Buch vorkommen.

Wie benutze ich das Dictionary?

1. Die blau gedruckten Stichwörter (z.B. **family, fan**) sind alphabetisch angeordnet, (also **f** vor **g**, **fa** vor **fe** und **fla** vor **flo**).

2. Beachte auch die Wörter, die schwarz hervorgehoben sind. Es sind:
- zusammengesetzte Wörter (z.B. **family tree**)
- abgeleitete Wörter (z.B. **finder** von **find**) oder
- längere Ausdrücke (z.B. **the first day**).

3. Zusammengesetzte Wörter und längere Ausdrücke findest du oft unter mehr als einem Stichwort, z.B. **so far** unter **so** und unter **far**.

4. In den eckigen Klammern hinter den Stichwörtern steht, wie das jeweilige Wort ausgesprochen und betont wird. Du bist bei den Lautschriftzeichen unsicher? Dann schau dir S. 145 an.

5. Bei manchen Stichwörtern findest du zusätzliche Hinweise, z.B. auf
- besondere Pluralformen
- Änderungen der Schreibweise, z.B. wenn Endungen wie -ing angefügt werden. In dem Beispiel wird **fit** zu **fitting** (mit Doppel-t).

6. Die Ziffern 1., 2. usw. zeigen, dass das englische Stichwort mehrere unterschiedliche Bedeutungen hat.

- Alles verstanden? Dann probier doch mal Aufgabe 10 auf S. 61.

family ['fæməli] Familie Welc (12/149) • **family tree** (Familien-)Stammbaum 2 (41)
fan [fæn] Fan 6 (106)
°**fancy-dress party** [ˌfænsi'dres] Kostümfest
fantastic [fæn'tæstɪk] fantastisch, toll 4 (81)
far [fɑː] weit (entfernt) 6 (102)
so far bis jetzt, bis hierher 6 (110)
find [faɪnd] finden Welc (10) • **find out (about)** herausfinden (über) 3 (65) • **finder** Finder 5 (91)
finger ['fɪŋgə] Finger 4 (74/169)
finish ['fɪnɪʃ] beenden, zu Ende machen; enden 6 (103)
first [fɜːst] **1.** erste(r, s) Welc (14)
the first day der erste Tag Welc (14)
be first der/die Erste sein 6 (105)
2. zuerst, als Erstes 1 (20)
fish, *pl* **fish** [fɪʃ] Fisch 2 (37/157)
fit (-tt-) [fɪt] *(in der Größe)* passen 3 (54)
flat [flæt] Wohnung Welc (14)
floor [flɔː] Fußboden 5 (98)
flow chart ['fləʊ tʃɑːt] Flussdiagramm 5 (90)
follow ['fɒləʊ] folgen; verfolgen 4 (71)
food [fuːd] **1.** Essen; Lebensmittel 1 (24); **2.** Futter 2 (39)

SF 5 Notizen machen (Unit 4)

Worum geht es beim Notizenmachen?

Oft liest du einen Text oder hörst du eine Geschichte und willst dich später daran erinnern – z.B. weil du etwas vortragen sollst. Dafür ist es hilfreich, wenn du dir in Stichworten *(key words)* Notizen machst.

Wie mache ich Notizen?

Am besten kannst du das an einem Beispiel sehen. Du sollst erzählen, wie jemand in England Halloween feiert. Du hast eine E-Mail mit deinen Fragen an eine englische Freundin geschrieben und diese Antwort bekommen. Schau dir an, wie du das Wichtige markieren und dir Notizen machen könntest.

Dear Maria

Do I have a Halloween party? Yes, I do – every year. I invite some girls from the hockey team and from my class, but I don't invite any boys. It's a girls' party. This year I'm a vampire – that's me in the photo. Mum is a poltergeist. The party usually starts at seven o'clock. We play games like Poltergeist Party or Dance of the Vampires. Then we eat pizza and chocolate cake. My mum always tells a scary story at the end of the party. I like scary stories like 'Dracula'. Mum tells the best scary stories in the world!

Your friend
Anne

Anne: ✔ Halloween party – every year
Invites some girls, but ~~boys~~
Anne: vampire
Starts: 7
Play games, eat pizza + chocolate cake
End of party: mum tells scary story

Tipp

- Verwende Ziffern (z.B. „7" statt „seven").
- Verwende Symbole und Abkürzungen, z.B. ✔ (für Ja) und + (für und). Du kannst auch deine eigenen Symbole erfinden.
- Verwende „not" oder ✗ statt „doesn't" oder „don't".

- Alles verstanden? Dann probier doch mal Aufgabe 8 auf S. 77.

SF 6 Unbekannte Wörter verstehen (Unit 5)

Worum geht es beim Verstehen unbekannter Wörter?

Du liest einen englischen Text und kennst ein paar Wörter nicht? Schlag sie nicht gleich im Wörterbuch nach. Das kostet viel Zeit und kann dir den Spaß am Lesen nehmen. Oft kannst du die Bedeutung von Wörtern selbst herausfinden.

Was hilft mir, unbekannte Wörter zu verstehen?

1. Bilder sind eine große Hilfe. Sie zeigen oft die Dinge, die du in einem Text nicht verstehst. Schau dir das Bild rechts an und lies dann den folgenden Textauszug:

On the fourth day the look-out saw a ship.

Was kann mit 'look-out' gemeint sein?

2. Es gibt viele englische Wörter, die im Deutschen ähnlich geschrieben werden oder ähnlich klingen. Was bedeuten wohl diese Wörter:

cabin • captain • deck • gold • kill • pistol • silver • Spanish • young

3. Manchmal stecken in unbekannten Wörtern bekannte Teile.

singer • **friend**ly • un**happy** • **end**less

4. Oft helfen dir auch die Wörter, die um das unbekannte Wort herum stehen. Kannst du im Beispiel aus dem Zusammenhang verstehen, was mit 'sail' gemeint ist?

'A great ship. Do many men sail on her?' asked the young man.

- Alles klar? Dann probier mal selbst herauszufinden, was **was asleep** in **He was very tired and soon he was asleep** bedeutet.

SF 7 Präsentation (Unit 6)

Worum geht es in einer Präsentation?

Du hast zu einem Thema viel herausgefunden und möchtest es deiner Klasse vorstellen? Du willst, dass deine Mitschüler/innen dir gern und aufmerksam zuhören? Du fragst dich, wie du das erreichen kannst? Die folgenden Hinweise helfen dir dabei.

Wie mache ich eine gute Präsentation?

Vorbereitung
Schreib die wichtigsten Gedanken für dich als Notizen auf (vgl. SF 5), z.B. auf nummerierte Karteikarten oder als Mindmap (vgl. SF 2).

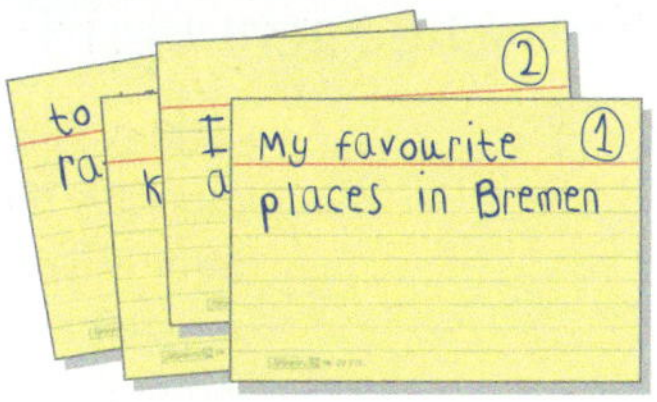

Bereite ein Poster (oder eine Folie) vor, wenn du deinen Vortrag interessanter gestalten willst. Schreib groß und für alle gut lesbar.

Übe deine Präsentation laut zu Hause, z.B. vor einem Spiegel. Das gibt Sicherheit. Sprich dabei laut und langsam.

Durchführung
Bevor du beginnst, häng das Poster auf und sortiere deine Vortragskarten. Stell dich vor deine Zuhörer und warte, bis es ruhig ist. Schau die Zuhörer an.

Erkläre zu Anfang, worüber du sprechen wirst. Lies nicht von deinen Karten ab, sondern sprich frei.

My presentation is about … First, I'd like to talk about … Second, …I'd like to talk about pirates…

Wenn du ein Poster benutzt, zeig während des Vortrags auch darauf.

This picture shows …

Schluss
Wenn du alles vorgestellt hast, was du sagen wolltest, beende deine Präsentation. Frag deine Mitschüler/innen, ob sie noch Fragen haben. Bedank dich fürs Zuhören.

Thank you.

That's the end of my presentation. Have you got any questions?

Die Regeln einer Sprache nennt man „Grammatik" (englisch: *grammar*). Im **Grammar File** (S. 126–144) findest du wichtige Regeln der englischen Sprache. Du kannst hier nachsehen, wenn
– du selbstständig etwas lernen oder wiederholen möchtest,
– du die Übungen aus dem Practice-Teil deines Englischbuchs oder aus dem *Workbook* machst,
– du dich auf einen Test oder eine Klassenarbeit vorbereiten willst.

Die **Abschnitte** 1–22 fassen zusammen, was du in den sechs Units über die englische Sprache gelernt hast.
In der **linken Spalte** findest du **Beispiele**, die dir zeigen, was richtig ist, und **Kästen mit Übersichten**, in denen das Wichtigste zusammengefasst ist.
In der **rechten Spalte** stehen **Erklärungen** und nützliche **Hinweise**.
Besonders wichtig sind die roten **Ausrufezeichen** (**!**). Sie zeigen, was im Deutschen anders ist, und machen auf Fehlerquellen aufmerksam.

Hinweise wie ► *Unit 1 (p. 20) • P 2–3 (pp. 25–26)* zeigen dir, zu welcher Unit und welcher Seite ein **Grammar File**-Abschnitt gehört und welche Übungen du dazu im Practice-Teil findest.

Am Ende eines Abschnitts stellt dir Polly oft eine kleine Aufgabe. Damit kannst du überprüfen, ob du alles richtig verstanden hast. Schreib die Lösungen in dein *exercise book*. Auf S. 144 kannst du deine Antworten überprüfen.

Grammatical terms (Grammatische Fachbegriffe)

adverb of frequency [ˌædvɜːb‿əv ˈfriːkwənsi]	Häufigkeitsadverb
imperative [ɪmˈperətɪv]	Imperativ (Befehlsform)
infinitive [ɪnˈfɪnətɪv]	Infinitiv (Grundform des Verbs)
irregular verb [ɪˌregjələ ˈvɜːb]	unregelmäßiges Verb
negative statement [ˌnegətɪv ˈsteɪtmənt]	verneinter Aussagesatz
noun [naʊn]	Nomen, Substantiv
object [ˈɒbdʒɪkt]	Objekt
object form [ˈɒbdʒɪkt fɔːm]	Objektform (der Personalpronomen)
past [pɑːst]	Vergangenheit
person [ˈpɜːsn]	Person
personal pronoun [ˌpɜːsənl ˈprəʊnaʊn]	Personalpronomen (persönliches Fürwort)
plural [ˈplʊərəl]	Plural, Mehrzahl
positive statement [ˌpɒzətɪv ˈsteɪtmənt]	bejahter Aussagesatz
possessive determiner [pəˌzesɪv dɪˈtɜːmɪnə]	Possessivbegleiter (besitzanzeigender Begleiter)
possessive form [pəˌzesɪv fɔːm]	*s*-Genitiv
present [ˈpreznt]	Gegenwart
present progressive [ˌpreznt prəˈgresɪv]	Verlaufsform der Gegenwart
pronoun [ˈprəʊnaʊn]	Pronomen, Fürwort
pronunciation [prəˌnʌnsiˈeɪʃn]	Aussprache
question [ˈkwestʃən]	Frage(satz)
question word [ˈkwestʃən wɜːd]	Fragewort
regular verb [ˌregjələ ˈvɜːb]	regelmäßiges Verb
short answer [ˌʃɔːt‿ˈɑːnsə]	Kurzantwort
simple past [ˌsɪmpl ˈpɑːst]	einfache Form der Vergangenheit
simple present [ˌsɪmpl ˈpreznt]	einfache Form der Gegenwart
singular [ˈsɪŋgjələ]	Singular, Einzahl
spelling [ˈspelɪŋ]	Schreibweise, Rechtschreibung
subject [ˈsʌbdʒɪkt]	Subjekt
subject form [ˈsʌbdʒɪkt fɔːm]	Subjektform (der Personalpronomen)
subordinate clause [səˌbɔːdɪnət ˈklɔːz]	Nebensatz
verb [vɜːb]	Verb
word order [ˈwɜːd‿ˌɔːdə]	Wortstellung
yes/no question	Entscheidungsfrage

Unit 1

GF 1 Personal pronouns Personalpronomen

Nomen:	boy	girl	pencil

Pronomen:	he	she	it

Nomen stehen für Personen *(boy, girl)*, für Dinge *(pencil)* und für alles, was man nicht sehen und anfassen kann, also für Begriffe wie *name* oder *love*.

Auch **Pronomen (Fürwörter)** können für Personen, Dinge und Begriffe stehen.
Personalpronomen sind:
I, you, he, she, it, we, you, they.

Jack is eleven.
Jack is nice.
▼
He's nice.

Where's my pencil?
My pencil is red.
▼
It's red.

◄ Statt *Jack* und *my pencil* stehen hier die Personalpronomen *he* und *it*.

You are nice. = Du bist nett.
Ihr seid nett.
Sie sind nett.

Übrigens, die deutschen Personalpronomen **du**, **ihr** und **Sie** heißen im Englischen alle ***you***.

Personalpronomen

Bei einer männlichen Person	– he
Bei einer weiblichen Person	– she
Bei einem Ding oder Begriff	– it
Bei einem Haustier	– he oder she
Bei einem Tier ohne Namen	– it
Bei mehreren Personen, Dingen, Tieren	– they

What colour is ...

... **the pencil**? **der** Bleistift
– It's green. = Er ist grün.

... **the school bag**? **die** Schultasche
– It's red. = Sie ist rot.

... **the ruler**? **das** Lineal
– It's brown. = Es ist braun.

! Das Pronomen ***it*** steht für **alle** Dinge.
(Deutsch: „er", „sie", „es")

▸ *Unit 1 (p. 20)* • *P 2–3 (pp. 25–26)*

Hast du alles verstanden? Dann kannst du jetzt die folgende Aufgabe lösen:
Suche die Personalpronomen. Wie viele sind es?

the • pencil • he • are • they • nice • you • your • I • we

Deine Antworten kannst du auf S. 144 überprüfen.

GF 2 The verb *(to) be* Das Verb *(to) be* („sein“)

a) Statements with *be*

Aussagen mit *be*

Wie du siehst, hat das Verb *be* in der Gegenwart *(present)* drei Formen: ***am***, ***are*** und ***is***.

Polly zeigt dir einige Lang- und Kurzformen von *be*.

***be* (present)**

Langformen: +	–	**Kurzformen:** +	–
I am	I am not	I'm	I'm not
you are	you are not	you're	you aren't
he/she/it is	he/she/it is not	he's/she's/it's	he/she/it isn't
we are	we are not	we're	we aren't
you are	you are not	you're	you aren't
they are	they are not	they're	they aren't

Beim Sprechen und in persönlichen Briefen werden meist die Kurzformen von *be* verwendet.

b) Questions with *be*

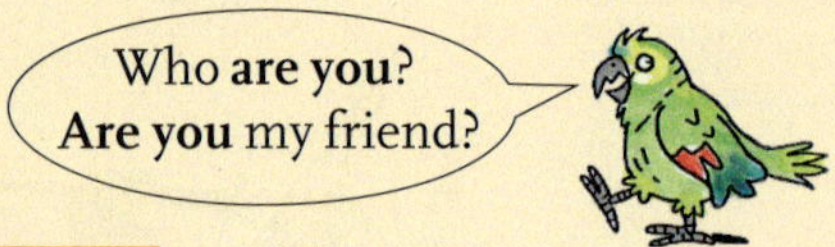

Fragen mit *be*

◄ Du kannst eine Frage **mit** oder **ohne** Fragewort stellen:

Are you my friend? (ohne Fragewort)
Who are you? (mit Fragewort *who*)

Nach einem Fragewort wird *is* oft verkürzt:
Who's that?
Where's my book?
What's your name?

***be* (present)**

Fragen:

Am I ...?	Are we ...?
Are you ...?	Are you ...?
Is he/she/it ...?	Are they ...?

c) Short answers with *be*

Well, are you my friend? Are you my friend?
– No, I'm not ... uhhh ... Yes, I am.

Kurzantworten mit *be*

◄ Fragen ohne Fragewort werden nicht nur mit *Yes* oder *No* beantwortet, das wäre unhöflich. Du solltest eine **Kurzantwort** benutzen, z.B. *Yes, I am* oder *No, I'm not.*

***be* (present)**

Kurzantworten: +	–
Yes, I am.	No, I'm not.
Yes, you are.	No, you aren't.
Yes, he/she/it is.	No, he/she/it isn't.
Yes, we/you/they are.	No, we/you/they aren't.

! Nach *Yes* darfst du keine Kurzform verwenden.
Also nur
Yes, I am.* / *Yes, we are.
usw.

► *Unit 1 (p. 21) • P 4–6 (p. 26)*

Alles klar? Dann löse jetzt diese Aufgabe:
Wie könntest du auf die folgende Frage antworten? Welche Antworten sind üblich?

Are you eleven? – 1 Yes. • 2 Yes, I'm. • 3 Yes, I am. • 4 No. • 5 No, I'm not.

GF 3 *can*

a) Statements with *can* ('können')

Polly can talk, but she can't (cannot) sing.

Jo can play football.
Jo kann Fußball spielen.
Ananda can't play football.
Ananda kann nicht Fußball spielen.

Aussagen mit *can* („können")

◄ Mit *can* und *can't* drückst du aus, was jemand tun kann oder nicht tun kann.
Es heißt immer *can* bzw. *can't*, egal, ob es um *I, you, he* oder *we* usw. geht.

Die Langform von *can't* heißt *cannot*.

! Anders als im Deutschen stehen *can/can't* und das Verb direkt hintereinander.

b) Questions with *can*

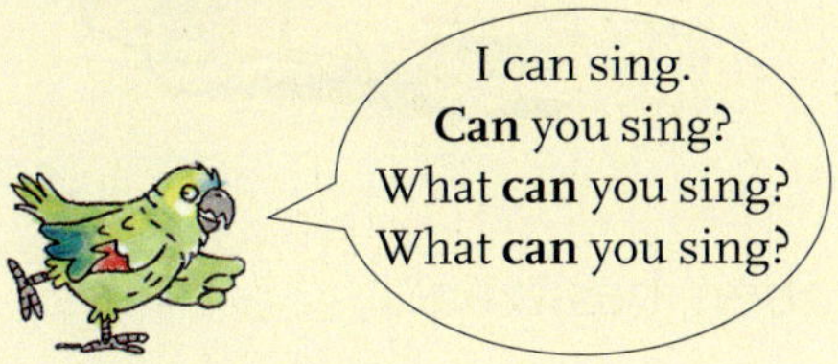

Fragen mit *can*

Fragen mit *can* bildest du so wie im Deutschen:

Can you sing? (ohne Fragewort)
What can you sing? (mit Fragewort *what*)

c) Short answers with *can*

Can you do tricks? – **Yes, I can. / No, I can't.**
Can Polly sing? – **No, she can't.**

can und can't

Bei *can* und *can't* gibt es nur eine Form für alle Personen:
I, you, he/she/it, we, you, they can
I, you, he/she/it, we, you, they can't

▸ *Unit 1 (p. 22) • P 7 (p. 27)*

Kurzantworten mit *can*

◄ So bildest du Kurzantworten mit *can* und *can't*.

d) *can* ('dürfen')

Room 14 is empty. Can we go in?
Raum 14 ist leer. Dürfen wir hineingehen?
We can go in, but we can't write on the board.
Wir dürfen hineingehen, aber wir dürfen nicht an die Tafel schreiben.

can („dürfen")

Mit *can* und *can't* kannst du auch ausdrücken, was jemand tun darf oder nicht tun darf.

Extra

May we go in?
Dürfen wir hineingehen?
May I write on the board?
Darf ich an die Tafel schreiben?

Wenn du besonders höflich um Erlaubnis bitten möchtest, kannst du statt *can* auch *may* benutzen.

GF 4 Imperatives Befehle, Aufforderungen

Come in, please.
Komm/Kommt/Kommen Sie bitte herein.

Write the words on the board, please.
Schreib die Wörter an die Tafel, bitte.

Polly, don't sing. And don't talk, please.
Polly, sing nicht. Und rede bitte nicht.

Befehlsformen

- \+ Sing.
- – Don't sing.

▸ *Unit 1 (p. 23)* • *P 11 (p. 29)*

Wie du siehst, ist die Befehlsform genauso wie der Infinitiv (die Grundform): *Walk*.

Bei einem Verbot (= einem verneinten Befehl) steht *don't* davor: *Don't walk*. (Langform: *Do not walk*.)

◂ Im Englischen gibt es nur eine Befehlsform, egal mit wem du sprichst.

Wenn du jemanden aufforderst, etwas zu tun, solltest du *please* verwenden. Das ist höflicher.

GF 5 The verb *have got* Das Verb *have got* („haben, besitzen")

a) Statements with *have got*

Jack has got a parrot.
Jack hat einen Papagei.

Sophie hasn't got a parrot. She's got a dog.
Sophie hat keinen Papagei. Sie hat einen Hund.

Jo and Dan have got pets too.
Jo und Dan haben auch Haustiere.

Aussagen mit *have got*

Die Form *have got* gilt für *I, you, we* und *they*.

Bei *he/she/it* heißt die Form *has got*.

! – *She's got a dog.* = *She has got a dog.*
(nicht: *She ~~is got~~ a dog.*)
– *She's very nice.* = *She is very nice.*

have got

Langformen: +	–	Kurzformen: +	–
I have got	I have not got	I've got	I haven't got
you have got	you have not got	you've got	you haven't got
he/she/it has got	he/she/it has not got	he's/she's/it's got	he/she/it hasn't got
we have got	we have not got	we've got	we haven't got
you have got	you have not got	you've got	you haven't got
they have got	they have not got	they've got	they haven't got

b) Questions with *have got*

Fragen mit *have got*

Have you got a pet? Has Jack got a pet?

What have you got next?
When have we got Maths today?

! In Fragen steht *got* nach dem Subjekt (*you, Jack, we*).

have got

Fragen:

Have I/you got ...?	Have we/you got ...?
Has he/she/it got ...?	Have they got ...?

c) Short answers with *have got*

Kurzantworten mit *have got*

Have you got a pet? – **Yes, I have. / No, I haven't.**
Has Jack got a pet? – **Yes, he has.**
Has Sophie got a parrot? – **No, she hasn't.**

! 1 Bei der Kurzantwort fällt das *got* weg.
2 Nach *Yes* musst du immer die Langform verwenden.

▸ *Unit 1 (p. 24)* • *P 13–14 (p. 30)*

Jetzt kannst du wieder eine Aufgabe lösen. Welche Sätze sind richtig?

1 Have you got a dog? – Yes, we have.
2 Has he got a pet? – Yes, he has got.
3 Have you got Maths now? – Yes, we've.
4 Has Jack got PE today? – No, he hasn't.

Unit 2

GF 6 The plural of nouns Der Plural der Nomen

a parrot (Singular)  two parrots [s] (Plural) 

Du bildest den Plural (die Mehrzahl) eines Nomens, indem du ein *s* anhängst: **Singular + *s* = Plural**.

Vorsicht bei der **Aussprache der Pluralendung**:

1 beds [bedz] • bags [bægz]
boys [bɔɪz] • trees [triːz]
sisters ['sɪstəz]

◂ 1 Nach **stimmhaften Konsonanten** (Mitlauten), z.B. [d], [g], [n], und nach **Vokalen** (Selbstlauten) klingt das Plural-*s* wie das Summen einer Biene: [z].

2 boxes ['bɒksɪz] • houses ['haʊzɪz]
hutches ['hʌtʃɪz] • cages ['keɪdʒɪz]

◂ 2 Nach **Zischlauten** wie [s], [z], [tʃ], [dʒ] ist die Aussprache [ɪz]. (Je nach Schreibung des Singulars wird ***es*** oder ***s*** angehängt: *box – boxes, cage – cages*.)

baby ▸ babies		family ▸ families	
activity ▸ activities		hobby ▸ hobbies	

! – ***y*** nach einem **Konsonanten** wird zu ***ies***.
(Aber ***y*** nach einem **Vokal** bleibt: *boy* → *boys*.)

one mouse ▸ two **mice** one **tooth** ▸ two **teeth**
one fish ▸ two fish

– Einige Nomen haben **unregelmäßige Pluralformen**.

▸ *Unit 2 (p. 38)* • *P 2 (p. 42)*

GF 7 The simple present Die einfache Form der Gegenwart

a) Positive statements

Bejahte Aussagesätze

I **get up** at 7.15 every morning. Then I **clean** my teeth.

Oh no, Jo. *I* **get up** at 7.15, *I* **clean** my teeth, you **sleep**.

Well, OK. But we **have** breakfast together, then we **go** to school together. Right?

◂ Jo und Dan reden hier über das, was sie regelmäßig tun (*every morning*, „jeden Morgen"). Ihre Sätze stehen im *simple present* (einfache Form der Gegenwart).

Dan and Jo **go** to school together.
Hamsters and rabbits **eat** carrots.

◂ Bei *I, you, we* und *they* haben Verben im *simple present* keine Endung.

Toby **helps** Sophie with Harry, the hamster.
He **cleans** his cage.
Sophie **gives** Sheeba meat and water.
Sheeba **eats** in the kitchen.

◂ Aber bei *he/she/it* (3. Person Singular) wird ein ***s*** angefügt.

He, she, it – das „s" muss mit!

! *can* und *can't* immer ohne ***s***:
*Toby/He **can help** Sophie.*

Simple present

Bejahte Aussagesätze:

I/You	like	apples and bananas.
He/She/It	likes	
We/You/They	like	

Simple present?
He, she, it?
YES, YES! An 's'!

▸ *Unit 2 (p. 39) • P 3, 6–7 (pp. 42–44)*

Versuche jetzt diese Aufgabe zu lösen:
Wo musst du ein **s** *hinzufügen?*

1 I like_ Maths.
2 Jo play_ football.
3 Ananda can_ play_ hockey.
4 Rabbits eat_ carrots.
5 Ben can_ climb_ trees.
6 Sophie feed_ the pets.

b) 3rd person singular: pronunciation and spelling

1 Toby **cleans** the cage. [-nz]
Jack **tells** his friends about Polly. [-lz]
Mrs Shaw **lives** in New Zealand. [-vz]
Ananda **plays** hockey. [-eɪz]

2 Prunella **pushes** Sophie's bed. [-ʃɪz]
After his homework Jack **watches** TV. [-tʃɪz]
Dan **uses** a blue pencil. [-zɪz]

Toby **tries** to help Sophie.
Ananda **copies** sentences from the board.

Sophie **goes** to Cotham School in Bristol.

She **does** her homework in her room. [dʌz]

Prunella **says**, 'Sophie, get up!' [sez]

▸ *Unit 2 (p. 39) • P 5 (p. 43)*

3. Person Singular:
Aussprache und Schreibweise

Wie beim Plural der Nomen (S. 131, GF 6) gibt es ein paar Besonderheiten:

◂ 1 [z] wie das Summen der Biene nach **stimmhaften Konsonanten**, z.B. [n], [l], [v], und nach **Vokalen**,

◂ 2 [ɪz] nach **Zischlauten**, z.B. [ʃ], [tʃ], [z].
(Je nach Schreibung des Infinitivs wird ***s*** oder ***es*** angehängt: *push – pushes, use – uses.*)

! – ***y*** nach einem **Konsonanten** wird zu ***ies***:
try → *tries*, ***copy*** → *copies*.
(Aber ***y*** nach einem **Vokal** bleibt: *play* → *plays*.)

– Die Verben ***do***, ***go*** und ***say*** sind unregelmäßig:
go + es → goes
do + es → does (*I do* [duː] – *she does* [dʌz])
say + s → says (*I say* [seɪ] – *she says* [sez]).

c) Negative statements

I **don't need** your help with the essay, Prunella.
You **don't like** me, Sophie.
We **don't write** essays every day.
Our teachers **don't give** homework every day.

Prunella **doesn't sleep**.
Ananda **doesn't like** the Drama teacher.
Toby **doesn't do** judo on Saturdays.
Dan **doesn't make** his bed every morning.

Verneinte Aussagesätze

◂ Bei *I, you, we* und *they* verneinst du eine Aussage im *simple present* mit ***don't*** **+ Infinitiv** (Grundform).
Die Langform von *don't* heißt *do not*.

◂ Bei *he/she/it* benutzt du jedoch ***doesn't*** **+ Infinitiv**.
Die Langform von *doesn't* heißt *does not*.

! Das ***s*** der 3. Person Singular steckt schon im *doesn't*.
Also nicht: *She doesn't ~~sleeps~~.*

Simple present

Verneinte Aussagesätze:

I	don't	like	apples and bananas.
You	don't	like	
He/She/It	doesn't	like	
We/You/They	don't	like	

Polly says,
In *doesn't* + verb
there's just one 's'!

▸ *Unit 2 (p. 40) • P 10–11 (p. 45)*

Jetzt kannst du diese Aufgabe lösen: Wie heißen die verneinten Formen?

1 We play hockey.
2 Toby does judo.
3 Parrots eat meat.
4 Sophie cleans the cage.

GF 8 Possessive determiners Possessivbegleiter

Sophie This is my room.
Prunella Your room, Sophie? No, it's our room.

Wörter wie *my* („mein") und *our* („unser") zeigen an, wem etwas gehört: ***my** room, **your** room, **our** room.*

Im Kasten findest du alle besitzanzeigenden Begleiter.

Possessivbegleiter (Besitzanzeigende Begleiter)

my	room	*mein Zimmer*	our	room	*unser Zimmer*
your	room	*dein/Ihr Zimmer*	your	room	*euer/Ihr Zimmer*
his	room	*sein Zimmer*	their	room	*ihr Zimmer*
her	room	*ihr Zimmer*			
its	room	*sein/ihr Zimmer*			

Your sister isn't nice. But you're nice.
Deine Schwester ... Aber du bist ...

Their name is Carter-Brown. They're new here.
Ihr Name ... Sie sind ...

▸ *Unit 2 (p. 41) • P 15 (p. 46)*

! Einige Possessivbegleiter kann man leicht mit Kurzformen von *be* verwechseln.
Beachte auch:

– *his* sein/e — *he's* er ist
– *its* sein/e, ihr/e — *it's* er/sie/es ist

GF 9 The possessive form Der *s*-Genitiv

Wenn du sagen willst, dass jemandem etwas gehört, benutzt du den ***s*-Genitiv**.

Englisch: **Jack**'s room
Deutsch: **Jacks** Zimmer

! Anders als im Deutschen wird im Englischen das ***s*** mit einem Apostroph (**'**) angehängt.

Singular: The **dog**'s basket is in the kitchen.
Der Korb des Hundes ...
Our **teacher**'s name is Mr Kingsley.

◂ Im Singular wird ***'s*** an das Nomen angehängt. Für die Aussprache gelten dieselben Regeln wie für das Plural-***s*** (siehe Seite 131, GF 6).

Plural: The **Kapoors**' flat is over the shop.
The **twins**' mum is in New Zealand.

◂ Wenn die Pluralform auf ***s*** endet, hängst du nur einen Apostroph an das Nomen.

This is **Jo and Dan**'s family tree.
Dies ist **Jos** und **Dans** Familienstammbaum.

◂ Bei zwei Personen hängst du nur einmal ***'s*** an, und zwar an das zweite Nomen.

Der *s*-Genitiv

Singular: Nomen + 's (the **dog**'s basket)
Plural: Pluralform des Nomens + ' (the **rabbits**' hutch)

▸ *Unit 2 (p. 41) • P 16 (p. 47)*

Alles klar? Dann löse jetzt diese Aufgabe:
*Wie viele Personen oder Tiere sind es? Sind es **ein** oder **mehrere** Brüder, Kaninchen, Papageien, ...?*

1 **my brother**'s room
2 **my brothers**' room
3 **the rabbits**' hutch
4 **the parrot**'s cage
5 **the twins**' teacher
6 **Jo**'s CDs

Unit 3

GF 10 The simple present Die einfache Form der Gegenwart

a) *Yes/No* questions

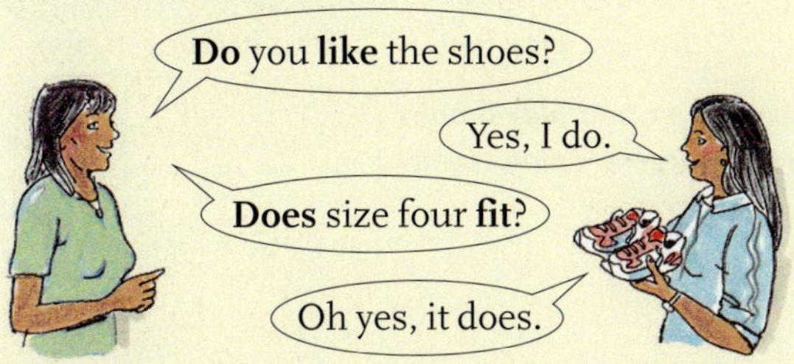

Do you **like** the colour, Ananda?
Do the shoes **look** OK, Mum?
Do we **need** help?

Does Ananda **want** the hockey shoes?
Does she **like** the T-shirt too?
Does it **fit**?

Entscheidungsfragen

Entscheidungsfragen sind Fragen, auf die man mit „Ja" oder „Nein" antworten kann.

◄ Fragen im *simple present* bildet man mit ***do*** oder ***does***:
- ***do*** bei *I, you, we* und *they*,
- ***does*** bei *he/she/it* (3. Person Singular).

Die Wortstellung ist wie beim Aussagesatz:

*We **need** help.* (Aussagesatz)
*Do we **need** help?* (Fragesatz)

! Das ***s*** der 3. Person Singular steckt jetzt im *Does*.
Das Verb steht ohne Endung:

*Size four **fits**.* (Aussagesatz)
Aber: ***Does** size four **fit**?* (Fragesatz)
Nicht: *Does it ~~fits~~?*

Simple present

Entscheidungsfragen:

Do	I	like ...?	Do	we	like ...?
Do	you	like ...?	Do	you	like ...?
Does	he/she/it	like ...?	Do	they	like ...?

Polly says,
In questions with *Does*
there's just one 's'!

► *Unit 3 (p. 54) • P 4–6 (p. 59)*

Stelle Fragen. Frage nach den Personen in Klammern.

1 Jack makes models. (Sophie?)
2 Dan and Jo go swimming. (Ananda and Dilip?)
3 Jack and Sophie like music. (Emily?)

b) Short answers

Do you **get up** early? – **Yes, I** do. / **No, I** don't.
Does Jack **like** computer games? – **Yes, he** does.
Does Ananda **play** football? – **No, she** doesn't.
Do we **need** a pen? – **Yes, we** do. / **No, we** don't.
Do the shoes **fit**? – **Yes, they** do.

► *Unit 3 (p. 54) • P 7 (p. 60)*

Kurzantworten

Entscheidungsfragen werden nicht nur mit *Yes* oder *No* beantwortet, sondern mit einer Kurzantwort:
- bei der Antwort *Yes* mit *do* oder *does*,
- bei der Antwort *No* mit *don't* oder *doesn't*.

Welche Kurzantwort ist richtig?

Does Jack like football? – 1 No, he don't. • 2 No, she doesn't. • 3 No, he doesn't.

c) Questions with question words

When do you **play** tennis, Prunella?
And **where do** you **play**?

How does Uncle Henry **play** without a head?
And **why does** he **take** my racket?

► *Unit 3 (p. 55) • P 8–9 (pp. 60–61)*

Fragen mit Fragewörtern

Fragen, die mit einem Fragewort *(When, Where, What, How, Why)* beginnen, bildest du wie Entscheidungsfragen (siehe Seite 135, GF 10 a):

	***Do** you **play** tennis?*	(Entscheidungsfrage)
When	***do** you **play** tennis?*	(Fragen mit Fragewort)
How	***does** he **play** tennis?*	

Wie heißen die Sätze richtig? Bringe die Wörter in die richtige Reihenfolge.

1 does – When – come – Uncle Henry?
2 Prunella – play – Where – tennis – does?
3 you – do – do – What – in your free time?

GF 11 Adverbs of frequency: word order Häufigkeitsadverbien: Wortstellung

I never **sleep**.
I usually **go** in all the rooms at night.
I sometimes **play** tennis.

Die Häufigkeitsadverbien *always, usually, often, sometimes, never* drücken aus, wie regelmäßig etwas geschieht oder nicht geschieht.

◄ Sie stehen gewöhnlich direkt **vor dem Vollverb** (z.B. *sleep, go, play*).

Jack always **writes** great stories.
Jack schreibt immer tolle Geschichten.

Prunella **can** often **help** Sophie.
Prunella kann Sophie oft helfen.

But Sophie **doesn't** always **need** her help.
Aber Sophie braucht ihre Hilfe nicht immer.

! Anders als im Deutschen stehen Häufigkeitsadverbien nie zwischen Verb und Objekt:

		Verb	Objekt
Jo	*often*	***plays***	***football*** .

	Verb		Objekt
Jo	***spielt***	*oft*	***Fußball*** .

I**'m** usually nice to Sophie.
Emily **is** never nice to her.

◄ Häufigkeitsadverbien stehen **hinter** *am/are/is*.

► *Unit 3 (p. 56) • P 13 (p. 63)*

Und wieder eine kleine Aufgabe: Welches **always** *steht an der richtigen Stelle,* **1** *oder* **2**?

Jay **always** (1) goes **always** (2) to basketball games.

GF 12 The verb *(to) have to* Das Verb *(to) have to* („müssen“)

I **have to** get up early every day.
I **have to** help in the kitchen.

Yes, Jack **has to** get up very early.
He **has to** help. Me too! Me too!

Jack's parents have to **make** breakfast for the guests. But they don't have to **make** lunch.
Jacks Eltern müssen das Frühstück ... machen. Aber sie müssen nicht das Mittagessen machen.

Every evening Jack has to **lay** the table.
But he doesn't have to **go** to yoga.

Do you have to **help** a lot, Jack? – **Yes, I** do.
And does Polly have to **work**? – **No, she** doesn't!

Wenn du ausdrücken willst, was du oder andere tun müssen, benutzt du *have to*.

Bei *he/she/it* (3. Person Singular) heißt es *has to*.

! Das ***to* nach *have*** und ***has*** muss immer dabeistehen.

◂ Verneinte Sätze, Fragen und Kurzantworten werden mit *do/does* gebildet – wie bei anderen Verben auch.

(to) have to

+	–	?
I/you have to	I/you don't have to	Do I/you have to ...?
he/she/it has to	he/she/it doesn't have to	Does he/she/it have to ...?
we/you/they have to	we/you/they don't have to	Do we/you/they have to ...?

▸ *Unit 3 (p. 57) • P 15–16 (pp. 63–64)*

Bringe die Wörter in die richtige Reihenfolge:

1 help – Jack – his mum – has to.
2 doesn't – He – have to – clean – the rooms.
3 he – make – Does – breakfast – have to?

Unit 4

GF 13 Personal pronouns: object forms Personalpronomen: Objektformen

I can't do this homework. You can help me.
You don't know me, but I know you.
There's Jack. **He**'s nice. Can you see him?
Ananda? **She**'s nice. We all like her.
It's my birthday cake. Do you like it?
We go swimming on Fridays. Come with us.
Dan and Jo, **you** like fruit. So this is for you.
The twins? **They** aren't here. I can't see them.

I like her.	Ich mag **sie**.	*(Sophie, meine Lehrerin, ...)*
I like it.	Ich mag **sie**.	*(meine Schule, die Stadt, ...)*
I like them.	Ich mag **sie**.	*(meine Eltern, die Stiefel, ...)*

▸ *Unit 4 (p. 70) • P 3–4 (pp. 75–76)*

◂ Bei den Personalpronomen unterscheiden wir die **Subjektformen** *(I, he, ...)* und die **Objektformen** *(me, him, ...)*.

Anders als im Deutschen gibt es für jede Person nur eine Objektform:
– *You can help me.* *Du kannst **mir** helfen.*
– *You can ask me.* *Du kannst **mich** fragen.*

! Das deutsche „sie“ (Objektform) kann auf Englisch *her*, *it* oder *them* heißen.

GF 14 *some* and *any* — *some* und *any*

We've got **some** crisps and **some** cheese.

Wir haben einige Kartoffelchips und etwas Käse.

◂ *some* steht vor allem in bejahten Aussagesätzen. Es kann „einige" oder „etwas" heißen.

But we haven't got **any** orange juice. Have we got **any** biscuits?

Aber wir haben keinen Orangensaft. Haben wir Kekse?

◂ In verneinten Aussagesätzen und in Fragen steht meist *any*.

! Im Deutschen kann man fragen „Haben wir Kekse?", aber im Englischen wird meist *any* eingefügt: *Have we got any biscuits?*

Yes, of course we've got **some** – with chocolate on.

Ja, natürlich haben wir welche – mit Schokolade.

Angebot: Would you like **some** biscuits?
Möchtest du ein paar Kekse?

Bitte: Can I have **some** juice, please?
Kann ich (etwas) Saft haben, bitte?

! Wenn du mit einer Frage etwas anbietest oder um etwas bittest, verwendest du *some*.

▸ *Unit 4 (p. 71) • P 6–7 (pp. 76–77)*

Sieh dir die Zeichnungen an:
Wo brauchst du some, *wo brauchst du* any?

Toby has got ..., but he hasn't got ...

GF 15 The present progressive — Die Verlaufsform der Gegenwart

a) The simple present and the present progressive

Die einfache Form der Gegenwart und die Verlaufsform der Gegenwart

simple present — I **help** in the kitchen **every day**.

present progressive — **I'm helping** in the kitchen **now**.

Mit dem ***simple present*** (einfache Form der Gegenwart) kannst du über die Gegenwart sprechen, z.B. über das, was jemand jeden Tag tut. (Siehe Seite 132/133, GF 7.)

Wenn du allerdings sagen möchtest, dass jemand **gerade in diesem Moment** etwas tut, musst du das ***present progressive*** (Verlaufsform der Gegenwart) verwenden.
Eine Verlaufsform gibt es im Deutschen nicht.
Wir sagen aber manchmal „Ich bin gerade dabei, fernzusehen" (= *I'm watching TV*).

b) The present progressive: positive and negative statements

Sophie is helping in the kitchen.
Sophie hilft (gerade) in der Küche.
Emily isn't helping.
Emily hilft (gerade) nicht.
Mr Carter-Brown and Toby are watching TV.
Mr Carter-Brown und Toby schauen (gerade) fern.

Sophie You're making a mess, Prunella.
Prunella I'm not making a mess, Sophie. I'm getting things ready for the party.
Sophie But you're dropping mum's plates ...

Die Verlaufsform der Gegenwart: bejahte und verneinte Aussagesätze

Du bildest das *present progressive* mit *am/are/is* + *-ing*-Form des Verbs:
*Sophie **is helping**. Emily **isn't helping**.*

Die *-ing*-Form ist der Infinitiv + *-ing*:
***help** + **ing** = **helping**.*

! Merke aber:

1 Ein stummes ***e*** fällt weg:
make → making, give → giving.

2 Nach einem einzelnen, betonten Vokal (a, e, i, o, u) wird der Konsonant (p, t, g, m, n, ...) verdoppelt:
drop → dropping, get → getting, run → running.

Present progressive

+		–	
I'm	working	I'm not	working
you're		you aren't	
he's/she's/it's		he isn't/she isn't/it isn't	
we're		we aren't	
you're		you aren't	
they're		they aren't	

▸ *Unit 4 (p. 72) • P 9–11 (pp. 78–79)*

Jetzt kannst du wieder eine Aufgabe lösen:
Wie bildest du die -ing-Formen dieser Verben?
*Ordne die Verben den Buchstaben **A** bis **C** zu, z.B. **1 A**.*

1 clean • 2 come • 3 eat • 4 run • 5 make • 6 sit

A: help → helping
B: ride → riding
C: swim → swimming

c) The present progressive: questions and short answers

Are you working, Dad?
– Yes, I am. / No, I'm not.
Is Sophie's mum making a salad?
– Yes, she is. / No, she isn't.
Are Dan and Jo running in the park?
– Yes, they are./ No, they aren't.
What are you doing? – I'm reading.
Where's Jack going? – To the park.

▸ *Unit 4 (pp. 73–74) • P 12 (p. 79)*

Die Verlaufsform der Gegenwart: Fragen und Kurzantworten

In Fragen sind Subjekt *(you, Sophie's mum)* und *am/are/is* vertauscht.

Die Kurzantworten sind genauso wie beim Verb *be* (siehe S. 128, Gf 2 c).

Ein Fragewort *(What, Where)* steht wie im Deutschen am Anfang der Frage.

Bringe die Wörter in die richtige Reihenfolge:

1 Sophie's dad – is – What – watching on TV?
2 What's – doing – Mr Green?

Unit 5

GF 16 The simple past Die einfache Form der Vergangenheit

Before the rehearsal the students were nervous.

Last week Ananda followed Mr Green to the station.
Letzte Woche ist Ananda Mr Green zum Bahnhof gefolgt. /
Letzte Woche folgte Ananda Mr Green zum Bahnhof.

Mit dem *simple past* kannst du über Vergangenes berichten – z.B. wenn du eine Geschichte erzählst.

Mit Zeitangaben wie *last week, yesterday, three days ago* sagst du, **wann** etwas geschehen ist oder **wann** jemand etwas getan hat.

GF 17 The simple past of the verb *(to) be*

Die einfache Form der Vergangenheit des Verbs *(to) be*

Beim *simple past* von *be* gibt es nur zwei Formen:
I, he/she/it *was*
you, we, they *were*

◂ Die verneinten Formen heißen ***wasn't*** und ***weren't***.

◂ Die Frage bildest du mit ***Was I ... / Were you...?*** usw.

◂ Die Kurzantworten heißen ***Yes, I was. / No, you weren't.*** usw.

Where were you after the dress rehearsal?

◂ Fragewörter stehen wie immer am Satzanfang.

► *Unit 5 (p. 86)* • *P 2–4 (pp. 90–91)*

Welche Kurzantwort ist richtig?

Was Sophie in the pirate scene at the end? –
1 No, she was. 2 Yes, she were.
3 Yes, she was. 4 Yes, she wasn't.

GF 18 The simple past: positive statements

Die einfache Form der Vergangenheit: bejahte Aussagesätze

a) Regular verbs

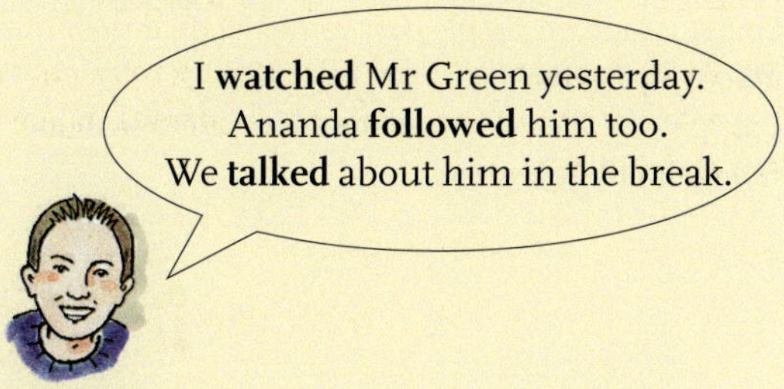

1 Ananda used her mobile a lot yesterday.

2 Jack stopped at Mr Green's door.

3 He tried to hear the woman's voice.

4 He wanted to see who the woman was. She sounded like his mother.

▸ *Unit 5 (p. 87) • P 6–8 (pp. 91–92)*

Regelmäßige Verben

Bei regelmäßigen Verben bildest du das *simple past* durch Anhängen von ***ed*** an den Infinitiv:
watch → *watched* [wɒtʃt],
follow → *followed* ['fɒləʊd],
talk → *talked* [tɔːkt].

Es gibt für **alle** Personen nur eine Form.

! Merke aber:

1 Ein stummes ***e*** fällt weg: *use* → *used*.

2 Einige Konsonanten werden verdoppelt: *stop* → *stopped*, *plan* → *planned* (vergleiche Seite 139, GF 15 b).

3 ***y*** nach einem Konsonanten wird zu ***ied***: ***try*** → *tried*, ***hurry*** → *hurried*. (Aber ***y*** nach einem **Vokal** bleibt: ***play*** → ***played***.)

4 Nach ***t*** und ***d*** wird die ***ed***-Endung [ɪd] ausgesprochen: *wanted*, *sounded*.

b) Irregular verbs

Lots of people went to the Spring Show.
(Infinitiv: **go**)

The Hansons came home late after the show.
(Infinitiv: **come**)

Mr Hanson said, 'The show was great!'
(Infinitiv: **say**)

After the show they had dinner very late.
(Infinitiv: **have**)
One of the pirates had a parrot.
(Infinitiv: **have got**)

▸ *Unit 5 (p. 88) • P 9 (p. 92)*

Unregelmäßige Verben

Wie im Deutschen gibt es auch im Englischen eine Reihe von unregelmäßigen Verben. Jedes unregelmäßige Verb hat eine eigene Form für das *simple past*, die du einzeln lernen musst.

▸ *Liste unregelmäßiger Verben (p. 175)*

! *had* ist die *simple past*-Form von *have* und von *have got*. Also nie: *One of the pirates ~~had got~~ a parrot*, sondern: ... *had a parrot*.

Welche dieser Formen sind simple past-*Formen?*

1 talked • 2 go • 3 had • 4 went • 5 say
6 were • 7 came • 8 tell • 9 looked • 10 told

GF 19 Extra The simple past: negative statements

Die einfache Form der Vergangenheit: verneinte Aussagesätze

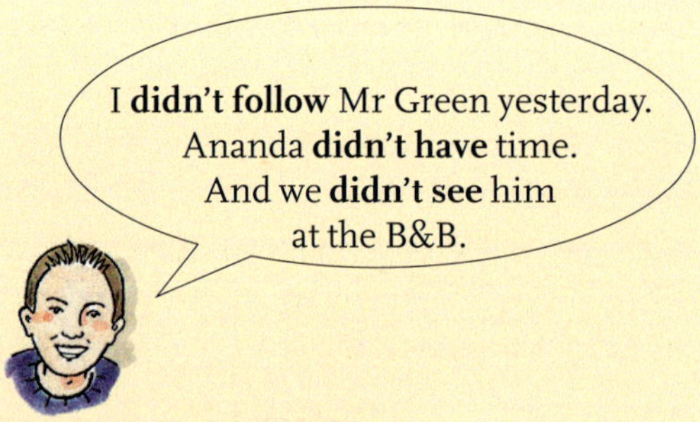

◄ Eine Aussage im *simple past* verneinst du immer mit ***didn't*** + **Infinitiv**.
Dies gilt für alle Personen und für regelmäßige und unregelmäßige Verben.

Verneinte Aussagesätze

Merke:

Simple present	I don't **play** the clarinet.	Jo doesn't **play** the clarinet.
Simple past	I didn't **play** the clarinet.	Jo didn't **play** the clarinet.

► *Unit 5 (p. 89) • P 12–14 (pp. 93–94)*

GF 20 Extra The simple past: questions and short answers

Die einfache Form der Vergangenheit: Fragen und Kurzantworten

Did your dad **go** to the Spring Show, Jo?
– **Yes, he** did. / **No, he** didn't.

Did your parents **like** the show, Jack?
– **Yes, they** did. / **No, they** didn't.

What did all the teachers **say**?
When did the show **finish**?

◄ Fragen im *simple past* bildest du immer mit ***did***:
Did he go?
(Nicht: *Did he ~~went~~?*)

Das Fragewort steht wie immer am Anfang.

Fragen

Merke:

Simple present	Do you **play** the clarinet?	Does Jo **play** the clarinet?
Simple past	Did you **play** the clarinet?	Did Jo **play** the clarinet?

► *Unit 5 (p. 89) • P 15 (p. 94)*

Und jetzt noch eine Aufgabe:
Frage nach den Personen in Klammern.

1 Jack's parents went to the show. (Mr Shaw?)
2 The Carter-Browns liked the show. (The Hansons?)

Unit 6

GF 21 Word order in subordinate clauses Die Wortstellung in Nebensätzen

▸ Unit 6 (p. 103) • P 5–6 (p. 107)

Nebensätze beginnen meist mit Wörtern wie *because, when, that*:
... *because it's quiet.*
... *when it's quiet.*

! Anders als im Deutschen ist die Wortstellung im Nebensatz genauso wie im Hauptsatz, nämlich **Subjekt – Verb (– Objekt)**:

Hauptsatz			Nebensatz			
S	V	O		S	V	O
I	*like*	*the library*	*because*	*I*	*like*	*books.*
		...,	*weil*	*ich*	*Bücher*	*mag.*

Wieder eine kleine Aufgabe: Welches ist der Nebensatz, **A** *oder* **B***?*

1 Jack doesn't go to football matches (A) because he hates sport. (B)

2 When it's hot (A) the Bristol kids often go swimming. (B)

GF 22 The simple present and the present progressive in contrast
Die einfache Form und die Verlaufsform der Gegenwart im Vergleich

◂ Dan redet über das, was die Zwillinge und ihr Vater **regelmäßig** tun. Er verwendet die einfache Form der Gegenwart *(simple present)*.

Wörter wie ***often, usually, on Saturdays, every day*** zeigen dir, dass du die einfache Form verwenden musst.

◂ Jo redet über das, was sie **im Moment** tun oder nicht tun. Er verwendet die Verlaufsform der Gegenwart *(present progressive)*.

Wörter wie ***now*** und ***today*** zeigen dir, dass du die Verlaufsform verwenden musst.

! Verben wie *know, want, need, like, hate, hear, see* werden normalerweise nicht im *present progressive* verwendet.

Simple present and present progressive

Simple present (Einfache Form der Gegenwart)

- Das ***simple present*** drückt aus, dass jemand etwas **wiederholt** tut:
  Dad usually washes the car on Saturdays.
- Das ***simple present*** wird auch verwendet, um **aufeinanderfolgende Handlungen** zu beschreiben, z.B. wenn man eine Geschichte erzählt (oft mit *First …, then …, after that …*):
  First Ananda follows Mr Green to the station, then she watches him. After that she calls Jack on her mobile.

Present progressive (Verlaufsform der Gegenwart)

Das ***present progressive*** drückt aus, dass jemand **gerade im Moment** etwas tut. Die Handlung ist **noch nicht abgeschlossen**:

Look, Polly is cleaning her cage now.

► *Unit 6 (p. 104) • P 8–11 (pp. 108–109)*

Polly is cleaning her cage.

Und jetzt noch eine Aufgabe: Welche Sätze drücken aus, dass jemand gerade etwas tut?

1 Jo sometimes goes to bed late.
2 I'm doing my homework now.
3 Look, you're making a mess with the glue.
4 Mum usually does yoga on Mondays.
5 Ananda is helping her mum and dad in the shop today.

Lösungen der Grammar-File-Aufgaben

p. 127 he, they, you, I, we (5)
p. 128 **3, 5**
p. 131 **1, 4**
p. 132 **2, 6**
p. 133 1 We **don't play** hockey.
2 Toby **doesn't do** judo.
3 Parrots **don't eat** meat.
4 Sophie **doesn't clean** the cage.
p. 134 1 Singular (eine Person)
2 Plural (mehrere Personen)
3 Plural (mehrere Tiere)
4 Singular (ein Tier)
5 Plural (mehrere Personen)
6 Singular (eine Person)
p. 135/1 1 **Does** Sophie **make** models?
2 **Do** Ananda and Dilip **go** swimming?
3 **Does** Emily **like** music?
p. 135/2 3

p. 136/1 1 When does Uncle Henry come?
2 Where does Prunella play tennis?
3 What do you do in your free time?
p. 136/2 1 (Jay always goes to basketball games.)
p. 137 1 Jack has to help his mum.
2 He doesn't have to clean the rooms.
3 Does he have to make breakfast?
p. 138 Toby has got **some** biscuits, but he hasn't got **any** orange juice.
p. 139/1 **1A, 2B, 3A, 4C, 5B, 6C**
p. 139/2 1 What is Sophie's dad watching on TV?
2 What's Mr Green doing?
p. 140 3
p. 141 **1, 3, 4, 6, 7, 9, 10**
p. 142 1 Did Mr Shaw go to the show?
2 Did the Hansons like the show?
p. 143 **1B, 2A**
p. 144 **2, 3, 5**

English sounds (Englische Laute)

Die Lautschrift in den eckigen Klammern zeigt dir, wie ein Wort ausgesprochen und betont wird.
In der folgenden Übersicht findest du alle Lautzeichen.

Vokale (Selbstlaute)

[iː]	gr**ee**n	[eɪ]	sk**a**te
[i]	happ**y**	[aɪ]	t**i**me
[ɪ]	**i**n	[ɔɪ]	b**oy**
[e]	y**e**s	[əʊ]	**o**ld
[æ]	bl**a**ck	[aʊ]	n**ow**
[ɑː]	p**ar**k	[ɪə]	h**ere**
[ɒ]	s**o**ng	[eə]	wh**ere**
[ɔː]	m**or**ning	[ʊə]	t**our**
[uː]	bl**ue**		
[ʊ]	b**oo**k		
[ʌ]	m**u**m		
[ɜː]	T-sh**ir**t		
[ə]	**a** partn**er**		

Konsonanten (Mitlaute)

[b]	**b**ox	[f]	**f**ull
[p]	**p**lay	[v]	**v**ery
[d]	**d**a**d**	[s]	**s**i**s**ter
[t]	**t**en	[z]	plea**s**e
[g]	**g**ood	[ʃ]	**sh**op
[k]	**c**at	[ʒ]	televi**s**ion
[m]	**m**u**m**	[tʃ]	tea**ch**er
[n]	**n**o	[dʒ]	**G**ermany
[ŋ]	si**ng**	[θ]	**th**anks
[l]	he**ll**o	[ð]	**th**is
[r]	**r**ed	[h]	**h**e
[w]	**w**e		
[j]	**y**ou		

Tipp

Am besten kannst du dir die Aussprache der einzelnen Lautzeichen einprägen, wenn du dir zu jedem Zeichen ein einfaches Wort merkst – das [iː] ist der **green**-Laut, das [eɪ] ist der **skate**-Laut usw.

Betonung

['] und [ˌ] sind **Betonungszeichen**.
Sie stehen immer vor der betonten Silbe.

['] zeigt die Hauptbetonung,
[ˌ] zeigt die Nebenbetonung.

Beispiel:
mobile phone [ˌməʊbaɪl 'fəʊn]
Hauptbetonung auf **phone**,
Nebenbetonung auf der ersten Silbe: **mobile**

Der „Bindebogen"

Der **Bindebogen** [‿] zeigt an, dass zwei Wörter beim Sprechen aneinandergebunden und wie ein Wort gesprochen werden.

Beispiele:
What colour is ...? [ˌwɒt 'kʌlər‿ɪz]
Mum and Dad [ˌmʌm‿ən 'dæd]
This is ... ['ðɪs‿ɪz]

The English alphabet (Das englische Alphabet)

a	[eɪ]	**h**	[eɪtʃ]	**o**	[əʊ]	**v**	[viː]
b	[biː]	**i**	[aɪ]	**p**	[piː]	**w**	['dʌbljuː]
c	[siː]	**j**	[dʒeɪ]	**q**	[kjuː]	**x**	[eks]
d	[diː]	**k**	[keɪ]	**r**	[ɑː]	**y**	[waɪ]
e	[iː]	**l**	[el]	**s**	[es]	**z**	[zed]
f	[ef]	**m**	[em]	**t**	[tiː]		
g	[dʒiː]	**n**	[en]	**u**	[juː]		

Diese Wörterverzeichnisse findest du in deinem Englischbuch:

- Das **Vocabulary** (Vokabelverzeichnis – S. 146–175) enthält alle Wörter und Wendungen, die du lernen musst. Sie stehen in der Reihenfolge, in der sie in den Units vorkommen.
- Das **Dictionary** besteht aus zwei alphabetischen Wörterlisten zum Nachschlagen:
  Englisch – Deutsch: S. 176–188
  Deutsch – Englisch: S. 189–197.

So ist das Vocabulary aufgebaut:

- Hier siehst du, wo die Wörter vorkommen.
  p. 21/A 3 = Seite 21, Abschnitt 3
  p. 27/P 7 = Seite 27, Übung 7
- Die Lautschrift zeigt dir, wie ein Wort ausgesprochen und betont wird. (→ Englische Laute: S. 145)
- Eingerückte Wörter lernst du am besten zusammen mit dem vorausgehenden Wort, weil die beiden zusammengehören.
- Diese Kästen solltest du dir besonders gut ansehen.
- In diesen Kästen findest du Wörter und Wendungen, die du sicher schon aus deinem bisherigen Englischunterricht kennst.

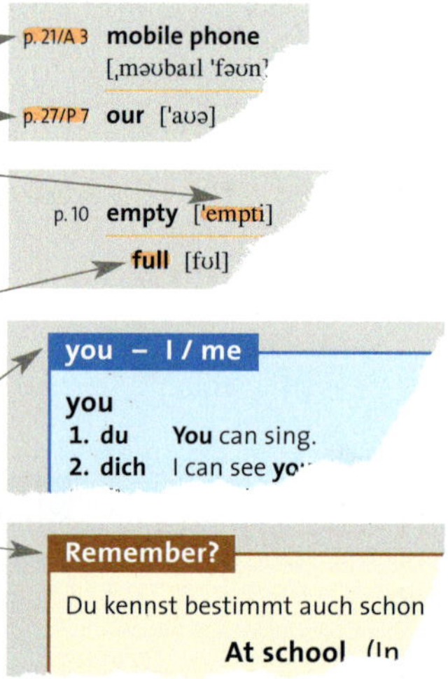

Abkürzungen / Symbole

p.	=	page (Seite)
pp.	=	pages (Seiten)
pl	=	*plural* (Mehrzahl)
no pl	=	*no plural*
jn.	=	jemanden
jm.	=	jemandem
◂▸		ist das „Gegenteil"-Zeichen. Beispiel: **full ◂▸ empty** (**full** ist das Gegenteil von **empty**)
!		Hier stehen Hinweise auf Besonderheiten, bei denen man leicht Fehler machen kann.

Tipps zum Wörterlernen findest du im Skills File auf den Seiten 118 und 119.

'Hello' and 'Welcome'

Remember? (Erinnerst du dich?)

pp. 6–8 Du kennst bestimmt schon viele englische Wörter und Sätze. Hier sind einige, die dir sicher schon begegnet sind.

Hi, I'm Tatjana.	Hallo, ich bin Tatjana.
What's your name?	Wie heißt du?
– Hello. My name is ...	– Hallo. Ich heiße ... / Mein Name ist ...
Where are you from?	Wo kommst du her?
– I'm from ...	– Ich komme aus ... / Ich bin aus ...
My mum and dad are from ...	Meine Mutter und mein Vater kommen aus ...
How old are you?	Wie alt bist du?
– I'm ... years old.	– Ich bin ... Jahre alt.
I've got a brother and a sister.	Ich habe einen Bruder und eine Schwester.
We live in Frankfurt, in ... Street.	Wir wohnen in Frankfurt, in der ...straße.
My favourite colour is ...	Meine Lieblingsfarbe ist ...
I like apples.	Ich mag Äpfel.
I don't like bananas.	Ich mag keine Bananen. / Ich mag Bananen nicht.
Can you sing a song in English?	Kannst du ein Lied auf Englisch singen?
– Yes, I can. / No, I can't.	– Ja, kann ich. / Nein, kann ich nicht.

p. 6	**pretty** [ˈprɪti]	hübsch	
	What about you? [ˌwɒt‿əˌbaʊt ˈjuː]	Und du? / Was ist mit dir?	I'm from Bristol in England. **What about you?**
p. 8	**Welcome (to Bristol).** [ˈwelkəm]	Willkommen (in Bristol).	
	I can talk to ... [tɔːk]	ich kann mit ... reden / ich kann mich mit ... unterhalten	
	my partner [ˈpɑːtnə]	mein Partner / meine Partnerin	

Aussprache

Wie ein englisches Wort ausgesprochen wird, zeigt dir die **Lautschrift**. Sie steht in eckigen Klammern:

- **welcome** ['welkəm]
- **talk** [tɔːk]
- **partner** ['pɑːtnə]

Zwei Dinge kannst du an diesen Beispielen sehen:
Erstens werden englische Wörter oft anders ausgesprochen, als man denkt.
Zweitens enthält die Lautschrift auch ein paar „komische" Zeichen wie [ə], [ɔː] oder [ɑː]:
[ə] ist ein schwaches „e" wie am Ende von „bitt**e**".
[ɔː] kennst du aus dem Wort „baseb**a**ll".
[ɑː] ist ein langes „a" wie in „Kr**a**m".

→ Übersicht über die englischen Laute und Lautschriftzeichen: S. 145

now [naʊ]	nun, jetzt	[aʊ] klingt wie das „au" in „bl**au**".
Meet Jack. [miːt]	Lerne Jack kennen. / Triff Jack.	
this is ['ðɪs‿ɪz]	dies ist	[ð] gibt es im Deutschen nicht. Der Laut klingt etwa so, als ob jemand die weichen „s"-Laute in „**S**en**s**e" lispelt.
he's [hiːz]	er ist	= he is [z] ist ein weiches „s" wie in „le**s**en".
she's [ʃiːz]	sie ist	= she is [ʃ] klingt wie das „sch" in „**sch**ön".
from Bristol **too** [tuː]	auch aus Bristol	! **too** steht am Ende des Satzes.
new [njuː]	neu	new ◄► old
with [wɪð]	mit	
his [hɪz]	sein, seine	
twin brother ['twɪn brʌðə]	Zwillingsbruder	Dan is Jo's **twin brother**. Dan and Jo are **twins**. [ʌ] klingt ähnlich wie das kurze „a" in „K**a**mm".
they're [ðeə] = **they are** [ðeɪ‿ɑː]	sie sind	This is Jo.  This is Dan. **They're** twins.
I can talk about ... [ə'baʊt]	ich kann über ... reden	
page [peɪdʒ]	(Buch-, Heft-)Seite	Abkürzung: **p.** 5 = **page** 5 • **pp.** 5–7 = **pages** 5–7

Remember?

p. 9 Erinnerst du dich an diese Wörter aus deinem bisherigen Englischunterricht?

	it's [ɪts]	er/sie/es ist	= it is
	a great place [ə greɪt 'pleɪs]	ein großartiger Ort/Platz, ein toller Ort/Platz	
	I can see a ... [siː]	ich kann ein/eine ... sehen	[s] ist ein hartes, scharfes „s“ wie in „la**ss**en“.
	photo ['fəʊtəʊ]	Foto	! **auf** dem Foto = **in** the photo [əʊ] kennst du aus dem Wort „Sh**ow**“.
	kite [kaɪt]	Drachen	[aɪ] klingt wie das „ei“ in „Kl**ei**d“.
p. 10	**Park Road** [ˌpɑːk 'rəʊd]	Parkstraße	

a **kite**

Betonung

['] und [ˌ] sind Betonungszeichen.
Sie stehen immer vor der betonten Silbe.

['] zeigt die Hauptbetonung,
[ˌ] zeigt die Nebenbetonung.

Betonungszeichen helfen, die Wörter richtig zu betonen:
– Im Deutschen heißt es ***Park****straße*.
– Im Englischen sagt man *Park* ***Road*** [ˌpɑːk 'rəʊd] (Hauptbetonung auf dem Wort „road“).

	when [wen]	wenn	Are you happy **when** the house is empty?
	empty ['empti]	leer	
	full [fʊl]	voll	full ◂▸ empty
	I close ... [kləʊz]	ich schließe ... / ich mache ... zu	
	thing [θɪŋ]	Ding, Sache	
	I open ... ['əʊpən]	ich öffne ... / ich mache ... auf	open ◂▸ close
	I push ... [pʊʃ]	ich drücke ... / ich schiebe ... / ich stoße ...	
	I pull ... [pʊl]	ich ziehe ...	push ◂▸ pull
	I drop ... [drɒp]	ich lasse ... fallen	[ɒ] klingt wie das „o“ in „B**o**ck“ oder „d**o**ch“.
	then [ðen]	dann, danach	
	I laugh [lɑːf]	ich lache	

you – I / me

you

1. du	**You** can sing.	=	**Du** kannst singen.
2. dich	I can see **you**.	=	Ich kann **dich** sehen.
3. dir	I can play with **you**.	=	Ich kann mit **dir** spielen.

I / me

1. ich	**I** can sing.	=	**Ich** kann singen.
2. mich	Can you see **me**?	=	Kannst du **mich** sehen?
3. mir	Play with **me**.	=	Spiel mit **mir**.

	you look [lʊk]	du schaust / du guckst	
	but [bət, bʌt]	aber	Sophie is a girl, **but** Jack is a boy.
	You can't find me. [faɪnd]	Du kannst mich nicht finden.	
	That's me. [ˌðæts 'miː]	Das bin ich.	
p. 11	**I think** [θɪŋk]	ich glaube / ich meine / ich denke	[θ] gibt es im Deutschen nicht. Der Laut klingt etwa so, als ob jemand den harten „s“-Laut in „be**ss**er“ lispelt. [ŋ] ist wie „ng“ in „Di**ng**“ oder das „n“ in „pi**n**k“.
	That's right. [ˌðæts 'raɪt]	Das ist richtig. / Das stimmt.	
	very nice [ˌveri 'naɪs]	sehr schön, sehr nett	! Das englische „v“ wird wie in „Vampir“ und „Vase“ gesprochen – nicht wie in „Vater“!

You can take the baby. [teɪk]	Du kannst das Baby nehmen.	
You can help me. [help]	Du kannst mir helfen.	
in here [ɪn 'hɪə]	hier drinnen	
Who are you? [hu:]	Wer bist du?	
there [ðeə]	da, dort	
picture ['pɪktʃə]	Bild	! **auf** dem Bild = **in** the picture [tʃ] klingt wie „tsch" in „**tsch**üs".

Remember?

p. 12 Du kennst bestimmt auch schon viele englische Wörter zu den Themen „Schule" und „Familie":

At school (In der Schule)

a classroom

A family [1]

Mr[2] Scott, the father (dad) — **Mrs[3] Scott, the mother (mum)**

Sally Scott, Philip's sister — **Philip Scott, Sally's brother**

Their pets: Bob, the dog — **Bella, the cat**

Their friends: Jennifer Ray — **Robbie Carter**

The Scotts live in Bristol.
Die Scotts leben/wohnen in Bristol.

[1] a family – two families • [2] Mr ['mɪstə] • [3] Mrs ['mɪsɪz]

at 7 Hamilton Street [stri:t]	in der Hamiltonstraße 7	
their father / their mother [ðeə]	ihr Vater / ihre Mutter	Dan and Jo and **their** father 
today [tə'deɪ]	heute	
the last day [ˌlɑ:st 'deɪ]	der letzte Tag	
of the summer holidays [əv ðə ˌsʌmə 'hɒlədeɪz]	der Sommerferien	
Sorry, I'm late. ['sɒri], [leɪt]	Entschuldigung, dass ich zu spät bin/komme.	
shopping list ['ʃɒpɪŋ lɪst]	Einkaufsliste	
Let's look at the list. [lets]	Sehen wir uns die Liste an. / Lasst uns die Liste ansehen.	
you need ... [ni:d]	du brauchst ... / du benötigst ...	
Me too. [tu:]	Ich auch.	I need a new school bag. – **Me too**.
pencil sharpener ['pensl ʃɑ:pnə]	Bleistiftanspitzer	a **pencil sharpener** 

exercise book ['eksəsaɪz bʊk]	Schulheft, Übungsheft	
exercise ['eksəsaɪz]	Übung, Aufgabe	
for school [fə, fɔː]	für die Schule	I need a glue stick **for school**, Dad.
Let's go. [ˌlets 'gəʊ]	Auf geht's! (*wörtlich:* Lass uns gehen.)	
you two	ihr zwei	
I can say ... [seɪ]	ich kann ... sagen	

Remember?

p. 13

What colour is ...? [ˌwɒt 'kʌlər‿ɪz]	Welche Farbe hat ...?	**What colour is** your pencil? – It's green. And **what colour is** your school bag? – It's red.

Aussprache

Der **Bindebogen** [‿] zeigt an, dass zwei Wörter beim Sprechen aneinandergebunden und wie ein Wort gesprochen werden.

What colour is ...? [ˌwɒt 'kʌlər‿ɪz]
Mum and Dad [ˌmʌm‿ən 'dæd]
This is ... ['ðɪs‿ɪz]

plate [pleɪt]	Teller	a **plate** 
Oh well ... [əʊ 'wel]	Na ja ... / Na gut ...	

Remember?

p. 14

The days of the week

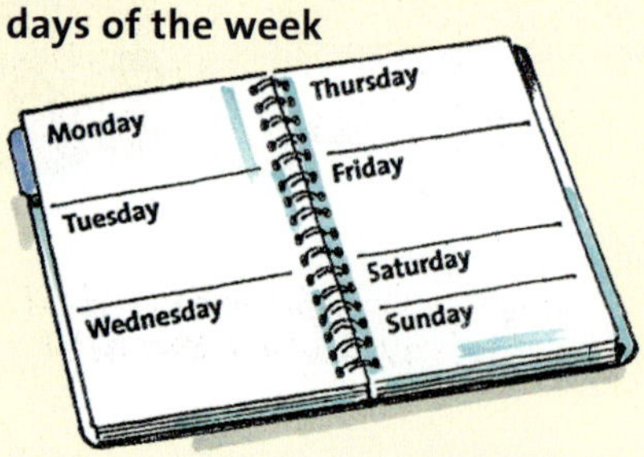

It's Monday morning ...

flat [flæt]	Wohnung	
over the shop [ˌəʊvə ðə 'ʃɒp]	über dem Laden / über dem Geschäft	
Well, ... [wel]	Nun, ... / Also, ...	**Well,** is your new school nice?
uniform ['juːnɪfɔːm]	Uniform	
tomorrow [tə'mɒrəʊ]	morgen	

	the first day [fɜ:st]	der erste Tag	[ɜ:] kennst du aus dem Wort „T-Sh**ir**t“. (Nicht das „r“ mitsprechen!)
	at the new school	an/auf der neuen Schule	
	Stop that! ['stɒp ðæt]	Hör auf damit! / Lass das!	
	You can go to the shop. [gəʊ]	Du kannst zum Laden gehen.	
	Why me? [waɪ]	Warum ich?	You can help your father now. – **Why me?**
	poem ['pəʊɪm]	Gedicht	
	week [wi:k]	Woche	
p. 15	**newspaper** ['nju:speɪpə]	Zeitung	
	I can have breakfast. [həv 'brekfəst]	Ich kann frühstücken.	
	o [əʊ], **zero** ['zɪərəʊ]	null	**!** Wenn man seine Telefonnummer sagt, benutzt man **o** [əʊ]: 5 0 7 9 ... = five **o** seven nine ...
	double ['dʌbl]	zweimal, doppelt, Doppel-	My phone number is 5 0 7 9 3 3 2. (five o seven nine **double** three two)
	I can do tricks. [du: 'trɪks]	Ich kann (Zauber-)Kunststücke (machen).	
p. 16	**Bed and Breakfast (B&B)** [ˌbed‿ən 'brekfəst]	Frühstückspension (*wörtlich:* Bett und Frühstück)	
	parrot ['pærət]	Papagei	
	They welcome you to ...	Sie heißen dich in ... willkommen	
	wheelchair ['wi:ltʃeə]	Rollstuhl	[eə] kennst du aus dem Wort „f**air**“. (Nicht das „r“ mitsprechen!)
	at work [wɜ:k]	bei der Arbeit / am Arbeitsplatz	

Remember?

What's the time? (Wie spät ist es?)

It's eleven o'clock.	**It's quarter past 11.** (*oder:* **11.15**)	**It's half past 11.** (*oder:* **11.30**)	**It's quarter to 12.** (*oder:* **11.45**)

! 
Englisch: **half <u>past</u> 11**
Deutsch: **halb <u>zwölf</u>**

p. 17	**Excuse me, ...** [ɪk'skju:z mi:]	Entschuldigung, ... / Entschuldigen Sie, ...

„Entschuldigung“

Excuse me, ...
sagt man, wenn man jemanden anspricht, z.B. wenn man um etwas bittet:
Excuse me, what's the time, please?

Sorry, ...
sagt man, wenn man sich für etwas entschuldigen möchte:
Sorry, I'm late.

You're welcome.	Gern geschehen. / Nichts zu danken.	

welcome

• Wenn du jemanden willkommen heißen willst:	**Welcome to** Germany!	**Willkommen in** Deutschland!
• Wenn sich jemand bei dir bedankt hat:	*A:* What's the time, please? *B:* Half past seven. *A:* Thank you. *B:* **You're welcome.**	*A:* Wie spät ist es, bitte? *B:* Halb acht. *A:* Danke. *B:* **Bitte, gern geschehen. / Nichts zu danken.**

! Nie: **Thank you. – ~~Please~~.** Sondern: **Thank you. – You're welcome.**

Good luck (with ...)! [ˌgʊd ˈlʌk]	Viel Glück (bei/mit ...)!	
trip [trɪp]	Reise; Ausflug	
back to Germany [ˌbæk tə ˈdʒɜːməni]	zurück nach Deutschland	[dʒ] kennst du aus „Job" und „Jeans".

Unit 1: New school, new friends

Remember?

p. 18 Hier sind wieder einige Wörter, die du wahrscheinlich schon kennst.

lots of [ˈlɒts‿əv]	eine Menge, viele, viel	
comic [ˈkɒmɪk]	Comic-Heft	I've got **lots of comics**. 
there's [ðəz, ðeəz]	es ist (vorhanden); es gibt	= there is
there are [ˈðər‿ə, ˈðeər‿ɑː]	es sind (vorhanden); es gibt	

There's ... / There are ...

Du kennst bereits **there** (= „da, dort"): **That's your room there.**

Mit **There's ...** und **There are ...** kannst du ausdrücken, ob etwas vorhanden ist oder nicht.
Im Deutschen sagt man meist „Es gibt ..." oder „Es ist/sind ...".

There's a football in my photo. But **there isn't a** skateboard in my photo.	Auf meinem Foto **ist ein** Fußball. Aber **es ist kein** Skateboard auf meinem Foto.
Are there skateboards in your photo? – Yes, **there are**. / No, **there aren't**.	**Gibt es** Skateboards auf deinem Foto? – Ja (, **gibt es**). / Nein (, **gibt es nicht**).
There are three books on the table.	**Es sind/Es liegen** drei Bücher auf dem Tisch.

! Nie: ~~It gives~~ ..., sondern immer: **There's ... / There are ...**

marmalade [ˈmɑːməleɪd]	(Orangen-)Marmelade	! Deutsch: Marmelade – Englisch: marmalade

p. 19	**in the morning**	am Morgen, morgens	
	word [wɜːd]	Wort	
	box [bɒks]	Kasten, Kästchen, Kiste	
	milk [mɪlk]	Milch	
	mobile phone [ˌməʊbaɪl ˈfəʊn]	Mobiltelefon, Handy	**!** Deutsch: **Handy** Englisch: **mobile phone** oder **mobile**
p. 20/A 1	**before** [bɪˈfɔː]	vor *(zeitlich)*	
	lessons [ˈlesnz]	Unterricht	
	lesson [ˈlesn]	(Unterrichts-)Stunde	
	student [ˈstjuːdənt]	Schüler/in; Student/in	
	nervous [ˈnɜːvəs]	nervös, aufgeregt	
	first [fɜːst]	zuerst, als Erstes	
	clever [ˈklevə]	klug, schlau	
	mad [mæd]	verrückt	
	Don't listen to Dan. [dəʊnt]	Hör nicht / Hört nicht auf Dan.	
	Come. [kʌm]	Komm. / Kommt.	
	Sit with me. [sɪt]	Setz dich / Setzt euch zu mir.	
p. 20/A 2	**wrong** [rɒŋ]	falsch, verkehrt	That's wrong. ◄► That's right.
	(It's) my turn. [tɜːn]	Ich bin dran / an der Reihe.	First it's **my turn**, then it's **your turn**.
p. 21/A 3	**our** [ˈaʊə]	unser, unsere	We're twins. **Our** names are Dan and Jo.
	her [hə, hɜː]	ihr, ihre	Ananda is from Bristol. **Her** dad is from Uganda.
	together [təˈgeðə]	zusammen	
	I'm sorry.	Entschuldigung. / Tut mir leid.	

sorry

Mit **sorry** kannst du ...

• dich entschuldigen:	**Sorry**, I'm late.	**Entschuldigung**, dass ich zu spät komme.
• sagen, dass dir etwas leidtut:	My mum and dad aren't together. – Oh, **I'm sorry.**	Meine Mutter und mein Vater sind nicht zusammen. – Oh, **das tut mir leid**.
• nachfragen, wenn du etwas nicht richtig verstanden hast:	It's eleven o'clock. – **Sorry?**	Es ist elf Uhr. – **Wie bitte?**

teacher [ˈtiːtʃə]	Lehrer/Lehrerin	Mr Keller is my English **teacher**.

Remember?

p. 22

p. 22/A 6	**form** [fɔːm]	(Schul-)Klasse	Ananda is in **Form** 7PK.
	Tell me your names. [tel]	Sagt mir eure Namen.	**Tell** your teacher **about** your pets. (= Erzähle ... von ... / Berichte ... über ...)
	PE [ˌpiː‿ˈiː]	Sportunterricht, Turnen	
	enough [ɪˈnʌf]	genug	
	quiet [ˈkwaɪət]	leise, still, ruhig	
	joke [dʒəʊk]	Witz	Can you tell me a **joke**? I like **jokes**.
	bad [bæd]	schlecht, schlimm	bad ◄► good
	Can you remember that? [rɪˈmembə]	Kannst du dir das merken?	
p. 22/A 8	**alphabet** [ˈælfəbet]	Alphabet	
	Throw a ball. [θrəʊ]	Wirf einen Ball.	
	Climb a tree. [klaɪm]	Klettere auf einen Baum.	Can cats **climb** trees? – Yes, they can. ! Das „b" wird nicht gesprochen: **climb** [klaɪm].
	Write ... [raɪt]	Schreibe ...	
	Do what I do. [duː]	Tue, was ich tue.	
p. 22/A 9	**Spell ...** [spel]	Buchstabiere ...	
p. 23/A 10	**timetable** [ˈtaɪmteɪbl]	Stundenplan	
	Take out ... [ˌteɪk‿ˈaʊt]	Nehmt ... heraus	**Take out** your English books, please.
	Write down ... [ˌraɪt ˈdaʊn]	Schreibt ... auf	
	at 8.45 [ət, æt]	um 8.45	
	on Tuesday	am Dienstag	

on

The first lesson **on Tuesday** is English.	Die erste Stunde **am** Dienstag ist Englisch.
Write the words **on the board**, please.	Schreib die Wörter **an** die Tafel, bitte.
Write your names **on your exercise books**, please.	Schreibt eure Namen **auf** eure Hefte, bitte.
Your ruler is **on your chair**.	Dein Lineal liegt **auf** deinem Stuhl.
Look at the pictures **on page 24**.	Seht euch die Bilder **auf** Seite 24 an.

with [wɪð]	bei	! **with** = **1.** mit – Look, there's Jo **with** his brother. **2.** bei – It's English **with** Mr Kingsley.

School subjects [1]

Art [ɑːt]	Kunst	**Maths** [mæθs]	Mathematik
Biology [baɪˈɒlədʒi]	Biologie	**Music** [ˈmjuːzɪk]	Musik
Drama [ˈdrɑːmə]	Schauspiel, darstellende Kunst	**PE** [2] [ˌpiː‿ˈiː]	Sportunterricht, Turnen
French [frentʃ]	Französisch	**RE** [3] [ˌɑːr‿ˈiː]	Religion, Religionsunterricht
Geography [dʒiˈɒgrəfi]	Geografie, Erdkunde	**Science** [ˈsaɪəns]	Naturwissenschaft
German [ˈdʒɜːmən]	Deutsch		
History [ˈhɪstri]	Geschichte		

[1] [ˈsʌbdʒɪkts] Schulfächer [2] Physical Education [ˌfɪzɪkəl‿edʒuˈkeɪʃn] [3] Religious Education [rɪˌlɪdʒəs‿edʒuˈkeɪʃn]

	after [ˈɑːftə]	nach *(zeitlich)*	after school ◄► before school
	break [breɪk]	Pause	Morning **break** is at 10.45 at Cotham School.
p. 23/A 11	**lunch** [lʌntʃ]	Mittagessen	**Lunch** is at 1.05.

p. 24/A 13	**food** [fu:d]	Essen; Lebensmittel	
	really ['rɪəli]	wirklich	
	I haven't got a chair. ['hævnt gɒt]	Ich habe keinen Stuhl.	I've got a sister, but **I haven't got a** brother.

at

Let's sit **at that table** there.	Setzen wir uns **an** den Tisch dort.
Look **at the board**, please.	Seht **an** die Tafel, bitte.
Let's look **at the list** now.	Sehen wir uns jetzt mal die Liste **an**.
The Shaws live **at 7 Hamilton Street**.	... **in** der Hamiltonstraße 7
Jo and Dan are **at school**, and Mrs Hanson is **at work**.	... **in** der Schule, ... **bei** der Arbeit
At 8.45 it's English with Mr Kingsley.	**Um** 8.45 ...

	bank robber ['bæŋk ˌrɒbə]	Bankräuber/in	
	all [ɔ:l]	alle; alles	Sophie, Ananda, Jack – they're **all** in Form 7PK. We need pens, felt tips and pencils. That's **all**.
	like [laɪk]	wie	My pencil case is **like** your pencil case.
	him [hɪm]	ihn; ihm	! **him** = **1.** ihn – There's Jack. Can you see **him**? **2.** ihm – Let's help **him**.
	idea [aɪ'dɪə]	Idee, Einfall	[ɪə] klingt wie das „ier" in „**hier**".
	What have we got next? [nekst]	Was haben wir als Nächstes?	
p. 24/A 14	**class** [klɑ:s]	(Schul-)Klasse	I'm in **class** 5 now, and my sister is in **class** 8.
p. 25/P 1	**different (from)** ['dɪfrənt]	verschieden, unterschiedlich; anders (als)	Cats and dogs are **different** – cats can climb, but dogs can't. Cats are **different from** dogs. ! anders **als** = different **from**

Classroom English

p. 28/P 9

Can we +work with a partner?	Können wir mit einem Partner/einer Partnerin arbeiten?
+What page are we on, please?	Auf welcher Seite sind wir, bitte?
+What's for homework? ['həʊmwɜ:k]	Was haben wir als Hausaufgabe auf?
Sorry, +I haven't got my exercise book.	Entschuldigung, ich habe mein Heft nicht dabei.
Can I help you with the +worksheets? ['wɜ:kʃi:ts]	Kann ich dir bei den Arbeitsblättern helfen?
Write +sentences in your exercise book. ['sentənsɪz]	Schreibt Sätze in euer Heft.
Can I open/close the +window, please? ['wɪndəʊ]	Kann ich bitte das Fenster öffnen/schließen?
Can I go to the +toilet, please? ['tɔɪlət]	Darf ich zur Toilette gehen, bitte?

+ = new words

	or [ɔ:]	oder	Is Sophie in Form 7PK **or** in Form 7BW?

How's the new school?

p. 32	**end** [end]	Ende	
	Hurry up. [ˌhʌri_'ʌp]	Beeil dich.	
	poor Sophie [pɔ:, pʊə]	(die) arme Sophie	[ʊə] klingt wie das „ur" in „**Kur**". (Nicht das „r" sprechen!)
	Come in. [ˌkʌm_'ɪn]	Komm rein/herein.	
	everything ['evriθɪŋ]	alles	

	tea [tiː]	Tee; *(auch:) leichte Nachmittags- oder Abendmahlzeit*	
	classmate ['klɑːsmeɪt]	Klassenkamerad/in, Mitschüler/in	
p. 33	How **was ...?** [wəz, wɒz]	Wie war ...?	How **was** the first day at your new school?
	world [wɜːld]	Welt	
	See you.	Bis bald. / Tschüs.	
	Go on. [ˌgəʊ_'ɒn]	Mach weiter. / Erzähl weiter.	
	a packet of mints [ə ˌpækɪt_əv 'mɪnts]	ein Päckchen/eine Packung Pfefferminzbonbons	
	little ['lɪtl]	klein	
	Bye. [baɪ]	Tschüs!	Bye./Goodbye. ◄► Hi./Hello.
	more [mɔː]	mehr	
	Dilip likes ...	Dilip mag ...	I like tennis, and my brother **likes** football.
	her [hə, hɜː]	sie; ihr	! **her** = **1.** sie – There's Sophie. I can see **her**. **2.** ihr – Let's help **her**. **3.** ihr, ihre – There's Ananda and **her** dad. Where's **her** mum?
	He likes her **a lot.** [ə 'lɒt]	Er mag sie sehr.	

Topic 1: Make a birthday calendar

Remember?

p. 35

The months[1] of the year

[1] [mʌnθs]

1 **January** ['dʒænjuəri]
2 **February** ['februəri]
3 **March** [mɑːtʃ]
4 **April** ['eɪprəl]
5 **May** [meɪ]

6 **June** [dʒuːn]
7 **July** [dʒu'laɪ]

8 **August** ['ɔːgəst]
9 **September** [sep'tembə]
10 **October** [ɒk'təʊbə]
11 **November** [nəʊ'vembə]

12 **December** [dɪ'sembə]

Make a calendar. [ˌmeɪk_ə 'kælɪndə]	Mache/Baue einen Kalender.	Let's **make a calendar** for our classroom. ! Deutsch: <u>K</u>alend<u>e</u>r – Englisch: <u>c</u>alend<u>a</u>r
birthday ['bɜːθdeɪ]	Geburtstag	! Deutsch: Ich **habe** im Mai Geburtstag. Englisch: My birthday **is** in May. (Nicht: ~~I've got birthday~~ ... / ~~I have birthday~~ ...)
when?	wann?	! **when** = **1.** wann; **2.** wenn

birthdays

My birthday **is** in May. **When's** your birthday?
– My birthday is in June. **On** 13th June.

Ich **habe** im Mai Geburtstag. **Wann hast** du Geburtstag?
– Ich habe im Juni Geburtstag. **Am** 13. Juni.

! Du schreibst: **on 13th June** – Du sagst: **on <u>the</u> thirteenth <u>of</u> June**

date [deɪt]	Datum

Unit 2: A weekend at home

p. 36	**weekend** [ˌwiːkˈend]	Wochenende	
	at home [ət ˈhəʊm]	daheim, zu Hause	

home

Dan is **at home**.	Dan ist **zu Hause**.
Jo, **come home**!	Jo, komm **nach Hause**!
Go home now.	Geh jetzt **nach Hause**.

Remember?

[1][ʃelf] • [2][ʃelvz]

I **share** a room **with ...** [ʃeə]	Ich teile mir ein Zimmer mit ...	
people [ˈpiːpl]	Menschen, Leute	The **people** in Bristol are very nice.
garden [ˈgɑːdn]	Garten	! Deutsch: Gar**t**en – Englisch: gar**d**en
desk [desk]	Schreibtisch	

Remember?

p. 37

[1][maɪs] • [2][maʊs] • [3][ˈgɪni pɪg]

	hutch [hʌtʃ]	(Kaninchen-)Stall	
	basket [ˈbɑːskɪt]	Korb	
	cage [keɪdʒ]	Käfig	
	budgie [ˈbʌdʒi]	Wellensittich	a **budgie** 
	tortoise [ˈtɔːtəs]	Schildkröte	a **tortoise** 
p. 38	**I can act** the song. [ækt]	Ich kann das Lied aufführen.	
	I **clean my teeth.** [kliːn], [tiːθ]	Ich putze mir die Zähne.	**Clean your teeth**, Jack. Dan, can you **clean** the bathroom, please?
	tooth [tuːθ], *pl* **teeth** [tiːθ]	Zahn	one **tooth**  lots of **teeth** 

I **wash my face**. [wɒʃ]	Ich wasche mir das Gesicht.	**Wash your face**, Jack. Dan, can you **wash** the car, please?
early ['ɜ:li]	früh	early ◄► late
p. 38/A 1 **afternoon** [ˌɑ:ftə'nu:n]	Nachmittag	

The day: morning – afternoon – evening – night

morning ['mɔ:nɪŋ]	Morgen, Vormittag	**evening** ['i:vnɪŋ]	Abend
afternoon [ˌɑ:ftə'nu:n]	Nachmittag	**night** [naɪt]	Nacht, später Abend

in the morning	morgens, am Morgen	**on Friday morning**	freitagmorgens, am Freitagmorgen
in the afternoon	nachmittags, am Nachmittag	**on Friday afternoon**	freitagnachmittags, am Freitagnachmittag
in the evening	abends, am Abend	**on Friday evening**	freitagabends, am Freitagabend
! **at night**	nachts, in der Nacht	**on Friday night**	freitagnachts, Freitagnacht
at the weekend	am Wochenende		

plan [plæn]	Plan	
essay (about, on) ['eseɪ]	Aufsatz (über)	Write an **essay about** Bristol.
life [laɪf], *pl* **lives** [laɪvz]	Leben	! We **live** in ... [lɪv] – Wir **leben/wohnen** in ... **life** in Bristol [laɪf] – **das Leben** in Bristol
easy ['i:zi]	leicht, einfach	
difficult ['dɪfɪkəlt]	schwierig, schwer	
I **get up** at ... [ˌget_'ʌp]	ich stehe um ... auf	
(to)[1] **get up**	aufstehen	
every ['evri]	jeder, jede, jedes	I get up at 6.45 **every** morning.
(to) **sleep** [sli:p]	schlafen	
hand [hænd]	Hand	
boring ['bɔ:rɪŋ]	langweilig	
bus [bʌs]	Bus	a **bus** 
(to) **read** [ri:d]	lesen	
p. 39/A 2 (to) **get dressed** [ˌget 'drest]	sich anziehen	First I clean my teeth, then I **get dressed**.
(to) **give** [gɪv]	geben	
(to) **feed** [fi:d]	füttern	
meat [mi:t]	Fleisch	Dogs eat **meat**.
carrot ['kærət]	Möhre, Karotte	
(to) **watch** [wɒtʃ]	beobachten, sich etwas ansehen; zusehen	
(to) **watch TV** [ti:'vi:]	fernsehen	TV = television ['telɪvɪʒn] ! **im** Fernsehen = **on** TV: a good film **on TV**

(to) look – (to) see – (to) watch

Look. Can you **see** Sheeba? – Yes, I can **see** her.	**Schau./Guck mal**. Kannst du Sheeba **sehen**? – ...
Toby **watches** Sophie.	Toby **beobachtet** Sophie. / Toby **schaut** Sophie **zu**.
Don't **watch TV** now, Dan. You've got homework.	**Sieh** jetzt nicht **fern**, Dan. ...

[1] Mit dem vorangestellten **(to)** kennzeichnen wir den Infinitiv (die Grundform) des Verbs.

	(to) **try to do** [traɪ]	versuchen, zu tun	Let's **try to play** my new game. (*or:* Let's **try and play** my new game.)
	(to) **put** [pʊt]	legen, stellen, *(etwas wohin)* tun	**Put** all the photos in the box. 
	after that	danach	First I feed the pets. **After that** I have my breakfast.
	food [fu:d]	Futter	**!** **food** = **1.** Essen, Lebensmittel; **2.** Futter
p. 39/A 3	**bowl** [bəʊl]	Schüssel; *hier:* Goldfischglas	a **bowl**  a goldfish **bowl**
	all day / all the time	den ganzen Tag (lang) / die ganze Zeit	
	(to) **drink** [drɪŋk]	trinken	
p. 40/A 5	**Thanks.** [θæŋks]	Danke.	= Thank you.
	help	Hilfe	**!** **help** = **1.** helfen; **2.** Hilfe
	of course [əv 'kɔ:s]	natürlich, selbstverständlich	Is Prunella a Poltergeist? – Yes, **of course** she is.
	Here you are. [ˌhɪə ju:‿'ɑ:]	Bitte sehr. / Hier bitte.	

„bitte"

– in Bitten und Aufforderungen:	**please**	→	What's the time, **please**? / Open the window, **please**.
– wenn du jemandem etwas gibst:	**Here you are.**	→	Can you give me that pen, please? – **Here you are.**
– wenn sich jemand bei dir bedankt:	**You're welcome.**	→	Thank you. – **You're welcome.**
– wenn du etwas nicht richtig verstanden hast (**„Wie bitte?"**):	**Sorry?**	→	Where are the twins? – **Sorry?**

	This is **all wrong.**	Das ist ganz falsch.	Can I see your homework? – Oh no, it's **all wrong**.
	sometimes ['sʌmtaɪmz]	manchmal	
	(to) **argue** ['ɑ:gju:]	sich streiten, sich zanken	Sophie sometimes **argues** with her sister.
	(to) **do judo** ['dʒu:dəʊ]	Judo machen	
	till [tɪl]	bis *(zeitlich)*	On Sundays I sleep **till** 11 o'clock.
p. 40/A 6	**letter** ['letə]	Buchstabe	lots of **letters** 
p. 41/A 7	**grandma** ['grænmɑ:]	Oma	= grandmother
	grandpa ['grænpɑ:]	Opa	= grandfather
	grandparents ['grænpeərənts]	Großeltern	Your grandmother and grandfather are your **grandparents**.
	parents ['peərənts]	Eltern	Your mother and father are your **parents**.
	at the top (of) [tɒp]	oben, am oberen Ende, an der Spitze (von)	
	because [bɪ'kɒz]	weil	Why are you late for school, Emily? – I'm late **because** the bus was late.
	dead [ded]	tot	

	child [tʃaɪld], *pl* **children** ['tʃɪldrən]	Kind	one **child** ! [tʃaɪld]  three **children** ! ['tʃɪldrən] 
	son [sʌn]	Sohn	
	daughter ['dɔːtə]	Tochter	
	uncle ['ʌŋkl]	Onkel	
	aunt [ɑːnt]	Tante	
	married (to) ['mærɪd]	verheiratet (mit)	! verheiratet **mit** = married **to**
	cousin ['kʌzn]	Cousin, Cousine	
	so [səʊ]	also; deshalb, daher	Polly is a parrot, **so** she lives in a cage.
	grandchild ['græntʃaɪld], *pl* **grandchildren** ['-tʃɪldrən]	Enkel/in	
	single ['sɪŋgl]	ledig, alleinstehend	not married
	divorced [dɪ'vɔːst]	geschieden	divorced ◄► married
	without [wɪ'ðaʊt]	ohne	without ◄► with
	just [dʒʌst]	(einfach) nur, bloß	Don't **just** sit there. Come and help me.

here – there – where

p. 42/P 1

	Ort		Richtung	
here	**Here**'s Dan.	**hier**	Come **here**, Jo.	**hierher**
there	**There**'s the ball.	**da, dort**	Paul Road is nice. Let's go **there**.	**dahin, dorthin**
where	**Where**'s Sheeba?	**wo?**	**Where** can we put the basket?	**wohin?**

p. 45/P 11	(to) **remember** [rɪ'membə]	sich erinnern (an)	! Kannst du dich **an ihren Namen erinnern**? = Can you **remember her name**?
	quiz [kwɪz], *pl* **quizzes** ['kwɪzɪz]	Quiz, Ratespiel	
p. 47/P 17	**guest** [gest]	Gast	

A day in the life of ...

p. 48	**by** [baɪ]	von	'A day in my life' – an essay **by** Jack Hanson.
	(to) **have a shower** ['ʃaʊə]	(sich) duschen	I get up at 7.15, then I **have a shower**.
	shower	Dusche	
	(to) **get things ready** ['redi]	Dinge fertig machen, Dinge vorbereiten	In the evening I **get my things ready** for school.
	ready	bereit, fertig	Are you **ready**? Can we go? Dan, Jo! Breakfast is **ready**.
	again [ə'gen]	wieder; noch einmal	Look, there's that little dog **again**. Can you say that **again**, please?
	(to) **do homework**	die Hausaufgabe(n) machen, die Schularbeiten machen	**Do** your **homework** first. Then you can play. ! **Hausaufgaben sind** langweilig. = **Homework is** boring. *(kein Plural)*
	interesting ['ɪntrəstɪŋ]	interessant	This book is great. It's very **interesting**.
	other ['ʌðə]	andere(r, s)	Jo is at home. The **other** children are at school.

country ['kʌntri]	Land	Germany is a big **country**.
spy [spaɪ]	Spion/in	
(to) **wear** [weə]	tragen, anhaben *(Kleidung)*	Can I **wear** your blue T-shirt, Dan? – Yes, OK.
sunglasses ['sʌnglɑːsɪz]	(eine) Sonnenbrille	! **glasses** und **sunglasses** sind Pluralwörter: I need my **glasses**. Where **are they**? Ich brauche meine **Brille**. Wo **ist sie**?
glasses ['glɑːsɪz]	(eine) Brille	
us [əs, ʌs]	uns	We're here. Can you see **us**?
(to) **fit** [fɪt]	passen	The T-shirt is too big. It doesn't **fit**.
story ['stɔːri]	Geschichte, Erzählung	

Der Plural von Wörtern auf „-y"

-y nach **Konsonant** wird im Plural zu **-ies**:

one	countr**y**	famil**y**	hobb**y**	sp**y**	stor**y**
lots of	countr**ies**	famil**ies**	hobb**ies**	sp**ies**	stor**ies**

-y nach **Vokal** bleibt:

one	b**oy**	d**ay**	ess**ay**
lots of	boy**s**	day**s**	essay**s**

Topic 2: My dream house

p. 50	**dream** [driːm]	Traum	
	downstairs [ˌdaʊn'steəz]	unten; nach unten	
	upstairs [ˌʌp'steəz]	oben; nach oben	
	stairs *(pl)* [steəz]	Treppe; Treppenstufen	My room is **upstairs**, but my sister's room is **downstairs**.

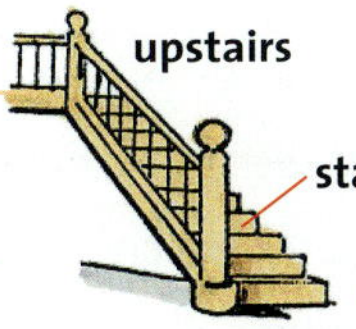

	sofa ['səʊfə]	Sofa	
	armchair ['ɑːmtʃeə]	Sessel	
	dining room ['daɪnɪŋ ruːm]	Esszimmer	
	fridge [frɪdʒ]	Kühlschrank	
	cooker ['kʊkə]	Herd	
	dishwasher ['dɪʃwɒʃə]	Geschirrspülmaschine	
	sink [sɪŋk]	Spüle, Spülbecken	
	cupboard ['kʌbəd]	(Küchen-)Schrank	
	bath [bɑːθ]	Badewanne	
p. 51	**tour (of the house)** [tʊə]	Rundgang, Tour (durch das Haus)	! ein **Rundgang durch** Bristol = a **tour of** Bristol
	visitor ['vɪzɪtə]	Besucher/in, Gast	
	(to) **look different/great/old**	anders/toll/alt aussehen	Ananda has got a new school bag. It **looks great**.
	a lot [ə 'lɒt]	viel	
	(to) **happen (to)** ['hæpən]	geschehen, passieren (mit)	Tell me what **happens to** Prunella in the story.
	swimming pool ['swɪmɪŋ puːl]	Schwimmbad, Schwimmbecken	

Unit 3: Sports and hobbies

Remember?

p. 52 **My hobbies** (Meine Hobbys)

On Mondays I go swimming.

On Tuesdays I play football.

On Wednesdays I ride my bike.

On Thursdays I play hockey.

On Fridays I play computer games.

And you?

	sport [spɔːt]	Sport; Sportart	I like **sport**. What are your favourite **sports**?
p. 53	**dancing lessons** ['dɑːnsɪŋ lesnz]	Tanzstunden, Tanzunterricht	
	(to) **dance** [dɑːns]	tanzen	
	guitar [gɪ'tɑː]	Gitarre	! Mike **spielt Gitarre**. = Mike **plays the guitar**.
	model ['mɒdl]	Modell*(-flugzeug, -schiff usw.)*	
	(to) **go riding** ['raɪdɪŋ]	reiten gehen	
	(to) **ride** [raɪd]	reiten	! (to) **ride** = reiten – (to) **ride a bike** = Rad fahren
	stamp [stæmp]	Briefmarke	
	card [kɑːd]	(Spiel-, Post-)Karte	
	(to) **collect** [kə'lekt]	sammeln	People **collect** stamps, cards, posters, comics, ...
	I **like swimming/dancing/...**	ich schwimme/tanze/... gern	I **like swimming**. And you? – I **don't like swimming**, but I **like riding**.

Sports

American football [əˌmerɪkən 'fʊtbɔːl]	Football
badminton ['bædmɪntən]	Badminton, Federball
baseball ['beɪsbɔːl]	Baseball
basketball ['bɑːskɪtbɔːl]	Basketball
dancing ['dɑːnsɪŋ]	Tanzen
football ['fʊtbɔːl]	Fußball
hockey ['hɒki]	Hockey
judo ['dʒuːdəʊ]	Judo
riding ['raɪdɪŋ]	Reiten, Reitsport
swimming ['swɪmɪŋ]	Schwimmen
table tennis ['teɪbl tenɪs]	Tischtennis
tennis ['tenɪs]	Tennis
volleyball ['vɒlibɔːl]	Volleyball

! Verschiedene Sportarten – verschiedene Verben:

You **play** football, badminton, hockey, ...
You **do** judo. / You **do** sport. („Sport treiben")
You **go** riding, swimming, ...

Remember?

p. 54/A 1

	shop assistant [ˈʃɒp_əˌsɪstənt]	Verkäufer, Verkäuferin	
	Good afternoon.	Guten Tag. *(nachmittags)*	! **Guten Tag.** = **Hello. / Good morning. / Good afternoon.** (Nicht: ~~Good day.~~)
	size [saɪz]	Größe	
	(to) **try on** [ˌtraɪ_ˈɒn]	anprobieren *(Kleidung)*	Can I **try on** your new dress? – Not now. You can **try** it **on** tomorrow.
	these [ðiːz]	diese, die (hier)	
	..., you know. [nəʊ]	..., wissen Sie. / ..., weißt du.	He's really good at football, **you know**.
	(to) **know**	wissen	Do you **know** where Jack is? – He's at school. ! Aussprache: (to) **know** [nəʊ] – **now** [naʊ]
	them [ðəm, ðem]	sie; ihnen	Look, the twins. Can you see **them**? Let's help **them**.
	(to) **want** [wɒnt]	(haben) wollen	I don't **want** these shoes. I **want** the red boots.
	(to) **buy** [baɪ]	kaufen	Can we **buy** the red boots, please?
	(to) **sell** [sel]	verkaufen	(to) sell ◄► (to) buy
p. 54/A 2	**top** [tɒp]	Top, Oberteil	
p. 55/A 3	**project (about, on)** [ˈprɒdʒekt]	Projekt (über, zu)	
	free [friː]	frei	
	free time [ˌfriː ˈtaɪm]	Freizeit, freie Zeit	
	(to) **ask** [ɑːsk]	fragen	
	piano [piˈænəʊ]	Klavier, Piano	! Sie **spielt Klavier**. = She **plays the piano**.
	alone [əˈləʊn]	allein	Does Prunella play tennis **alone**?
	head [hed]	Kopf	
	always [ˈɔːlweɪz]	immer	Prunella **always** plays tennis with her uncle.
	(to) **win** [wɪn]	gewinnen	And she always **wins**!
	neighbour [ˈneɪbə]	Nachbar, Nachbarin	
	anyway [ˈeniweɪ]	sowieso	I don't like that shirt. And it doesn't fit **anyway**.

p. 56/A 6	**often** ['ɒfn]	oft, häufig	I **often** ride my bike to school.
	Dear Jay ... [dɪə]	Lieber Jay, ...	
	quick [kwɪk]	schnell	
	some [səm, sʌm]	einige, ein paar	There are **some** apples for you in the kitchen.
	question ['kwestʃn]	Frage	You ask lots of **questions**. **!** Fragen stellen = (to) ask questions
	(to) **answer** ['ɑːnsə]	antworten; beantworten	
	answer (to) ['ɑːnsə]	Antwort (auf)	Here's a quick **answer to** your question.
	match [mætʃ]	Spiel, Wettkampf	Football **matches** are often on Saturdays.
	Love ... [lʌv]	Liebe Grüße, ... *(Briefschluss)*	
	the next morning/day [nekst]	am nächsten Morgen/Tag	
	never ['nevə]	nie, niemals	never ◄► always
	usually ['juːʒuəli]	meistens, gewöhnlich, normalerweise	never – sometimes – often – usually – always
	(to) **walk** [wɔːk]	(zu Fuß) gehen	I never ride my bike to school. I always **walk**.
	Say hi to Dilip **for me.**	Grüß Dilip von mir.	
p. 57/A 8	(to) **hate** [heɪt]	hassen, gar nicht mögen	My sister likes cats a lot, but she **hates** dogs.
	(to) **have to** do ['hæv tə, 'hæf tə]	tun müssen	I can't help you with your homework, I **have to** feed the rabbits.
	at least [ət 'liːst]	zumindest, wenigstens	These shoes aren't cool, but **at least** they fit.
	most people [məʊst]	die meisten Leute	**Most** children like hamsters and rabbits. **!** <u>die</u> **meisten** Kinder = **most** children
	(to) **understand** [ˌʌndə'stænd]	verstehen, begreifen	In English, please. I don't **understand** German.
	(to) **lay the table** [leɪ]	den Tisch decken	I always **lay the table** for breakfast on Sundays.
	dinner ['dɪnə]	Abendessen, Abendbrot	We usually have **dinner** at 7 o'clock.
p. 57/A 9	**right now** [raɪt 'naʊ]	jetzt sofort; jetzt gerade	I need your help **right now**. Sorry, I can't help you **right now**.
	right after lunch	direkt/gleich nach dem Mittagessen	On Tuesdays I play hockey **right after school**.
	(to) **teach** [tiːtʃ]	unterrichten, lehren	Mr Kingsley is a teacher. He **teaches** English.
	(to) **learn** [lɜːn]	lernen	
	(to) **shout** [ʃaʊt]	schreien, rufen	Some teachers **shout** a lot. Don't **shout at** me. (= Schrei mich nicht an.)
p. 58/P 2	**snake** [sneɪk]	Schlange	
p. 60/P 7	(to) **know** [nəʊ]	kennen	**!** (to) **know** = **1.** wissen; **2.** kennen
	appointment [ə'pɔɪntmənt]	Termin, Verabredung	
	(to) **meet** [miːt]	sich treffen	**!** (to) **meet**: **1.** Can **we meet** at 8 o'clock? (Können **wir uns** ... **treffen**?) **2.** Can **you meet us** after school? (Kannst **du uns** ... **treffen**?)

p. 61/P 10	**under** ['ʌndə]	unter	Oh, there's my book – **under** the desk.
p. 62/P 11	(to) **skate** [skeɪt]	Inliner/Skateboard fahren	
	skates [skeɪts]	Inliner	
p. 62/P 12	**on the radio** ['reɪdiəʊ]	im Radio	
p. 63/P 13	**virus** ['vaɪrəs]	Virus	! Aussprache: **virus** ['vaɪrəs]
p. 63/P 14	(to) **link** [lɪŋk]	verbinden, verknüpfen	Can you **link** the words and the pictures?
p. 63/P 15	**car** [kɑː]	Auto	a **car** 
p. 64/P 17	**opposite** ['ɒpəzɪt]	Gegenteil	What's the **opposite** of 'full'? – 'Empty'.

The SHoCK Team

p. 65	**man** [mæn], *pl* **men** [men]	Mann	
	woman ['wʊmən], *pl* **women** ['wɪmɪn]	Frau	
	the only guest ['əʊnli]	der einzige Gast	Dan and Jo are **the only** twins in 7PK.
	suddenly ['sʌdnli]	plötzlich, auf einmal	**Suddenly** everything was quiet.
	noise [nɔɪz]	Geräusch; Lärm	Listen! There's a **noise** at the window. What's all that **noise**? I can't do my homework.
	outside his room [ˌaʊt'saɪd]	vor seinem Zimmer; außerhalb seines Zimmers	Sophie's rabbits live **outside** the house – in a hutch in the garden.
	scary ['skeəri]	unheimlich; gruselig	
	(to) **run** [rʌn]	laufen, rennen	
	out of ... ['aʊt_əv]	aus ... (heraus/hinaus)	
	into ... ['ɪntə, 'ɪntʊ]	in ... (hinein)	**into** the house – **out of** the house
	(to) **call** [kɔːl]	rufen; anrufen; nennen	Please **call** your dog. It's in our garden. **Call** me tomorrow. Here's my phone number. Her name is Elizabeth, but we **call** her Liz.
	police (*pl*) [pə'liːs]	Polizei	! **police** ist immer Plural: Where **are** the **police**? We have to call **them**. (Wo ist die Polizei? Wir müssen sie holen.)
	maybe ['meɪbi]	vielleicht	**Maybe** Mr Green is a bank robber?
	This is about Mr Green.	Es geht um Mr Green.	**This is about** the SHoCK Team, not about Jack.
	(to) **find out (about)** [ˌfaɪnd_'aʊt]	herausfinden (über)	
	detective [dɪ'tektɪv]	Detektiv, Detektivin	! Deutsch: Dete**k**tiv – Englisch: dete**c**tive
p. 66	**a piece of paper** [ə ˌpiːs_əv 'peɪpə]	ein Stück Papier	**a piece of paper** 
	(to) **add (to)** [æd]	hinzufügen, ergänzen, addieren (zu)	**Add** blue **to** yellow and you've got green.
	(to) **start** [stɑːt]	starten, anfangen, beginnen (mit)	

watch [wɒtʃ]	Armbanduhr	**!** **watch** = **1.** *(verb)* beobachten, sich ansehen **2.** *(noun)* Armbanduhr
clock [klɒk]	(Wand-, Stand-, Turm-)Uhr	

Topic 3: An English jumble sale

p. 67 **jumble sale** ['dʒʌmbl seɪl]	Wohltätigkeitsbasar	
money ['mʌni]	Geld	
pound (£) [paʊnd]	Pfund *(britische Währung)*	
pence (p) *(pl)* [pens]	Pence *(Mehrzahl von „penny")*	10**p** [pi:] = 10 **pence**
penny ['peni]	*kleinste britische Münze*	1**p** [pi:] = 1 **penny**
euro (€) ['jʊərəʊ]	Euro	
cent (c) [sent]	Cent	
What about ...?	Wie wär's mit ...?	
too much [tu: 'mʌtʃ]	zu viel	**!** **too** = **1.** auch – The flat is big, and the garden is big **too**. („auch groß") **2.** zu – The house is **too** big. („zu groß")
How much is/are ...? [ˌhaʊ 'mʌtʃ]	Was kostet/kosten ...? / Wie viel kostet/kosten ...?	**How much is** the felt tip? And **how much are** the pencils?
It's £1.	Er/Sie/Es kostet 1 Pfund.	The felt tip **is** £1.75, and the pencils **are** 35p.
only ['əʊnli]	nur, bloß	There aren't two books on the desk, there's **only** one.
(to) **take** 10c **off** [ˌteɪk_'ɒf]	10 Cent abziehen	£3? That's too much. Can you **take 50p off**?
I'll take it. [aɪl 'teɪk_ɪt]	Ich werde es (ihn, sie) nehmen. / Ich nehme es (ihn, sie).	How much is the pencil case? – £2.50. – OK, **I'll take it**.
change [tʃeɪndʒ]	Wechselgeld	

Unit 4: Party, party!

Remember?

pp. 68/69 **Food and drink**

(to) **have ... for breakfast**	... zum Frühstück essen/ trinken	I usually **have** toast and orange juice **for breakfast**.
chips *(pl)* [tʃɪps]	Pommes frites	
biscuit ['bɪskɪt]	Keks, Plätzchen	
crisps *(pl)* [krɪsps]	Kartoffelchips	! **crisps** = Kartoffelchips – **chips** = Pommes frites
fruit salad ['fru:t ˌsæləd]	Obstsalat	
sausage ['sɒsɪdʒ]	(Brat-, Bock-)Würstchen, Wurst	**sausages** and **chips** 
sweets *(pl)* [swi:ts]	Süßigkeiten	
sweet [swi:t]	süß	I don't like bananas. They're too **sweet**.
bottle ['bɒtl]	Flasche	 a milk **bottle**  a **bottle of** milk
glass [glɑ:s]	Glas	
jug [dʒʌg]	Krug	

a bottle of ..., a glass of ...

next to	neben	**next to** the bottle 
hungry ['hʌŋgri]	hungrig	! Ich habe Hunger. = I'm hungry.
thirsty ['θɜ:sti]	durstig	! Ich habe Durst. = I'm thirsty.
Would you like ...? [wəd, wʊd]	Möchtest du ...? / Möchten Sie ...?	**Would you like** a piece of pizza? – Yes, please.
something to eat ['sʌmθɪŋ]	etwas zu essen	
I'd like ... (= I would like ...)	Ich hätte gern ... / Ich möchte gern ...	What would you like? – **I'd like** a hamburger, please.
some cheese/juice/money [səm, sʌm]	etwas Käse/Saft/Geld	! **some** = **1.** einige – **some** apples, chips, bottles, ... **2.** etwas – **some** cheese, milk, money, ...
p. 70/A 1 **invitation (to)** [ˌɪnvɪ'teɪʃn]	Einladung (zu)	
(to) **invite (to)** [ɪn'vaɪt]	einladen (zu)	Can I **invite** all my friends to my party?
long [lɒŋ]	lang	Ananda's essay is very **long**.
short [ʃɔ:t]	kurz	Dan's essay is very **short**. short ◂▸ long
(to) **want to** do [wɒnt]	tun wollen	Do you really **want to** invite all your friends? ! (to) **want** = haben wollen: I **want** a new skateboard. (to) **want to do** = tun wollen: I **want to** buy it now.
both [bəʊθ]	beide	Do you want to listen to **both** CDs? We **both** like hamsters. I like **both** these T-shirts. Can we buy **both**?

	real [rɪəl]	echt, wirklich	It's a party for **real** people, not for poltergeists.
p. 71/A 4	**present** ['preznt]	Geschenk	! **present** = **1.** Gegenwart; **2.** Geschenk
	still [stɪl]	(immer) noch	After dinner Jo was **still** hungry.
	soap [səʊp]	Seife	a piece of **soap** 
	funny ['fʌni]	witzig, komisch	
	expensive [ɪk'spensɪv]	teuer	£60 for a T-shirt? That's too **expensive**.
	any ...? ['eni]	(irgend)welche ...?	! **any** bleibt oft unübersetzt: Are there **any** oranges**?** (= Gibt es Apfelsinen?) Do you need **any** help**?** (= Brauchst du Hilfe?)
	earring ['ɪərɪŋ]	Ohrring	
	not (...) any	kein, keine	There is**n't any** milk in the fridge. We have**n't** got **any** pets. What about you?
	(to) **be in a hurry** ['hʌri]	in Eile sein, es eilig haben	! **hurry**: **1. I'm in a hurry**. (= Ich habe es eilig.) **2. Hurry up**, please. (= Beeil dich, bitte.)
	(to) **follow** ['fɒləʊ]	folgen; verfolgen	My dog always **follows** me. The police **are following** the man to his house.
p. 71/A 5	**key word** ['ki: wɜ:d]	Stichwort, Schlüsselwort	
p. 71/A 6	**another** [ə'nʌðə]	ein(e) andere(r, s); noch ein(e)	I can't write with this pen. I need **another** pen. I'm still hungry. Let's eat **another** sandwich.
	reason ['ri:zn]	Grund, Begründung	Can you give a **reason** why you are late, Jo?
p. 72/A 7	(to) **tidy** ['taɪdi]	aufräumen	On Saturdays I have to **tidy** my room.
	(to) **make a mess** [mes]	alles durcheinanderbringen, alles in Unordnung bringen	When the house is empty, Prunella often **makes a mess**.
	away [ə'weɪ]	weg, fort	Go **away**, Prunella. I have to do my homework.
	(to) **take** [teɪk]	(weg-, hin)bringen	Please **take** the plates into the kitchen, Sophie.
	up [ʌp]	hinauf, herauf, nach oben	Please take your books **up** to your room, Toby.
	down [daʊn]	hinunter, herunter, nach unten	down ◄► up
	to Jenny's	zu Jenny	Can we go **to Jenny's** now? (= to Jenny's house/flat)
	later ['leɪtə]	später	
p. 73/A 9	(to) **hear** [hɪə]	hören	! (to) **hear** = hören (können) (to) **listen (to)** = zuhören, horchen **Listen**. Can you **hear** the dogs in the park?
	train [treɪn]	Zug	! There was a funny man **on the train**. (= **im Zug**)
	station ['steɪʃn]	Bahnhof	Ananda sees Mr Green at the **station**.
	(to) **wait (for)** ['weɪt fɔ:]	warten (auf)	Don't **wait for** Prunella – she's always late.
	somebody ['sʌmbədi]	jemand	Mr Green is talking to **somebody**.
	(to) **get off (the train/bus)** [ˌget_'ɒf] **(-tt-)**[1]	(aus dem Zug/Bus) aussteigen	This is where I live. We have to **get off** here.
	(to) **get on (the train/bus)** [ˌget_'ɒn] **(-tt-)**	(in den Zug/Bus) einsteigen	! **in** den Bus **einsteigen** = (to) **get on** the bus **aus** dem Bus **aussteigen** = (to) **get off** the bus
	parcel ['pɑ:sl]	Paket	

[1] Die Angabe **(-tt-)** zeigt, dass der Endkonsonant bei der Bildung der *-ing*-Form verdoppelt wird: **get** – **getting**.

	(to) **look round** [ˌlʊk ˈraʊnd]	sich umsehen	Mr Green **looks round**, then he starts to run.
	(to) **hide** [haɪd]	sich verstecken; *(etwas)* verstecken	Prunella often **hides** in the wardrobe. Can you **hide** this parcel for me, please?
p. 74/A 10	**Which** picture ...? [wɪtʃ]	Welches Bild ...?	**Which** cake would you like? The chocolate cake?

Remember?

My body[1] (Mein Körper)

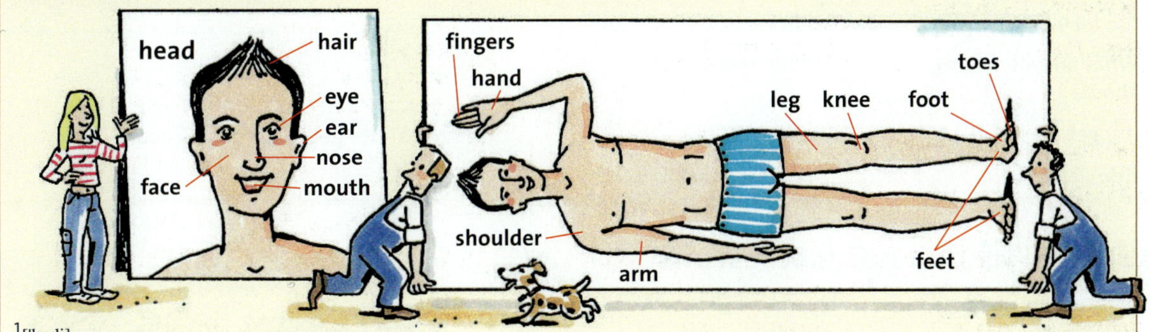

[1] [ˈbɒdi]

p. 80/P 15	**roll** [rəʊl]	Brötchen	

Sophie's party – a play

p. 81	**play** [pleɪ]	Theaterstück	! **play** = **1.** *(verb)* spielen; **2.** *(noun)* Theaterstück
	scene [siːn]	Szene	! Das „c" wird nicht gesprochen: **scene** [siːn].
	... pm [ˌpiː‿ˈem]	... Uhr nachmittags/abends	! Man verwendet **am** oder **pm** nicht mit **o'clock**. Also nur: **at two pm** (nicht: ~~at two o'clock pm~~)
	... am [ˌeɪ‿ˈem]	... Uhr morgens/vormittags	
	Don't worry. [ˈwʌri]	Mach dir keine Sorgen.	
	(to) **worry (about)**	sich Sorgen machen (wegen, um)	When I come home late my mum always **worries about** me.
	minute [ˈmɪnɪt]	Minute	It's three **minutes** to six. 
	doorbell [ˈdɔːbel]	Türklingel	
	door [dɔː]	Tür	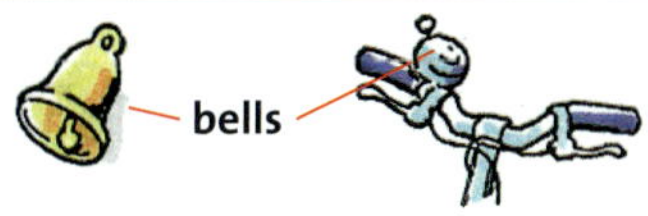
	bell [bel]	Klingel, Glocke	
	front door [ˌfrʌnt ˈdɔː]	Wohnungstür, Haustür	
	inside [ˌɪnˈsaɪd]	innen (drin), drinnen	Sophie isn't in the garden. She's **inside**.
	outside [ˌaʊtˈsaɪd]	draußen	Where's Sheeba? – She's **outside**, in the garden.
	hole [həʊl]	Loch	a **hole** in my shoe 
	fantastic [fænˈtæstɪk]	fantastisch, toll	
	so sweet [səʊ]	so süß	
	(to) **be afraid (of)** [əˈfreɪd]	Angst haben (vor)	My brother **is afraid of** big dogs. I**'m afraid of** mice.
	(to) **pass** [pɑːs]	(herüber)reichen, weitergeben	Can you **pass** me the milk, please? You have to **pass** the parcel to the next student.
	(to) **pass round** [ˌpɑːs ˈraʊnd]	herumgeben	Now Sophie **is passing round** the party food.

	no more music	keine Musik mehr	
	no	kein, keine	I can't do my homework now. I've got **no** time.
p. 82	**note** [nəʊt]	Mitteilung, Notiz	Here's a **note** from Jack. Can you read it? I can't.
	(to) **take notes**	sich Notizen machen	
	(to) **choose** [tʃuːz]	(sich) aussuchen, (aus)wählen	We have to **choose** a name for our new dog.
	prize [praɪz]	Preis, Gewinn	There's a **prize** for the best story.
	(to) **be over**	vorbei sein, zu Ende sein	
	What are you talking about?	Wovon redest du?	
	(to) **get** [get] **(-tt-)**	gelangen, (hin)kommen	How can we **get** to Cotham School?
	title ['taɪtl]	Titel, Überschrift	

Unit 5: School: not just lessons

pp. 84/85	**phrase** [freɪz]	Ausdruck, (Rede-)Wendung	
	spring [sprɪŋ]	Frühling	
	autumn ['ɔːtəm]	Herbst	
	winter ['wɪntə]	Winter	**spring** **summer** **autumn** **winter**
	show [ʃəʊ]	Show, Vorstellung	
	(to) **show**	zeigen	Can you **show** me your new computer?
	programme ['prəʊgræm]	Programm	
	(to) **paint** [peɪnt]	malen, anmalen	Let's **paint** our faces for the party!
	ship [ʃɪp]	Schiff	
	may [meɪ]	dürfen	**May** I come in? (*höflich für:* Can I come in?)
	(to) **bring** [brɪŋ]	(mit-, her)bringen	 ! **Bring** me the newspaper. („herbringen“)  Now **take** it to Dad. („hinbringen“)
	(to) **use** [juːz]	benutzen, verwenden	May I **use** your phone, please?
	result [rɪ'zʌlt]	Ergebnis, Resultat	
	rehearsal [rɪ'hɜːsl]	Probe *(am Theater)*	
	(to) **rehearse** [rɪ'hɜːs]	proben *(am Theater)*	
	junior ['dʒuːniə]	Junioren-, Jugend-	
	choir ['kwaɪə]	Chor	! Schreibung: choir – Aussprache: ['kwaɪə]
	(to) **practise** ['præktɪs]	üben; trainieren	
	pirate ['paɪrət]	Pirat, Piratin	! Betonung auf der 1. Silbe: **pirate** ['paɪrət]
p. 86/A 1	(we/you/they) **were** [wə, wɜː]	*Vergangenheitsform von „be“*	I was at home last night. Where **were** you?
	Miss White [mɪs]	Frau White *(unverheiratet)*	
	group [gruːp]	Gruppe	

	(to) **sound** [saʊnd]	klingen, sich *(gut usw.)* anhören	A party in the park? That **sounds** very nice.
	sound	Laut; Klang	
	kid [kɪd]	Kind, Jugendliche(r)	
	ticket ['tɪkɪt]	Eintrittskarte	**Tickets** for the party are £2.50.
p. 86/A 2	**yesterday** ['jestədeɪ, 'jestədi]	gestern	**Yesterday** I was home late.
p. 87/A 3	**terrible** ['terəbl]	schrecklich, furchtbar	
	mistake [mɪ'steɪk]	Fehler	There are three **mistakes** in your essay.
	I can't wait to see ...	ich kann es kaum erwarten, ... zu sehen	The band is great. **I can't wait** to see their next show.
	a minute **ago** [ə'gəʊ]	vor einer Minute	Where's Dan? – He was here **a minute ago**. **!** **ago** steht hinter dem Nomen.
	voice [vɔɪs]	Stimme	Can he sing? – Yes, he's got a great **voice**.
	clear [klɪə]	klar, deutlich	Is that **clear**? – Yes, I understand now.
	part [pɑːt]	Teil	Cornwall is a pretty **part** of England.
p. 88/A 6	**king** [kɪŋ]	König	
p. 88/A 7	**diary** ['daɪəri]	Tagebuch; Terminkalender	
	had [hæd]	*Vergangenheitsform von „have" und von „have got"*	Yesterday I **had** breakfast at 6 o'clock. In 1998 we **had** a dog. Now we've got two cats. **!** Nie: ... we ~~had got~~ a dog.
	came [keɪm]	*Vergangenheitsform von „come"*	The teacher **came** into the classroom, and the students were quiet.
	did [dɪd]	*Vergangenheitsform von „do"*	Tell your partner what you **did** last Sunday.

Unregelmäßige Vergangenheitsformen

(to) get up	**got up** [gɒt]	aufstehen	(to) make	**made** [meɪd]	machen, bauen, bilden
(to) go	**went** [went]	gehen	(to) say	**said** [sed]	sagen

	tired ['taɪəd]	müde	
	this morning/afternoon/ evening	heute Morgen/Nachmittag/ Abend	I can meet you at two o'clock **this afternoon**.
	to [tə, tu]	um zu	Dan and Jo went to the park **to** play football.
	sure [ʃʊə, ʃɔː]	sicher	Ananda's dad is from Uganda? Are you **sure**?
p. 89/A 9	**article** ['ɑːtɪkl]	(Zeitungs-)Artikel	There was an **article** in the school magazine about the Spring Show.
	we **didn't go** ['dɪdnt]	wir gingen nicht / wir sind nicht gegangen	My friends went to the Spring Show, but we **didn't go**.
	stage [steɪdʒ]	Bühne	At 9 o'clock the band went on **stage** and started to play.
	on the right [raɪt]	rechts, auf der rechten Seite	Here are my pets. Alice, my dog, is **on the right**. My cat Morris is **on the left**.
	on the left [left]	links, auf der linken Seite	
	twin town [ˌtwɪn 'taʊn]	Partnerstadt	
	town [taʊn]	Stadt	

	(to) **mail** [meɪl]	schicken, senden *(per Post oder E-Mail)*	Ananda **mailed** her friends some photos of the Spring Show.
	information (about/on) *(no pl)* [ˌɪnfə'meɪʃn]	Information(en) (über)	**!** • Hier sind die **Informationen** über die Show. = Here's the **information** about/on the show. *Nie:* ... the information~~s~~ • **eine** interessante Information = **some** interesting information
	for example [ˌfər_ɪg'zɑ:mpl]	zum Beispiel	Toby likes ball games – football, **for example**.
	Did you know ...?	Wusstest du ...?	
p. 90/P 1	**flow chart** ['fləʊ tʃɑ:t]	Flussdiagramm	
p. 90/P 2	**phone call** ['fəʊn kɔ:l]	Anruf, Telefongespräch	
p. 92/P 8	**extra** ['ekstrə]	zusätzlich	Oh, here's Sophie. We need an **extra** plate.
	syllable ['sɪləbl]	Silbe	There are two **syllables** in *mistake*: *mis* and *take*.
p. 92/P 9	**report (on)** [rɪ'pɔ:t]	Bericht, Reportage (über)	There was a **report on** the Spring Show on the radio.
p. 95/P 16	**elephant** ['elɪfənt]	Elefant	

A pirate story

Unregelmäßige Vergangenheitsformen

(to) run	**ran** [ræn]	laufen, rennen	(to) take	**took** [tʊk]	nehmen; (weg-, hin)bringen
(to) see	**saw** [sɔ:]	sehen	(to) tell	**told** [təʊld]	sagen; erzählen
(to) sit	**sat** [sæt]	sitzen; sich setzen			

p. 96	**dark** [dɑ:k]	dunkel	It's very **dark** in here. I can't find my pen.
	windy ['wɪndi]	windig	
	wind [wɪnd]	Wind	
	young [jʌŋ]	jung	young ◄► old
	many ['meni]	viele	Poor Peter. He hasn't got **many** friends.
	how many ...?	wie viele ...?	**How many** kids are in the SHoCK Team? – Five.

„viel“, „viele“

viel	**How much** orange juice have we got? – We haven't got **much** orange juice, but we've got **lots of** milk. **Wie viel** Orangensaft ...? – ... nicht **viel** Orangensaft, ... **viel** Milch.
viele	**How many** CDs have you got? – I haven't got **many** CDs, but I've got **lots of** computer games. **Wie viele** CDs ...? – ... nicht **viele** CDs, ... **viele** Computerspiele.

	(to) **kill** [kɪl]	töten	
	tonight [tə'naɪt]	heute Nacht, heute Abend	**!** heute Morgen = **this morning** heute Nachmittag = **this afternoon** heute Abend = **this evening** heute Nacht = **tonight**
p. 97	**for** three **days**	drei Tage (lang)	Sophie was in London **for five days** last year.

	that [ðət, ðæt]	dass	Prunella says **that** she never sleeps. Ananda doesn't think **that** Jack's mum is a spy.
	(to) **be scared (of)** [skeəd]	Angst haben (vor)	My little brother is **scared of** poltergeists.
	at last [ət 'lɑːst]	endlich, schließlich	Jack waited for a long time. **At last** Ananda came.
	danger ['deɪndʒə]	Gefahr	
	soon [suːn]	bald	It's my birthday **soon**. Let's have a party.
	(to) **be asleep** [ə'sliːp]	schlafen	
	when	als	

when

wann	**When**'s your birthday?	**Wann** hast du Geburtstag?
wenn	We can play cards **when** you come home.	Wir können Karten spielen, **wenn** du nach Hause kommst.
als	Jonah was scared **when** Mr Bonny saw him.	Jonah hatte Angst, **als** Mr Bonny ihn sah.

	beautiful ['bjuːtɪfl]	schön	Ann Bonny was a **beautiful** woman.
	sea [siː]	Meer, *(die)* See	
p. 98	(to) **be cold** [kəʊld]	frieren	It was very windy, and I **was cold**. (= Ich fror. / Mir war kalt.)
	cold	kalt	cold ◄► hot
	floor [flɔː]	Fußboden	Jo, put your books on the desk, not on the **floor**.
	I don't think so.	Das finde/glaube ich nicht.	This is a great book. – **I don't think so.** I think it's boring.
	I think so.	Ich glaube (ja).	Is he from Germany? – **I think so**, but I'm not sure.

Unit 6: Great places for kids

p. 100	**city** ['sɪti]	Stadt, Großstadt	
	village ['vɪlɪdʒ]	Dorf	
	church [tʃɜːtʃ]	Kirche	
	near [nɪə]	in der Nähe von, nahe (bei)	
	bridge [brɪdʒ]	Brücke	
	free	kostenlos	
	tower ['taʊə]	Turm	

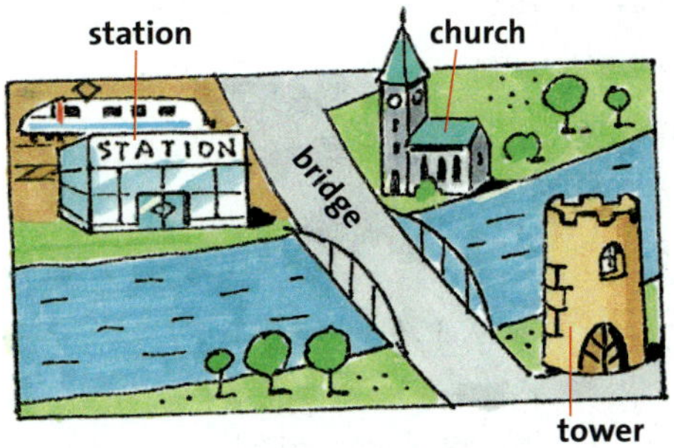

The church is **near** the station.
! in der Nähe (von) = **near** (nicht: ~~in the near of~~)

p. 101	(to) **explore** [ɪk'splɔː]	erkunden, erforschen	It's very interesting to **explore** new places.
	I'd like to go (= I would like to go)	ich würde gern gehen / ich möchte gehen	**I'd like to go** to the park this afternoon. What **would** you **like to do**?
	I wouldn't like to go	ich würde nicht gern gehen / ich möchte nicht gehen	**I wouldn't like to go** to the park. I'd like to watch a film on TV.
	museum [mju'ziːəm]	Museum	
	price [praɪs]	(Kauf-)Preis	

fun [fʌn] Spaß

fun

Riding **is fun**. (*Nicht:* ... ~~makes fun~~.)	Reiten **macht Spaß**.
Prunella **has fun** with Sophie.	Prunella **hat viel Spaß / amüsiert sich** mit Sophie.
Have fun!	**Viel Spaß!**
Just **for fun**.	Nur **zum Spaß**.

! The play was **fun**. Das Theaterstück **hat Spaß gemacht**.
The play was **funny**. Das Theaterstück **war lustig/witzig**.

p. 102/A 1	**each** [iːtʃ]	jeder, jede, jedes (einzelne)	There are six guests at the party, so we need six little presents – one for **each** of them.
	must [mʌst]	müssen	**!** **müssen** = **1.** have to; **2.** must (*have to* wird häufiger verwendet als *must*.)
	corner ['kɔːnə]	Ecke	
	(to) **agree (on)** [ə'griː]	sich einigen (auf)	We have to **agree on** a day for our party.
	middle (of) ['mɪdl]	Mitte	
	library ['laɪbrəri]	Bibliothek, Bücherei	
p. 102/A 2	**far** [fɑː]	weit (entfernt)	Is it **far** to the station? – Yes, it is. It's too **far** to walk.
	(to) **be right**	Recht haben	**!** Ananda **hat Recht**. = Ananda **is right**.
	against [ə'genst]	gegen	against ◄► for
	(to) be/look **the same** [seɪm]	gleich sein/aussehen	All the cars in this museum **look the same**. the same ◄► different
	the same ...	der-/die-/dasselbe ...; dieselben	Sophie and her friends are at **the same** school.
	step [step]	Schritt	The first **step** is to choose an interesting place.
p. 103/A 3	(to) **whisper** ['wɪspə]	flüstern	'I think there's a poltergeist in this house!' Jo **whispered**.
	that's why	deshalb, darum	She's a poltergeist. **That's why** you can't see her.
	loud [laʊd]	laut	loud ◄► quiet
p. 103/A 5	(to) **take photos**	Fotos machen, fotografieren	Learn to **take photos** at the camera club!
	over there [ˌəʊvə 'ðeə]	da drüben, dort drüben	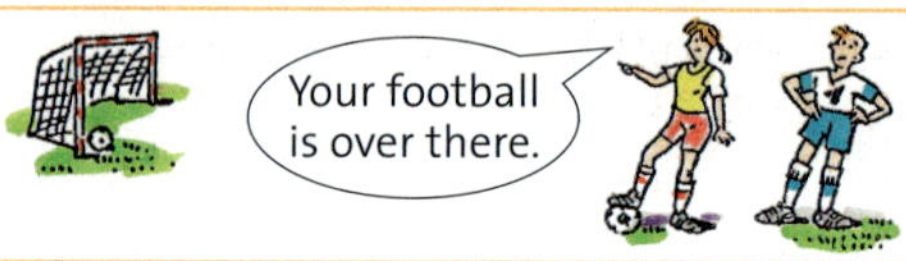
	in front of [ɪn 'frʌnt_əv]	vor	**in front of** the box 
	better ['betə]	besser	Your essay is good, but my essay is **better**.
	those [ðəʊz]	die (da), jene (dort)	

this, that – these, those

Wenn etwas **näher beim Sprecher** ist, verwendet man eher **this** und **these**.

Wenn etwas **weiter entfernt** ist, verwendet man eher **that** und **those**.

	(to) **finish** ['fɪnɪʃ]	beenden, zu Ende machen; enden	Let's **finish** the exercise and read the text again. Lessons **finish** at 3.30 pm. (to) finish ◄► (to) start
	(to) **smile** [smaɪl]	lächeln	
p. 104/A 7	**glue** [gluː]	Klebstoff	
	everywhere ['evriweə]	überall	Oh no, now there's glue **everywhere**.
	(to) **grumble** ['grʌmbl]	murren, nörgeln	
	presentation [ˌprezn'teɪʃn]	Präsentation, Vorstellung	
	(to) **present (to)** [prɪ'zent]	*(jm. etwas)* präsentieren, vorstellen	**Present** your ideas **to** the class. ! Aussprache: (to) **present** [prɪ'zent] = präsentieren **the present** ['preznt] = **1.** das Geschenk; **2.** die Gegenwart
p. 104/A 8	**city centre** [ˌsɪti 'sentə]	Stadtzentrum, Innenstadt	
p. 105/A 9	**one more**	noch ein(e), ein(e) weitere(r, s)	We need **two more** photos for the poster.
	to the front [frʌnt]	nach vorn	Go **to the front** and start your presentation.
	for lots of reasons	aus vielen Gründen	I ride my bike **for lots of reasons** – it's quick, it's fun, and it isn't expensive.

The Mr Green mystery

p. 110	**so far** [səʊ 'fɑː]	bis jetzt, bis hierher	Do you like the book? – Yes, it's great **so far**.
	key [kiː]	Schlüssel	I can't open the door. I can't find my **keys**.
	(to) **be out** [bi‿'aʊt]	nicht da sein, weg sein	Dan **is out** – can you call back later?
	(to) **knock (on)** [nɒk]	(an)klopfen (an)	He **knocked on** the door and went in.
p. 111	**hall** [hɔːl]	Flur, Diele	
	How do you know ...?	Woher weißt/kennst du ...?	**How do you know** my phone number?
	(to) **turn on** the computer [ˌtɜːn‿'ɒn]	den Computer einschalten	
	(to) **hurt** [hɜːt], *simple past:* **hurt**	wehtun; verletzen	Poor Ananda. She **hurt** her leg in a hockey match yesterday.
	(to) **hit** [hɪt] **(-tt-)**, *simple past:* **hit**	schlagen	Jo often argues with Dan, but he never **hits** him.

Irregular verbs (Unregelmäßige Verben)

Infinitive	Simple past		Infinitive	Simple past	
(to) **be**	**was/were**	sein	(to) **hurt**	**hurt**	wehtun; verletzen
(to) **come**	**came**	kommen	(to) **make**	**made**	machen; bauen; bilden
(to) **do**	**did**	tun, machen	(to) **run**	**ran**	laufen, rennen
(to) **get up**	**got up**	aufstehen	(to) **say**	**said**	sagen
(to) **go**	**went**	gehen	(to) **see**	**saw**	sehen
(to) **have** **(have got)**	**had**	haben	(to) **sit**	**sat**	sitzen; sich setzen
			(to) **take**	**took**	nehmen; (weg-, hin)bringen
(to) **hit**	**hit**	schlagen	(to) **tell**	**told**	sagen; erzählen

to spend, spent - verbringen

Das Dictionary besteht aus zwei alphabetischen Wörterlisten:

Englisch – Deutsch (S. 176–188)
Deutsch – Englisch (S. 189–197).

Das **English – German Dictionary** enthält den gesamten Wortschatz dieses Bandes.
Wenn du wissen möchtest, was ein Wort bedeutet, wie man es ausspricht, wie es genau geschrieben wird oder wo es zum ersten Mal in *English G 21* vorkommt, kannst du hier nachschlagen.

Es werden folgende **Abkürzungen** und **Symbole** verwendet:

jm. = jemandem	sb. = somebody	pl = plural *(Mehrzahl)*
jn. = jemanden	sth. = something	no pl = no plural

° Mit diesem Kringel sind Wörter markiert, die nicht zum Lernwortschatz gehören.
► Der Pfeil verweist auf Kästchen im Vocabulary (S. 146–175), in denen du weitere Informationen findest.

Die **Fundstellenangaben** geben an, wo ein Wort zum ersten Mal vorkommt
(Ziffern in Klammern bezeichnen immer Seitenzahlen):

Welc (8)	= 'Hello' and 'Welcome', Seite 8
Welc (8/146)	= 'Hello' and 'Welcome', Seite 146 (im Vocabulary, zu Seite 8)
1 (33)	= Unit 1, Seite 33
1 (18/152)	= Unit 1, Seite 152 (im Vocabulary, zu Seite 18)
TOP 2 (51)	= Topic 2, Seite 51
TOP 2 (50/161)	= Topic 2, Seite 161 (im Vocabulary, zu Seite 50)

Tipps zur Arbeit mit dem Dictionary findest du im Skills File auf Seite 122.

A

a [ə] ein, eine Welc (8/146) • **a lot** viel TOP 2 (51) • **He likes her a lot.** Er mag sie sehr. 1 (33)

about [ə'baʊt] über Welc (8) • **ask about sth.** nach etwas fragen 5 (87) • **This is about Mr Green.** Es geht um Mr Green. 3 (65) • **What about ...?** **1.** Was ist mit ...? / Und ...? Welc (6); **2.** Wie wär's mit ...? TOP 3 (67) • **What are you talking about?** Wovon redest du? 4 (82) **°Say what you like about ...** Sag, was du an ... magst

act [ækt] aufführen, spielen 2 (38) **°Act out ...** Spiele/Spielt ... vor.

activity [æk'tɪvəti] Aktivität, Tätigkeit (3)

add (to) [æd] hinzufügen, ergänzen, addieren (zu) 3 (66)

afraid [ə'freɪd]: **be afraid (of)** Angst haben (vor) 4 (81)

after ['ɑ:ftə] **1.** nach *(zeitlich)* 1 (23) **after that** danach 2 (39) **°2.** nachdem

afternoon [ˌɑ:ftə'nu:n] Nachmittag 2 (38) • **in the afternoon** nachmittags, am Nachmittag 2 (38/158) **on Friday afternoon** freitagnachmittags, am Freitagnachmittag 2 (38/158)

again [ə'gen] wieder; noch einmal 2 (48)

against [ə'genst] gegen 6 (102)

ago [ə'gəʊ]: **a minute ago** vor einer Minute 5 (87)

agree (on) [ə'gri:] sich einigen (auf) 6 (102)

°ahoy [ə'hɔɪ]: **Ship ahoy!** Schiff ahoi!

°alarm clock [ə'lɑ:m klɒk] Wecker

°algebra ['ældʒɪbrə] Algebra

all [ɔ:l] alle; alles 1 (24) • **all day** den ganzen Tag (lang) 2 (39) • **all the time** die ganze Zeit 2 (39) **This is all wrong.** Das ist ganz falsch. 2 (40)

alone [ə'ləʊn] allein 3 (55)

alphabet ['ælfəbet] Alphabet 1 (22)

°alphabetical [ˌælfə'betɪkl] alphabetisch

°also ['ɔ:lsəʊ] auch

always ['ɔ:lweɪz] immer 3 (55)

am [ˌeɪ‿'em]: **7 am** 7 Uhr morgens/vormittags 4 (81/169)

American football [əˌmerɪkən 'fʊtbɔ:l] Football 3 (53/162)

an [ən] ein, eine 1 (18/152)

and [ənd, ænd] und Welc (8/146)

another [ə'nʌðə] ein(e) andere(r, s); noch ein(e) 4 (71)

answer ['ɑ:nsə] **1.** antworten; beantworten 3 (56); **2. answer (to)** Antwort (auf) 3 (56/164)

any ['eni]: **any ...?** (irgend)welche ...? 4 (71) • **not (...) any** kein, keine 4 (71)

anyway ['eniweɪ] sowieso 3 (55)

apple ['æpl] Apfel Welc (8/146)

appointment [ə'pɔɪntmənt] Termin, Verabredung 3 (60)

April ['eɪprəl] April TOP 1 (35/156)

are [ɑ:] bist; sind; seid Welc (8/146) **The pencils are 35p.** Die Bleistifte kosten 35 Pence. TOP 3 (67/166)

argue ['ɑ:gju:] sich streiten, sich zanken 2 (40)

arm [ɑ:m] Arm 4 (74/169)

armchair ['ɑ:mtʃeə] Sessel TOP 2 (50)

art [ɑ:t] Kunst 1 (23/154)

article ['ɑ:tɪkl] (Zeitungs-)Artikel 5 (89)

ask [ɑ:sk] fragen 3 (55) • **ask about sth.** nach etwas fragen 5 (87) • **ask questions** Fragen stellen 3 (56/164)

asleep [ə'sli:p]: **be asleep** schlafen 5 (97)

°assembly [ə'sembli] Schulversammlung

at [ət, æt]: **at 7 Hamilton Street** in der Hamiltonstraße 7 Welc (12) • **at 8.45** um 8.45 1 (23) • **at home** daheim, zu Hause 2 (36) • **at last** endlich, schließlich 5 (97) • **at least** zumindest, wenigstens 3 (57) **at night** nachts, in der Nacht

2 (38/158) • **at school** in der Schule Welc (12/149) • **at that table** an dem Tisch (dort) / an den Tisch (dort) 1 (24/155) • **at the end (of)** am Ende (von) 5 (86) • **at the Shaws' house** im Haus der Shaws / bei den Shaws zu Hause 2 (41) • **at the station** am Bahnhof 4 (73/168) • **at the top (of)** oben, am oberen Ende, an der Spitze (von) 2 (41) • **at the weekend** am Wochenende 2 (38/158)
at work bei der Arbeit / am Arbeitsplatz Welc (16)
°**audience** ['ɔːdiəns] Zuschauer/innen, Zuhörer/innen, Publikum
August ['ɔːgəst] August TOP 1 (35/156)
aunt [ɑːnt] Tante 2 (41)
autumn ['ɔːtəm] Herbst 5 (84/85/170)
°**avocado** [ˌævə'kɑːdəʊ] Avocado
away [ə'weɪ] weg, fort 4 (72)

B

baby ['beɪbi] Baby Welc (11)
back (to) [bæk] zurück (nach) Welc (17)
bad [bæd] schlecht, schlimm 1 (22)
°**bad luck** Pech
badminton ['bædmɪntən] Badminton, Federball 1 (22)
bag [bæg] Tasche, Beutel, Tüte Welc (12/149)
ball [bɔːl] Ball 1 (22/153)
banana [bə'nɑːnə] Banane Welc (8/146)
band [bænd] Band, (Musik-)Gruppe Welc (9/147)
°**Bang!** [bæŋ] Peng!
bank [bæŋk] Bank, Sparkasse 1 (24)
bank robber ['bæŋk ˌrɒbə] Bankräuber/in 1 (24)
°**barbecue** ['bɑːbɪkjuː] Grillparty
baseball ['beɪsbɔːl] Baseball 3 (53/162)
basket ['bɑːskɪt] Korb 2 (37) • **a basket of apples** ein Korb Äpfel 4 (69/167)
basketball ['bɑːskɪtbɔːl] Basketball 1 (22)
bath [bɑːθ] Badewanne TOP 2 (50)
bathroom ['bɑːθruːm] Badezimmer 2 (36/157)
be [biː] sein 1 (21)
beautiful ['bjuːtɪfl] schön 5 (97)
because [bɪ'kɒz] weil 2 (41)
bed [bed] Bett Welc (16) • **Bed and Breakfast (B&B)** [ˌbed‿ən 'brekfəst] Frühstückspension (*wörtlich:* Bett und Frühstück) Welc (16) • **go to bed** ins Bett gehen 2 (38)
bedroom ['bedruːm] Schlafzimmer 2 (36/157)
before [bɪ'fɔː] **1.** vor *(zeitlich)* 1 (20); °**2.** bevor
bell [bel] Klingel, Glocke 4 (81/169)
°**below** [bɪ'ləʊ] unten
°**bend** [bend] beugen
best [best]**: the best ...** der/die/das beste ...; die besten ... 6 (102)
better ['betə] besser 6 (103)
°**between** [bɪ'twiːn] zwischen
big [bɪg] groß Welc (9/147)
bike [baɪk] Fahrrad 3 (53/162) • **ride a bike** Rad fahren 3 (53/162)
biology [baɪ'ɒlədʒi] Biologie 1 (23/154)
bird [bɜːd] Vogel 2 (37/157)
birthday ['bɜːθdeɪ] Geburtstag TOP 1 (35) • **Happy birthday.** Herzlichen Glückwunsch zum Geburtstag. 4 (77) • **My birthday is in May.** Ich habe im Mai Geburtstag. TOP 1 (35/156) • **My birthday is on 13th June.** Ich habe am 13. Juni Geburtstag. TOP 1 (35/156) • **When's your birthday?** Wann hast du Geburtstag? TOP 1 (35/156)
► S.156 birthdays
biscuit ['bɪskɪt] Keks, Plätzchen 4 (69)
black [blæk] schwarz Welc (13/150)
°**blow sth. up** [ˌbləʊ‿'ʌp] etwas in die Luft sprengen
blue [bluː] blau Welc (13/150)
board [bɔːd] **1.** (Wand-)Tafel 1 (22/153) • **on the board** an der/die Tafel 1 (22/153)
°**2.** Brett
boat [bəʊt] Boot, Schiff Welc (9/147)
body ['bɒdi] Körper 4 (74/169)
book [bʊk] Buch Welc (12)
boot [buːt] Stiefel 3 (54/163)
boring ['bɔːrɪŋ] langweilig 2 (38)
both [bəʊθ] beide 4 (70)
bottle ['bɒtl] Flasche 4 (69) • **a bottle of milk** eine Flasche Milch 4 (69/167)
°**bottom** ['bɒtəm] Grund, Boden
°**bough of holly** [ˌbaʊ‿əv 'hɒlɪ] Stechpalmenast
bowl [bəʊl] Schüssel 2 (39) • **a bowl of cornflakes** eine Schale Cornflakes 4 (69/167)
box [bɒks] Kasten, Kästchen, Kiste 1 (19)
boy [bɔɪ] Junge Welc (9/147)
°**bracket** ['brækɪt] Klammer *(in Texten)*
°**brainy** ['breɪni] intelligent
bread *(no pl)* [bred] Brot 4 (69/166)
break [breɪk] Pause 1 (23)
breakfast ['brekfəst] Frühstück Welc (15) • **have breakfast** frühstücken Welc (15)
bridge [brɪdʒ] Brücke 6 (100)
bring [brɪŋ] (mit-, her)bringen 5 (84/85)
brother ['brʌðə] Bruder Welc (8/146)
brown [braʊn] braun Welc (13/150)
budgie ['bʌdʒi] Wellensittich 2 (37)
°**build** [bɪld] bauen
bus [bʌs] Bus 2 (38)
but [bət, bʌt] aber Welc (10)
°**butter** ['bʌtə] Butter
buy [baɪ] kaufen 3 (54)
by [baɪ] von 2 (48)
Bye. [baɪ] Tschüs! 1 (33)

C

°**cabbage** ['kæbɪdʒ] Kohl
°**cabin boy** ['kæbɪn bɔɪ] Schiffsjunge
café ['kæfeɪ] *(kleines)* Restaurant, Imbissstube, Café 4 (77)
cage [keɪdʒ] Käfig 2 (37)
cake [keɪk] Kuchen, Torte 4 (69/166)
calendar ['kælɪndə] Kalender TOP 1 (35)
call [kɔːl] **1.** rufen; anrufen; nennen 3 (65); **2.** Anruf, Telefongespräch 5 (90)
came [keɪm] *Vergangenheitsform von „come“* 5 (88)
camera ['kæmərə] Kamera, Fotoapparat 5 (84/85)
can [kən, kæn] **1.** können Welc (8/146)
I can't ... [kɑːnt] ich kann nicht ... Welc (8/146) • **Can I help you?** Kann ich Ihnen helfen? / Was kann ich für Sie tun? *(im Geschäft)* 3 (54)
2. dürfen 1 (22/129)
°**captain** ['kæptɪn] Kapitän/in
°**caption** ['kæpʃn] Bildunterschrift
car [kɑː] Auto 3 (63)
°**caravan** ['kærəvæn] Wohnwagen
card [kɑːd] (Spiel-, Post-)Karte 3 (53)
°**Caribbean** [ˌkærə'biːən]**: in the Caribbean** in der Karibik
carrot ['kærət] Möhre, Karotte 2 (39)
cat [kæt] Katze Welc (12/149)
CD [ˌsiː'diː] CD 1 (19) • **CD player** CD-Spieler 4 (78)
cent (c) [sent] Cent TOP 3 (67)
centre ['sentə] Zentrum, Mitte 6 (104)
°**chain** [tʃeɪn] Kette
chair [tʃeə] Stuhl 1 (18/152)
champion ['tʃæmpiən] Meister/in, Champion 6 (106)
°**championship** ['tʃæmpiənʃɪp] Meisterschaft

change [tʃeɪndʒ] **1.** Wechselgeld TOP 3 (67); **°2.** (ver)ändern
°chant [tʃɑːnt] Sprechchor *(z.B. von Fußballfans)*
°charity ['tʃærəti] Wohltätigkeitsorganisation
°chart [tʃɑːt] Schaubild, Diagramm, Tabelle
°chase [tʃeɪs] jagen
check [tʃek] (über)prüfen, kontrollieren 1 (31)
checkpoint ['tʃekpɔɪnt] Kontrollpunkt *(hier: zur Selbstüberprüfung)* (3)
°Cheers. [tʃɪəz] Prost!
cheese [tʃiːz] Käse 4 (69/166)
chicken ['tʃɪkɪn] Huhn; (Brat-)Hähnchen 4 (69/166)
child [tʃaɪld], *pl* **children** ['tʃɪldrən] Kind 2 (41)
chips *(pl)* [tʃɪps] Pommes frites 4 (69)
chocolate ['tʃɒklət] Schokolade 4 (69/166)
choir ['kwaɪə] Chor 5 (84/85)
choose [tʃuːz] (sich) aussuchen, (aus)wählen 4 (82)
°chorus ['kɔːrəs] Refrain
°Christmas ['krɪsməs] Weihnachten **°Father Christmas** der Weihnachtsmann • **°Merry Christmas.** Frohe Weihnachten.
church [tʃɜːtʃ] Kirche 6 (100)
°chutney ['tʃʌtni] Chutney *(Paste aus Früchten und Gewürzen)*
°circle ['sɜːkl] Kreis
city ['sɪti] Stadt, Großstadt 6 (100) **city centre** [ˌsɪti 'sentə] Stadtzentrum, Innenstadt 6 (104)
°clap (-pp-) [klæp]**: Clap your hands.** Klatsch(t) in die Hände.
°clarinet [ˌklærə'net] Klarinette
class [klɑːs] (Schul-)Klasse 1 (24) **class teacher** Klassenlehrer/in 1 (24)
classmate ['klɑːsmeɪt] Klassenkamerad/in, Mitschüler/in 1 (32)
classroom ['klɑːsruːm] Klassenzimmer Welc (12/149)
clean [kliːn] sauber machen, putzen 2 (38) • **I clean my teeth.** Ich putze mir die Zähne. 2 (38)
clear [klɪə] klar, deutlich 5 (87)
clever ['klevə] klug, schlau 1 (20)
climb [klaɪm] klettern; hinaufklettern (auf) 1 (22) • **Climb a tree.** Klettere auf einen Baum. 1 (22)
clock [klɒk] (Wand-, Stand-, Turm-)Uhr 3 (66/166)
close [kləʊz] schließen, zumachen Welc (10)
°clothes *(pl)* [kləʊðz] Kleidung, Kleidungsstücke
club [klʌb] Klub; Verein 5 (84/85)
°cocktail stick ['kɒkteɪl stɪk] Cocktailspieß(chen)
cola ['kəʊlə] Cola 4 (69)
cold [kəʊld] kalt 5 (98) • **be cold** frieren 5 (98)
°collage ['kɒlɑːʒ] Collage
collect [kə'lekt] sammeln 3 (53)
colour ['kʌlə] Farbe Welc (8/146) **What colour is ...?** Welche Farbe hat ...? Welc (13)
°combine [kəm'baɪn] kombinieren, verbinden
come [kʌm] kommen 1 (20) • **come home** nach Hause kommen 2 (36/157) • **come in** hereinkommen 1 (32)
comic ['kɒmɪk] Comic-Heft 1 (18)
°compare [kəm'peə] vergleichen
°complete [kəm'pliːt] vervollständigen, ergänzen
computer [kəm'pjuːtə] Computer 1 (22/153)
cooker ['kʊkə] Herd TOP 2 (50)
cool [kuːl] cool 4 (82)
°copy ['kɒpi] **1.** kopieren, übertragen, abschreiben; **2.** Kopie
corner ['kɔːnə] Ecke 6 (102)
cornflakes ['kɔːnfleɪks] Cornflakes 2 (42)
°correct [kə'rekt] **1.** korrigieren, verbessern; **°2. the correct times** die richtigen/korrekten Zeiten
country ['kʌntri] Land 2 (48)
course: of course [əv 'kɔːs] natürlich, selbstverständlich 2 (40)
cousin ['kʌzn] Cousin, Cousine 2 (41)
cover ['kʌvə] (CD-)Hülle 5 (89)
°Crash. [kræʃ] Krach!
°crisp [krɪsp] knackig
crisps *(pl)* [krɪsps] Kartoffelchips 4 (69)
°cross [krɒs] Kreuz
°cucumber ['kjuːkʌmbə] (Salat-)Gurke
cupboard ['kʌbəd] (Küchen-)Schrank TOP 2 (50)
°cut (-tt-) [kʌt] schneiden

D

dad [dæd] Papa, Vati; Vater Welc (8/146)
dance [dɑːns] **1.** tanzen 3 (53/162); **2.** Tanz 5 (84/85) • **°dancer** Tänzer/in • **dancing** Tanzen 3 (53/162) • **dancing lessons** Tanzstunden, Tanzunterricht 3 (53)
danger ['deɪndʒə] Gefahr 5 (97)
dark [dɑːk] dunkel 5 (96)
date [deɪt] Datum TOP 1 (35)
daughter ['dɔːtə] Tochter 2 (41)
day [deɪ] Tag Welc (12) • **one day** eines Tages 5 (90) • **days of the week** Wochentage Welc (14/150)
dead [ded] tot 2 (41)
dear [dɪə] **1.** Schatz, Liebling 4 (72); **2. Dear Jay ...** Lieber Jay, ... 3 (56)
December [dɪ'sembə] Dezember TOP 1 (35/156)
°decide (on) [dɪ'saɪd] sich entscheiden (für), beschließen
°deck [dek] Deck
°deck [dek] schmücken
°decorations *(pl)* [ˌdekə'reɪʃnz] (Fest-)Schmuck
°describe [dɪ'skraɪb] beschreiben
desk [desk] Schreibtisch 2 (36)
detective [dɪ'tektɪv] Detektiv/in 3 (65)
°dialogue ['daɪəlɒg] Dialog
diary ['daɪəri] Tagebuch; Terminkalender 5 (88)
dictionary ['dɪkʃənri] Wörterbuch, *(alphabetisches)* Wörterverzeichnis (3)
did [dɪd] *Vergangenheitsform von „do“* 5 (88) • **Did you know ...?** Wusstest du ...? 5 (89) • **we didn't go** ['dɪdnt] wir gingen nicht / wir sind nicht gegangen 5 (89)
different (from) ['dɪfrənt] verschieden, unterschiedlich; anders (als) 1 (25)
difficult ['dɪfɪkəlt] schwierig, schwer 2 (38/158)
dining room ['daɪnɪŋ ruːm] Esszimmer TOP 2 (50)
dinner ['dɪnə] Abendessen, Abendbrot 3 (57) • **have dinner** Abendbrot essen 3 (57/164)
disco ['dɪskəʊ] Disko 4 (70)
dishwasher ['dɪʃwɒʃə] Geschirrspülmaschine TOP 2 (50)
divorced [dɪ'vɔːst] geschieden 2 (41)
do [duː] tun, machen 1 (22) • **Do what I do.** Tue, was ich tue. 1 (22) **Do you like ...?** Magst du ...? 1 (18/152) • **do sport** Sport treiben 3 (53/162)
dog [dɒg] Hund Welc (12/149)
don't [dəʊnt]**: Don't listen to Dan.** Hör/Hört nicht auf Dan. 1 (20) • **I don't like ...** Ich mag ... nicht. / Ich mag kein(e) ... Welc (8/146)
door [dɔː] Tür 4 (81/169)
doorbell ['dɔːbel] Türklingel 4 (81)
°doorstopper ['dɔːstɒpə] Türstopper; *hier:* mehrschichtiges Sandwich

dossier ['dɒsieɪ] Mappe, Dossier *(des Sprachenportfolios)* (3)
°**dot** [dɒt] Pünktchen
double ['dʌbl] zweimal, doppelt, Doppel- Welc (15)
down [daʊn] hinunter, herunter, nach unten 4 (72/168)
downstairs [ˌdaʊn'steəz] unten; nach unten TOP 2 (50)
drama ['drɑːmə] Schauspiel, darstellende Kunst 1 (23/154)
°**draw** [drɔː] zeichnen
dream [driːm] Traum TOP 2 (50) **dream house** Traumhaus TOP 2 (50)
dress [dres] Kleid 3 (54/163)
°**dress rehearsal** ['dres rɪˌhɜːsl] Generalprobe, Kostümprobe
dressed [drest]**: get dressed** sich anziehen 2 (39)
drink [drɪŋk] **1.** trinken 2 (39); **2.** Getränk 4 (69)
drop (-pp-) [drɒp] **1.** fallen lassen Welc (10); **2.** fallen 6 (111)
°**drum** [drʌm] Trommel
DVD [ˌdiː viː' diː] DVD 4 (71)

E

each [iːtʃ] jeder, jede, jedes (einzelne) 6 (102) • °**Ask each other questions.** Stellt euch gegenseitig Fragen.
ear [ɪə] Ohr 4 (74/169)
early ['ɜːli] früh 2 (38)
earring ['ɪərɪŋ] Ohrring 4 (71)
easy ['iːzi] leicht, einfach 2 (38)
eat [iːt] essen 1 (18/152)
e-friend ['iːfrend] Brieffreund/in *(im Internet)* 5 (89)
elephant ['elɪfənt] Elefant 5 (95)
e-mail ['iːmeɪl] E-Mail 2 (42)
empty ['empti] leer Welc (10)
end [end] Ende 1 (32) • **at the end (of)** am Ende (von) 5 (86)
English ['ɪŋglɪʃ] Englisch; englisch Welc (8/146)
enough [ɪ'nʌf] genug 1 (22)
essay (about, on) ['eseɪ] Aufsatz (über) 2 (38)
°**etc.** [et'setərə] usw.
euro (€) ['jʊərəʊ] Euro TOP 3 (67)
evening ['iːvnɪŋ] Abend 2 (38/158) **in the evening** abends, am Abend 2 (38/158) • **on Friday evening** freitagabends, am Freitagabend 2 (38/158)
every ['evri] jeder, jede, jedes 2 (38)
everything ['evriθɪŋ] alles 1 (32)
everywhere ['evriweə] überall 6 (104)
example [ɪg'zɑːmpl] Beispiel 5 (89) **for example** zum Beispiel 5 (89)

Excuse me, ... [ɪk'skjuːz miː] Entschuldigung, ... / Entschuldigen Sie, ... Welc (17)
► S.151 „Entschuldigung"
exercise ['eksəsaɪz] Übung, Aufgabe Welc (12/150) • **exercise book** ['eksəsaɪz bʊk] Schulheft, Übungsheft Welc (12)
expensive [ɪk'spensɪv] teuer 4 (71)
explore [ɪk'splɔː] erkunden, erforschen 6 (101)
°**explosive** [ɪk'spləʊsɪv] Sprengstoff
extra ['ekstrə] zusätzlich 5 (92)
eye [aɪ] Auge 4 (74/169)

F

face [feɪs] Gesicht 1 (22/153)
family ['fæməli] Familie Welc (12/149) • **family tree** (Familien-)Stammbaum 2 (41)
fan [fæn] Fan 6 (106)
°**fancy-dress party** [ˌfænsi'dres] Kostümfest
fantastic [fæn'tæstɪk] fantastisch, toll 4 (81)
far [fɑː] weit (entfernt) 6 (102) **so far** bis jetzt, bis hierher 6 (110)
°**Fast away the old year passes.** [fɑːst] *etwa:* Schnell vergeht das alte Jahr.
father ['fɑːðə] Vater Welc (12/149) °**Father Christmas** der Weihnachtsmann
favourite ['feɪvərɪt] Lieblings- Welc (8/146) • **my favourite colour** meine Lieblingsfarbe Welc (8/146)
February ['februəri] Februar TOP 1 (35/156)
feed [fiːd] füttern 2 (39)
feet [fiːt] *Plural von „foot"* 4 (74/169)
felt tip ['felt tɪp] Filzstift Welc (12/149)
file [faɪl]**: grammar file** *Grammatikanhang* (3/126) • **skills file** *Anhang mit Lern- und Arbeitstechniken* (3/118)
°**fill in** [ˌfɪl‿'ɪn] einsetzen
film [fɪlm] Film 2 (48) • **film star** Filmstar 2 (48)
find [faɪnd] finden Welc (10) • **find out (about)** herausfinden (über) 3 (65) • **finder** Finder 5 (91)
finger ['fɪŋgə] Finger 4 (74/169)
finish ['fɪnɪʃ] beenden, zu Ende machen; enden 6 (103)
first [fɜːst] **1.** erste(r, s) Welc (14) **the first day** der erste Tag Welc (14) **be first** der/die Erste sein 6 (105) **2.** zuerst, als Erstes 1 (20)
fish, *pl* **fish** [fɪʃ] Fisch 2 (37/157)

fit (-tt-) [fɪt] passen 2 (48)
flat [flæt] Wohnung Welc (14)
floor [flɔː] Fußboden 5 (98)
flow chart ['fləʊ tʃɑːt] Flussdiagramm 5 (90)
follow ['fɒləʊ] folgen; verfolgen 4 (71)
food [fuːd] **1.** Essen; Lebensmittel 1 (24); **2.** Futter 2 (39)
foot [fʊt], *pl* **feet** [fiːt] Fuß 4 (74/169)
football ['fʊtbɔːl] Fußball Welc (9/147) • **football boots** Fußballschuhe, -stiefel 3 (54/163)
for [fə, fɔː] **1.** für Welc (12) • **for breakfast/lunch/dinner** zum Frühstück/Mittagessen/Abendbrot 4 (69) • **for example** zum Beispiel 5 (89) • **for lots of reasons** aus vielen Gründen 6 (105) • **for three days** drei Tage (lang) 5 (97) • **just for fun** nur zum Spaß 6 (101/174) **What's for homework?** Was haben wir als Hausaufgabe auf? 1 (28/155) • °**for a long time** eine lange Zeit, lange °**2.** denn
form [fɔːm] **1.** (Schul-)Klasse 1 (22) **form teacher** Klassenlehrer/in 1 (22) °**2.** Form
free [friː] **1.** frei 3 (55) • **free time** Freizeit, freie Zeit 3 (55) **2.** kostenlos 6 (100)
°**freeze** [friːz] einfrieren, gefrieren; *hier:* stillstehen, erstarren
French [frentʃ] Französisch 1 (23/154)
Friday ['fraɪdeɪ, 'fraɪdi] Freitag Welc (14/150)
fridge [frɪdʒ] Kühlschrank TOP 2 (50)
friend [frend] Freund/in Welc (12/149)
from [frəm, frɒm] **1.** aus Welc (8/146); **2.** von 2 (46) • **I'm from ...** Ich komme aus ... / Ich bin aus ... Welc (8/146) • **Where are you from?** Wo kommst du her? Welc (8/146)
front [frʌnt]**: in front of** vor *(räumlich)* 6 (103) • **to the front** nach vorn 6 (105) • **front door** [ˌfrʌnt 'dɔː] Wohnungstür, Haustür 4 (81)
fruit [fruːt] Obst, Früchte; Frucht 4 (69) • **fruit salad** ['fruːt ˌsæləd] Obstsalat 4 (69)
full [fʊl] voll Welc (10)
fun [fʌn] Spaß 6 (101) • **have fun** Spaß haben, sich amüsieren 6 (101/174) • **Have fun!** Viel Spaß! 6 (101/174) • **just for fun** nur zum Spaß 6 (101/174) • **Riding is fun.**

Reiten macht Spaß. 6 (101/174)
► S.174 fun
funny ['fʌni] witzig, komisch 4 (71)

G

°**galleon** ['gæliən] Galeone
game [geɪm] Spiel (3)
garden ['gɑːdn] Garten 2 (36)
geography [dʒi'ɒgrəfi] Geografie, Erdkunde 1 (23/154)
German ['dʒɜːmən] Deutsch; deutsch; Deutsche(r) 1 (23/154)
Germany ['dʒɜːməni] Deutschland Welc (17)
get (-tt-) [get] **1.** gelangen, (hin-)kommen 4 (82) • **get home** nach Hause kommen 6 (106)
2. get dressed sich anziehen 2 (39)
3. get off (the train/bus) (aus dem Zug/Bus) aussteigen 4 (73) • **get on (the train/bus)** (in den Zug/Bus) einsteigen 4 (73/168)
4. get ready (for) sich fertig machen (für), sich vorbereiten (auf) 4 (72) • **get things ready** Dinge fertig machen, vorbereiten 2 (48)
5. get up aufstehen 2 (38)
getting by in English [ˌgetɪŋ 'baɪ] *etwa:* auf Englisch zurechtkommen (3)
girl [gɜːl] Mädchen Welc (9/147)
give [gɪv] geben 2 (39)
glass [glɑːs] Glas 4 (69) • **a glass of water** ein Glas Wasser 4 (69/167)
glasses *(pl)* ['glɑːsɪz] (eine) Brille 2 (48/161)
°**glorious** ['glɔːriəs] herrlich; ruhmreich
glue [gluː] **1.** Klebstoff 6 (104); °**2.** (auf-, ein)kleben • **glue stick** ['gluː stɪk] Klebestift Welc (12/149)
go (to) [gəʊ] gehen (zu, nach) Welc (14) • **go home** nach Hause gehen 2 (36/157) • **go on** weitermachen 1 (33) • **Go on.** Mach weiter. / Erzähl weiter. 1 (33) • **go out** weg-, raus-, ausgehen 4 (79)
go riding reiten gehen 3 (53) • **go shopping** einkaufen gehen 3 (63)
go swimming schwimmen gehen 3 (52/162) • **go to bed** ins Bett gehen 2 (38) • **Let's go.** Auf geht's! Welc (12) • °**go with** passen zu
°**gold** [gəʊld] Gold
good [gʊd] gut Welc (14/150)
Good afternoon. Guten Tag. *(nachmittags)* 3 (54) • **Good luck (with ...)!** Viel Glück (bei/mit ...)! Welc (17) • **Good morning.** Guten Morgen. Welc (14/150)
Goodbye. [ˌgʊd'baɪ] Auf Wiedersehen. Welc (14/150) • **say goodbye** sich verabschieden Welc (17)
got [gɒt]: **I've got ...** Ich habe ... Welc (8/146) • **I haven't got a chair.** Ich habe keinen Stuhl. 1 (24)
got up [ˌgɒt_'ʌp] *Vergangenheitsform von „get up"* 5 (88/171)
grammar ['græmə] Grammatik (3)
grammar file *Grammatikanhang* (3/126)
grandchild ['græntʃaɪld], *pl* **grandchildren** ['-tʃɪldrən] Enkel/in 2 (41)
grandfather ['grænfɑːðə] Großvater 2 (41/159)
grandma ['grænmɑː] Oma 2 (41)
grandmother ['grænmʌðə] Großmutter 2 (41/159)
grandpa ['grænpɑː] Opa 2 (41)
grandparents ['grænpeərənts] Großeltern 2 (41)
great [greɪt] großartig, toll Welc (9)
green [griːn] grün Welc (13/150)
°**ground** [graʊnd] (Erd-)Boden, Erde
group [gruːp] Gruppe 5 (86)
grumble ['grʌmbl] murren, nörgeln 6 (104)
°**guess** [ges] raten, erraten
guest [gest] Gast 2 (47)
guinea pig ['gɪni pɪg] Meerschweinchen 2 (37/157)
guitar [gɪ'tɑː] Gitarre 3 (53) • **play the guitar** Gitarre spielen 3 (53/162)

H

had [hæd] *Vergangenheitsform von „have" und von „have got"* 5 (88)
°**hail** [heɪl] *(das neue Jahr)* begrüßen
hair *(no pl)* [heə] Haar, Haare 4 (74/169)
half [hɑːf]: **half past 11** halb zwölf (11.30 / 23.30) Welc (16/151)
hall [hɔːl] **1.** Flur, Diele 6 (111); °**2.** Halle, Saal
°**ham** [hæm] Schinken
hamburger ['hæmbɜːgə] Hamburger 4 (69/166)
hamster ['hæmstə] Hamster 2 (37/157)
hand [hænd] Hand 2 (38)
happen (to) ['hæpən] geschehen, passieren (mit) TOP 2 (51)
happy ['hæpi] glücklich, froh Welc (9/147) • **Happy birthday.** Herzlichen Glückwunsch zum Geburtstag. 4 (77)
°**harbour** ['hɑːbə] Hafen
°**hat** [hæt] Hut
hate [heɪt] hassen, gar nicht mögen 3 (57)
have [hæv]: **have a shower** (sich) duschen 2 (48) • **have breakfast** frühstücken Welc (15) • **have dinner** Abendbrot essen 3 (57/164)
have ... for breakfast ... zum Frühstück essen/trinken 4 (69)
have fun Spaß haben, sich amüsieren 6 (101/174) • **Have fun!** Viel Spaß! 6 (101/174) • **have to do** tun müssen 3 (57)
have got: I've got ... [aɪv 'gɒt] Ich habe ... Welc (8/146) • **I haven't got a chair.** ['hævnt gɒt] Ich habe keinen Stuhl. 1 (24)
°**hay** [heɪ] Heu
he [hiː] er Welc (8)
head [hed] Kopf 3 (55)
hear [hɪə] hören 4 (73)
°**heat** [hiːt] Hitze
Hello. [hə'ləʊ] Hallo. / Guten Tag. Welc (8/146)
help [help] **1.** helfen Welc (11) • **Can I help you?** Kann ich Ihnen helfen? / Was kann ich für Sie tun? *(im Geschäft)* 3 (54)
2. Hilfe 2 (40)
her [hə, hɜː] **1.** ihr, ihre 1 (21); **2.** sie; ihr 1 (33)
here [hɪə] **1.** hier Welc (11); **2.** hierher 2 (42/160) • **Here you are.** Bitte sehr. / Hier bitte. 2 (40)
► S.159 „bitte"
Hi! [haɪ] Hallo! Welc (8/146) • **Say hi to Dilip for me.** Grüß Dilip von mir. 3 (56)
hide [haɪd] sich verstecken; *(etwas)* verstecken 4 (73)
°**highlight** ['haɪlaɪt] Höhepunkt
him [hɪm] ihn; ihm 1 (24)
his [hɪz] sein, seine Welc (8)
history ['hɪstri] Geschichte 1 (23/154)
hit (-tt-) [hɪt] **1.** schlagen 6 (111); **2.** *Vergangenheitsform von „hit"* 6 (111)
hobby ['hɒbi] Hobby 3 (52/162)
hockey ['hɒki] Hockey 1 (22)
hockey shoes Hockeyschuhe 3 (54/163)
°**hold** [həʊld]: **hold hands** sich an den Händen halten • **hold up** hochhalten
hole [həʊl] Loch 4 (81)
holidays ['hɒlədeɪz] Ferien Welc (12)
home [həʊm] Heim, Zuhause 2 (36)
at home daheim, zu Hause 2 (36)
come home nach Hause kommen 2 (36/157) • **get home** nach Hause kommen 6 (106) • **go home** nach Hause gehen 2 (36/157)
homework *(no pl)* ['həʊmwɜːk] Hausaufgabe(n) 1 (28/155) • **do homework** die Hausaufgabe(n)

machen 2 (48) • **What's for homework?** Was haben wir als Hausaufgabe auf? 1 (28/155)
°**Hooray!** [hu'reɪ] Hurra!
horse [hɔːs] Pferd 2 (37/157)
°**hospital** ['hɒspɪtl] Krankenhaus
hot [hɒt] heiß 4 (69/166) • **hot chocolate** heiße Schokolade 4 (69/166)
house [haʊs] Haus Welc (9/147) **at the Shaws' house** im Haus der Shaws / bei den Shaws zu Hause 2 (41)
how [haʊ] wie Welc (8/146) • **How do you know ...?** Woher weißt/kennst du ...? 6 (111) • **how many?** wie viele? 5 (96/172) • **how much?** wie viel? 5 (96/172) • **How much is/are ...?** Was kostet/kosten ...? / Wie viel kostet/kosten ...? TOP 3 (67) **How old are you?** Wie alt bist du? Welc (8/146) • **How was ...?** Wie war ...? 1 (33)
hundred ['hʌndrəd] hundert Welc (15)
hungry ['hʌŋgri] hungrig 4 (69) **be hungry** Hunger haben, hungrig sein 4 (69)
°**hurrah** [hə'rɑː] hurra
hurry ['hʌri]: **1. hurry up** sich beeilen 1 (32); **2. be in a hurry** in Eile sein, es eilig haben 4 (71)
hurt [hɜːt] **1.** wehtun; verletzen 6 (111); **2.** *Vergangenheitsform von „hurt"* 6 (111)
hutch [hʌtʃ] (Kaninchen-)Stall 2 (37)

I

I [aɪ] ich Welc (8/146) • **I'm** [aɪm] ich bin Welc (8/146) • **I'm from ...** Ich komme aus ... / Ich bin aus ... Welc (8/146) • **I'm ... years old.** Ich bin ... Jahre alt. Welc (8/146) • **I'm sorry.** Entschuldigung. / Tut mir leid. 1 (21)
ice: ice cream [ˌaɪs 'kriːm] (Speise-)Eis 4 (69/166) • °**ice rink** ['aɪs rɪŋk] Schlittschuhbahn
idea [aɪ'dɪə] Idee, Einfall 1 (24)
°**if** [ɪf] falls, wenn • °**if you're happy** wenn du glücklich bist
°**imagine sth.** [ɪ'mædʒɪn] sich etwas vorstellen
in [ɪn] in Welc (8/146) • **in ... Street** in der ...straße Welc (8/146) • **in English** auf Englisch Welc (8/146) **in front of** vor *(räumlich)* 6 (103) **in here** hier drinnen Welc (11) • **in the afternoon** nachmittags, am Nachmittag 2 (38/158) • **in the evening** abends, am Abend 2 (38/158) • **in the morning** am Morgen, morgens 1 (19) • **in the photo** auf dem Foto Welc (9/148) **in the picture** auf dem Bild Welc (11/149) • **in there** dort drinnen 5 (87)
°**Indian** ['ɪndiən] indisch
°**industrial museum** [ɪnˌdʌstriəl mju'ziːəm] Industriemuseum
infinitive [ɪn'fɪnətɪv] Infinitiv *(Grundform des Verbs)* 5 (88)
information (about/on) *(no pl)* [ˌɪnfə'meɪʃn] Information(en) (über) 5 (89)
°**ingredient** [ɪn'griːdiənt] Zutat *(beim Kochen)*
inside [ˌɪn'saɪd] innen (drin), drinnen 4 (81)
interesting ['ɪntrəstɪŋ] interessant 2 (48)
internet ['ɪntənet] Internet 5 (89)
°**interview** ['ɪntəvjuː] **1.** interviewen, befragen; **2.** Interview
into ['ɪntə, 'ɪntʊ] in ... (hinein) 3 (65/165)
°**invent** [ɪn'vent] erfinden
invitation (to) [ˌɪnvɪ'teɪʃn] Einladung (zu) 4 (70)
invite (to) [ɪn'vaɪt] einladen (zu) 4 (70/167)
is [ɪz] ist Welc (8/146)
it [ɪt] er/sie/es Welc (9) • **It's £1.** Er/Sie/Es kostet 1 Pfund. TOP 3 (67)
its [ɪts] sein/seine; ihr/ihre 2 (41/134)

J

January ['dʒænjuəri] Januar TOP 1 (35/156)
jazz [dʒæz] Jazz 5 (91)
jeans *(pl)* [dʒiːnz] Jeans 3 (54/163)
job [dʒɒb] Aufgabe, Job 5 (93)
joke [dʒəʊk] Witz 1 (22)
°**jolly** ['dʒɒli] fröhlich
judo ['dʒuːdəʊ] Judo 2 (40) • **do judo** Judo machen 2 (40)
jug [dʒʌg] Krug 4 (69) • **a jug of orange juice** ein Krug Orangensaft 4 (69/167)
juice [dʒuːs] Saft 4 (69/166)
July [dʒu'laɪ] Juli TOP 1 (35/156)
°**jumble** ['dʒʌmbl] gebrauchte Sachen, Trödel
jumble sale ['dʒʌmbl seɪl] Wohltätigkeitsbasar TOP 3 (67)
°**jump** [dʒʌmp] springen
June [dʒuːn] Juni TOP 1 (35/156)
junior ['dʒuːniə] Junioren-, Jugend- 5 (84/85)
just [dʒʌst] (einfach) nur, bloß 2 (41)

K

key [kiː] Schlüssel 6 (110) • **key word** Stichwort, Schlüsselwort 4 (71)
°**kickboxing** ['kɪkbɒksɪŋ] Kickboxen
kid [kɪd] Kind, Jugendliche(r) 5 (86)
kill [kɪl] töten 5 (96)
king [kɪŋ] König 5 (88)
kitchen ['kɪtʃɪn] Küche 2 (36/157)
kite [kaɪt] Drachen Welc (9)
knee [niː] Knie 4 (74/169)
°**knife** [naɪf], *pl* **knives** [naɪvz] Messer
knock (on) [nɒk] (an)klopfen (an) 6 (110)
know [nəʊ] **1.** wissen 3 (54/163); **2.** kennen 3 (60) • **How do you know ...?** Woher weißt du ...? / Woher kennst du ...? 6 (111) **..., you know.** ..., wissen Sie. / ..., weißt du. 3 (54) • **You know what, Sophie?** Weißt du was, Sophie? 6 (104)

L

°**label** ['leɪbl] beschriften, etikettieren
°**ladder** ['lædə] *(die)* Leiter
°**lads and lasses** [ˌlædz‿ənd 'læsəz] *(umgangssprachlich)* Jungs und Mädels
lamp [læmp] Lampe 2 (36/157)
language ['læŋgwɪdʒ] Sprache (3)
lasagne [lə'zænjə] Lasagne 1 (24)
last [lɑːst] letzte(r, s) Welc (12) **the last day** der letzte Tag Welc (12) **at last** endlich, schließlich 5 (97)
late [leɪt] spät; zu spät Welc (12) **be late** zu spät sein/kommen Welc (12) • **Sorry, I'm late.** Entschuldigung, dass ich zu spät bin/komme. Welc (12)
later ['leɪtə] später 4 (72)
laugh [lɑːf] lachen Welc (10)
lay the table [leɪ] den Tisch decken 3 (57)
°**lazy** ['leɪzi] faul
learn [lɜːn] lernen 3 (57)
least: at least [ət 'liːst] zumindest, wenigstens 3 (57)
°**leave** [liːv] verlassen
°**leaves** *(pl)* [liːvz] Laub, Blätter
left [left]: **on the left** links, auf der linken Seite 5 (89/171)

leg [leg] Bein 4 (74/169)
lemonade [ˌleməˈneɪd] Limonade 4 (69/166)
lesson [ˈlesn] (Unterrichts-)Stunde 1 (20) • **lessons** *(pl)* [ˈlesnz] Unterricht 1 (20)
Let's ... [lets] Lass uns ... / Lasst uns ... Welc (12) • **Let's go.** Auf geht's! Welc (12) • **Let's look at the list.** Sehen wir uns die Liste an. / Lasst uns die Liste ansehen. Welc (12)
letter [ˈletə] **1.** Buchstabe 2 (40); **°2. letter (to)** Brief (an)
°lettuce [ˈletɪs] (grüner) Salat
library [ˈlaɪbrəri] Bibliothek, Bücherei 6 (102)
life [laɪf], *pl* **lives** [laɪvz] Leben 2 (38)
like [laɪk] wie 1 (24) • **°like this** so
like [laɪk] mögen, gernhaben Welc (8/146) • **I like ...** Ich mag ... Welc (8/146) • **I don't like ...** Ich mag ... nicht. / Ich mag kein(e) ... Welc (8/146) • **Do you like ...?** Magst du ...? 1 (18/152) • **Dilip likes ...** Dilip mag ... 1 (33) • **I like swimming/dancing/...** Ich schwimme/tanze/... gern. 3 (53) • **I'd like ... (= I would like ...)** Ich hätte gern ... / Ich möchte gern ... 4 (69) • **I'd like to go (= I would like to go)** Ich würde gern gehen / Ich möchte gehen 6 (101) **I wouldn't like to go** Ich würde nicht gern gehen / Ich möchte nicht gehen 6 (101) • **Would you like ...?** Möchtest du ...? / Möchten Sie ...? 4 (69) • **°Say what you like about ...** Sag, was du an ... magst
°line [laɪn] Linie
link [lɪŋk] verbinden, verknüpfen 3 (63) • **°link up (with)** sich *(über das Internet)* in Verbindung setzen (mit)
list [lɪst] Liste Welc (12)
listen (to) [ˈlɪsn] zuhören; sich *etwas* anhören Welc (9/147)
little [ˈlɪtl] klein 1 (33)
live [lɪv] leben, wohnen Welc (8/146)
lives [laɪvz] *Plural von „life"* 2 (38)
living room [ˈlɪvɪŋ ruːm] Wohnzimmer 2 (36/157)
°local [ˈləʊkl] lokal, örtlich, Lokal-
°locked [lɒkt] abgeschlossen, verschlossen
long [lɒŋ] lang 4 (70)
look [lʊk] schauen, gucken Welc (10) • **look at** ansehen, anschauen Welc (12/149) • **Look at the board.** Sieh/Seht an die Tafel. 1 (24/155) • **look different/great/old** anders/toll/alt aussehen TOP 2 (51) **look round** sich umsehen 4 (73) **°look for** suchen • **°look up words** Wörter nachschlagen ► S.158 (to) look – (to) see – (to) watch
°look-out [ˈlʊkaʊt] Ausguck
lot: a lot [ə ˈlɒt] viel TOP 2 (51) **Thanks a lot!** Vielen Dank! 3 (56) **He likes her a lot.** Er mag sie sehr. 1 (33) • **lots more** [lɒts] viel mehr 6 (101) • **lots of ...** eine Menge ..., viele ..., viel ... 1 (18)
loud [laʊd] laut 6 (103)
°love [lʌv] lieben
Love ... [lʌv] Liebe Grüße, ... *(Briefschluss)* 3 (56)
luck [lʌk]: **Good luck (with ...)!** Viel Glück (bei/mit ...)! Welc (17) • **°bad luck** Pech
°luggage van [ˈlʌgɪdʒ væn] Gepäckwagen
lunch [lʌntʃ] Mittagessen 1 (23) **lunch break** Mittagspause 1 (23)

M

mad [mæd] verrückt 1 (20)
made [meɪd] *Vergangenheitsform von „make"* 5 (88/171)
magazine [ˌmægəˈziːn] Zeitschrift, Magazin 4 (79)
mail [meɪl] schicken, senden *(per Post oder E-Mail)* 5 (89)
make [meɪk] machen; bauen TOP 1 (35) • **make a mess** alles durcheinanderbringen, alles in Unordnung bringen 4 (72)
man [mæn], *pl* **men** [men] Mann 3 (65)
many [ˈmeni] viele 5 (96) • **how many?** wie viele? 5 (96/172) ► S.172 „viel", „viele"
March [mɑːtʃ] März TOP 1 (35/156)
°mark [mɑːk] markieren, kennzeichnen
marmalade [ˈmɑːməleɪd] (Orangen-)Marmelade 1 (18)
married (to) [ˈmærɪd] verheiratet (mit) 2 (41)
match [mætʃ] Spiel, Wettkampf 3 (56)
°match [mætʃ] **1.** passen zu; **2.** zuordnen • **°Match the letters and numbers.** Ordne die Buchstaben den Zahlen zu.
maths [mæθs] Mathematik 1 (23/154)
may [meɪ] dürfen 5 (84/85)
May [meɪ] Mai TOP 1 (35/156)
maybe [ˈmeɪbi] vielleicht 3 (65)
me [miː] mir; mich Welc (10) • **Me too.** Ich auch. Welc (12) • **That's me.** Das bin ich. Welc (10) • **Why me?** Warum ich? Welc (14)
meat [miːt] Fleisch 2 (39)
meet [miːt] **1.** treffen; kennenlernen Welc (8); **2.** sich treffen 3 (60)
men [men] *Plural von „man"* 3 (65)
°Merry Christmas. [ˌmeri ˈkrɪsməs] Frohe Weihnachten.
mess [mes]: **make a mess** alles durcheinanderbringen, alles in Unordnung bringen 4 (72)
°miaow [miˈaʊ] miauen
mice [maɪs] *Plural von „mouse"* 2 (37/157)
middle (of) [ˈmɪdl] Mitte 6 (102)
milk [mɪlk] Milch 1 (19)
°mime [maɪm] **1.** vorspielen, pantomimisch darstellen; **2.** Pantomime
mind map [ˈmaɪnd mæp] Mindmap („Gedankenkarte", „Wissensnetz") 2 (38)
mints *(pl)* [mɪnts] Pfefferminzbonbons 1 (33)
minute [ˈmɪnɪt] Minute 4 (81)
°mirror [ˈmɪrə] Spiegel
Miss White [mɪs] Frau White *(unverheiratet)* 5 (86)
°missing [ˈmɪsɪŋ]: **the missing information/words** die fehlenden Informationen/Wörter
mistake [mɪˈsteɪk] Fehler 5 (87)
°mix (with) [mɪks] sich vermischen (mit) • **°mix up** durcheinanderbringen
°mobile [ˈməʊbaɪl] Mobile
mobile (phone) [ˈməʊbaɪl] Mobiltelefon, Handy 1 (19)
model [ˈmɒdl] Modell*(-flugzeug, -schiff usw.)* 3 (53)
Monday [ˈmʌndeɪ, ˈmʌndi] Montag Welc (14/150) • **Monday morning** Montagmorgen Welc (14/150)
money [ˈmʌni] Geld TOP 3 (67)
month [mʌnθ] Monat TOP 1 (35/156)
more [mɔː] mehr 1 (33) • **lots more** viel mehr 6 (101) • **no more music** keine Musik mehr 4 (81) **one more** noch ein(e), ein(e) weitere(r, s) 6 (105)
morning [ˈmɔːnɪŋ] Morgen, Vormittag Welc (14/150) • **in the morning** morgens, am Morgen 1 (19) • **Monday morning** Montagmorgen Welc (14/150) • **on Friday morning** freitagmorgens, am Freitagmorgen 2 (38/158)
most [məʊst]: **most people** die meisten Leute 3 (57)
°mostly [ˈməʊstli] hauptsächlich
mother [ˈmʌðə] Mutter Welc (12/149)
°mountain [ˈmaʊntən] Berg
mouse [maʊs], *pl* **mice** [maɪs] Maus 2 (37/157)
mouth [maʊθ] Mund 4 (74/169)

°**mozzarella** [ˌmɒtsəˈrelə] Mozzarella
MP3 player [ˌempiːˈθriː ˌpleɪə] MP3-Spieler Welc (12)
Mr ... [ˈmɪstə] Herr ... Welc (12/149)
Mrs ... [ˈmɪsɪz] Frau ... Welc (12/149)
much [mʌtʃ] viel TOP 3 (67) • **how much?** wie viel? 5 (96/172) • **How much is/are ...?** Was kostet/kosten ...? / Wie viel kostet/kosten ...? TOP 3 (67)
► S.172 „viel", „viele"
mum [mʌm] Mama, Mutti; Mutter Welc (8/146)
museum [mjuˈziːəm] Museum 6 (101)
music [ˈmjuːzɪk] Musik 1 (23/154)
musical [ˈmjuːzɪkl] **1.** Musical 5 (86); °**2.** musikalisch
must [mʌst] müssen 6 (102)
my [maɪ] mein/e Welc (8/146) • **My name is ...** Ich heiße ... / Mein Name ist ... Welc (8/146) • **It's my turn.** Ich bin dran / an der Reihe. 1 (20)
°**mystery** [ˈmɪstri] Rätsel, Geheimnis

N

name [neɪm] Name Welc (8/146) **My name is ...** Ich heiße ... / Mein Name ist ... Welc (8/146) • **What's your name?** Wie heißt du? Welc (8/146)
near [nɪə] in der Nähe von, nahe (bei) 6 (100)
°**necklace** [ˈnekləs] Halskette
need [niːd] brauchen, benötigen Welc (12)
neighbour [ˈneɪbə] Nachbar/in 3 (55)
nervous [ˈnɜːvəs] nervös, aufgeregt 1 (20)
°**network** [ˈnetwɜːk] (Wörter-)Netz
never [ˈnevə] nie, niemals 3 (56)
new [njuː] neu Welc (8)
°**news** [njuːz]: **no news** keine Neuigkeiten
newspaper [ˈnjuːspeɪpə] Zeitung Welc (15)
next [nekst]: **be next** der/die Nächste sein 6 (105) • **the next morning/day** am nächsten Morgen/Tag 3 (56) • **the next photo** das nächste Foto 6 (104) **What have we got next?** Was haben wir als Nächstes? 1 (24)
next to [nekst] neben 4 (69)
nice [naɪs] schön, nett Welc (11)
°**nickname** [ˈnɪkneɪm] Spitzname
night [naɪt] Nacht, später Abend 2 (38/158) • **at night** nachts, in der Nacht 2 (38/158) • **on Friday night** freitagnachts, Freitagnacht 2 (38/158)
no [nəʊ] **1.** nein Welc (8/146); **2.** kein, keine 4 (81/170) • **no more music** keine Musik mehr 4 (81)
noise [nɔɪz] Geräusch; Lärm 3 (65)
nose [nəʊz] Nase 4 (74/169)
not [nɒt] nicht Welc (9/147) • **not (...) any** kein, keine 4 (71)
note [nəʊt] Mitteilung, Notiz 4 (82) **take notes** sich Notizen machen 4 (82/170)
°**notice** [ˈnəʊtɪs] Notiz, Mitteilung
November [nəʊˈvembə] November TOP 1 (35/156)
now [naʊ] nun, jetzt Welc (8)
number [ˈnʌmbə] Zahl, Ziffer, Nummer Welc (9/147)

O

o [əʊ] null Welc (15)
o'clock [əˈklɒk]: **eleven o'clock** elf Uhr Welc (16/151)
October [ɒkˈtəʊbə] Oktober TOP 1 (35/156)
°**odd** [ɒd]: **What word is the odd one out?** Welches Wort passt nicht dazu? / Welches Wort gehört nicht dazu?
°**ode** [əʊd] Ode *(feierliches Gedicht)*
of [əv, ɒv] von 2 (38) • **of the summer holidays** der Sommerferien Welc (12)
of course [əv ˈkɔːs] natürlich, selbstverständlich 2 (40)
off [ɒf]: **take 10c off** 10 Cent abziehen TOP 3 (67)
often [ˈɒfn] oft, häufig 3 (56)
Oh well ... [əʊ ˈwel] Na ja ... / Na gut ... Welc (13)
OK [əʊˈkeɪ] okay, gut, in Ordnung Welc (12)
old [əʊld] alt Welc (8/146) • **How old are you?** Wie alt bist du? Welc (8/146) • **I'm ... years old.** Ich bin ... Jahre alt. Welc (8/146)
on [ɒn] auf 1 (23/154) • **on 13th June** am 13. Juni TOP 1 (35/156) • **on Friday** am Freitag 1 (23) • **on Friday afternoon** freitagnachmittags, am Freitagnachmittag 2 (38/158) • **on Friday evening** freitagabends, am Freitagabend 2 (38/158) • **on Friday morning** freitagmorgens, am Freitagmorgen 2 (38/158) • **on Friday night** freitagnachts, Freitagnacht 2 (38/158) **on the board** an die Tafel 1 (22/153) **on the left** links, auf der linken Seite 5 (89/171) • **on the phone** am Telefon 4 (78) • **on the radio** im Radio 3 (62) • **on the right** rechts, auf der rechten Seite 5 (89) • **on the train** im Zug 4 (73/168) • **on TV** im Fernsehen 2 (39/158) • **What page are we on?** Auf welcher Seite sind wir? 1 (28/155)
one [ˈwʌn] eins, ein, eine Welc (14) **one day** eines Tages 5 (90) • **one more** noch ein/e, ein/e weitere(r, s) 6 (105)
only [ˈəʊnli] **1.** nur, bloß TOP 3 (67); **2. the only guest** der einzige Gast 3 (65)
°**onto** [ˈɒntə, ˈɒntu] auf (... hinauf)
open [ˈəʊpən] **1.** öffnen, aufmachen Welc (10); **2.** sich öffnen 6 (111)
opposite [ˈɒpəzɪt] Gegenteil 3 (64)
or [ɔː] oder 1 (28)
orange [ˈɒrɪndʒ] **1.** orange(farben) Welc (13/150); **2.** Orange, Apfelsine 4 (69/166) • **orange juice** [ˈɒrɪndʒ dʒuːs] Orangensaft 4 (69/166)
°**order** [ˈɔːdə] Reihenfolge • °**in the right order** in der richtigen Reihenfolge • °**word order** Wortstellung
other [ˈʌðə] andere(r, s) 2 (48) **the others** die anderen 3 (66)
Ouch! [aʊtʃ] Autsch! 4 (82)
our [ˈaʊə] unser, unsere 1 (21)
out [aʊt]: **be out** weg sein, nicht da sein 6 (110)
out of ... [ˈaʊt‿əv] aus ... (heraus/hinaus) 3 (65)
outside [ˌaʊtˈsaɪd] draußen 4 (81/169) • **outside his room** vor seinem Zimmer; außerhalb seines Zimmers 3 (65)
over [ˈəʊvə] **1.** über, oberhalb von Welc (14) • **over there** da drüben, dort drüben 6 (103) **2. be over** vorbei sein, zu Ende sein 4 (82)
°**own** [əʊn]: **your own song** dein eigenes Lied
°**owner** [ˈəʊnə] Besitzer/in
°**Oxfam** [ˈɒksfæm] *bekannteste Wohltätigkeitsorganisation Großbritanniens mit einer Kette von Gebrauchtwarengeschäften*

P

packet [ˈpækɪt] Päckchen, Packung, Schachtel 1 (33) • **a packet of mints** ein Päckchen/eine Packung Pfefferminzbonbons 1 (33)
page [peɪdʒ] (Buch-, Heft-)Seite Welc (8) • **What page are we on?** Auf welcher Seite sind wir? 1 (28/155)

paint [peɪnt] malen, anmalen 5 (84/85)
°**pair** [peə]: **ten pairs of opposites** zehn Gegenteil-Paare
paper ['peɪpə] Papier 3 (66)
parcel ['pɑːsl] Paket 4 (73)
parents ['peərənts] Eltern 2 (41/159)
park [pɑːk] Park Welc (10)
parrot ['pærət] Papagei Welc (16)
part [pɑːt] Teil 5 (87)
partner ['pɑːtnə] Partner/in Welc (8)
party ['pɑːti] Party 4 (68)
pass [pɑːs] (herüber)reichen, weitergeben 4 (81) • **pass round** herumgeben 4 (81)
°**past** [pɑːst] Vergangenheit
past [pɑːst]: **half past 11** halb zwölf (11.30 / 23.30) Welc (16/151) **quarter past 11** Viertel nach 11 (11.15 / 23.15) Welc (16/151)
PE [ˌpiː_'iː], **Physical Education** [ˌfɪzɪkəl_edʒu'keɪʃn] Sportunterricht, Turnen 1 (23/154)
pen [pen] Kugelschreiber, Füller Welc (12/149)
pence (p) *(pl)* [pens] Pence *(Plural von „penny")* TOP 3 (67)
pencil ['pensl] Bleistift Welc (12/149) **pencil case** ['pensl keɪs] Federmäppchen Welc (12/149) • **pencil sharpener** ['pensl ʃɑːpnə] Bleistiftanspitzer Welc (12)
penny ['peni] *kleinste britische Münze* TOP 3 (67/166)
people ['piːpl] Menschen, Leute 2 (36)
°**pepper** ['pepə] Pfeffer
°**perfect** ['pɜːfɪkt] perfekt; ideal
°**person** ['pɜːsn] Person
pet [pet] Haustier Welc (12/149) **pet shop** Tierhandlung 2 (44)
phone [fəʊn] Telefon 1 (19) • **on the phone** am Telefon 4 (78) **phone call** Anruf, Telefongespräch 5 (90) • **phone number** Telefonnummer Welc (15)
photo ['fəʊtəʊ] Foto Welc (9) • **in the photo** auf dem Foto Welc (9/148) • **take photos** Fotos machen, fotografieren 6 (103)
phrase [freɪz] Ausdruck, (Rede-)Wendung 5 (84/85)
piano [pi'ænəʊ] Klavier, Piano 3 (55) **play the piano** Klavier spielen 3 (55/163)
picture ['pɪktʃə] Bild Welc (11) • **in the picture** auf dem Bild Welc (11/149)
piece [piːs]: **a piece of** ein Stück 3 (66) • **a piece of paper** ein Stück Papier 3 (66)
pink [pɪŋk] pink(farben), rosa Welc (13/150)
pirate ['paɪrət] Pirat, Piratin 5 (84/85)
°**pistol** ['pɪstl] Pistole
pizza ['piːtsə] Pizza 1 (24)
place [pleɪs] Ort, Platz Welc (9)
°**placemat** ['pleɪsmæt] Set, Platzdeckchen
plan [plæn] **1.** Plan 2 (38); °**2. plan to do (-nn-)** planen zu tun
°**plank** [plæŋk] Brett, Planke
°**plastic explosive** [ˌplæstɪk ɪk'spləʊsɪv] Plastiksprengstoff
plate [pleɪt] Teller Welc (13) • **a plate of chips** ein Teller Pommes frites 4 (69/167)
play [pleɪ] **1.** spielen Welc (9/147) **play football** Fußball spielen Welc (9/147) • **play the guitar** Gitarre spielen 3 (53/162) • **play the piano** Klavier spielen 3 (55/163) **2.** Theaterstück 4 (81)
player ['pleɪə] Spieler/in 6 (106)
please [pliːz] bitte *(in Fragen und Aufforderungen)* Welc (12/149) ► S.159 „bitte"
pm [ˌpiː_'em]: **7 pm** 7 Uhr nachmittags/abends 4 (81)
poem ['pəʊɪm] Gedicht Welc (14)
°**poetry** ['pəʊətri] *hier:* Gedichte
°**point** [pɔɪnt] **1.** Punkt; °**2. point to** zeigen auf, deuten auf
police *(pl)* [pə'liːs] Polizei 3 (65)
poltergeist ['pəʊltəgaɪst] Poltergeist Welc (10)
poor [pɔː, pʊə] arm 1 (32) • **poor Sophie** (die) arme Sophie 1 (32)
poster ['pəʊstə] Poster 1 (24)
potato [pə'teɪtəʊ], *pl* **potatoes** Kartoffel 4 (69/166)
pound (£) [paʊnd] Pfund *(britische Währung)* TOP 3 (67)
practice ['præktɪs] *hier:* Übungsteil (3)
practise ['præktɪs] üben; trainieren 5 (84/85)
°**prepare** [prɪ'peə] vorbereiten
present ['preznt] **1.** Gegenwart 4 (71/168); **2.** Geschenk 4 (71)
present (to) [prɪ'zent] *(jm. etwas)* präsentieren, vorstellen 6 (104/175)
presentation [ˌprezn'teɪʃn] Präsentation, Vorstellung 6 (104)
pretty ['prɪti] hübsch Welc (6)
price [praɪs] (Kauf-)Preis 6 (101)
prize [praɪz] Preis, Gewinn 4 (82)
programme ['prəʊgræm] Programm 5 (84/85)
project (about, on) ['prɒdʒekt] Projekt (über, zu) 3 (55)
pronunciation [prəˌnʌnsi'eɪʃn] Aussprache (3)
pull [pʊl] ziehen Welc (10)
purple ['pɜːpl] violett; lila Welc (13/150)
push [pʊʃ] drücken, schieben, stoßen Welc (10)
put (-tt-) [pʊt] legen, stellen, *(etwas wohin)* tun 2 (39) • °**Put up your hand.** Heb deine Hand. / Hebt eure Hand.

Q

quarter ['kwɔːtə]: **quarter past 11** Viertel nach 11 (11.15 / 23.15) Welc (16/151) • **quarter to 12** Viertel vor 12 (11.45 / 23.45) Welc (16/151)
question ['kwestʃn] Frage 3 (56) **ask questions** Fragen stellen 3 (56/164) • °**question word** Fragewort
quick [kwɪk] schnell 3 (56)
quiet ['kwaɪət] leise, still, ruhig 1 (22)
quiz [kwɪz], *pl* **quizzes** ['kwɪzɪz] Quiz, Ratespiel 2 (45)

R

rabbit ['ræbɪt] Kaninchen 2 (37/157)
°**racket** ['rækɪt] (Tennis-, Federball-, Squash-)Schläger
radio ['reɪdiəʊ] Radio 3 (62) • **on the radio** im Radio 3 (62)
°**rainy** ['reɪni] verregnet
°**ram (-mm-)** [ræm] rammen
ran [ræn] *Vergangenheitsform von „run"* 5 (96/172)
rap [ræp] Rap *(rhythmischer Sprechgesang)* 1 (22)
RE [ˌɑːr_'iː], **Religious Education** [rɪˌlɪdʒəs_edʒu'keɪʃn] Religion, Religionsunterricht 1 (23/154)
read [riːd] lesen 2 (38) • °**read on** weiterlesen • °**read out** vorlesen °**Read out loud.** Lies laut vor. °**Read the poem to a partner.** Lies das Gedicht einem Partner/einer Partnerin vor.
ready ['redi] bereit, fertig 2 (48) **get ready (for)** sich fertig machen (für), sich vorbereiten (auf) 4 (72) **get things ready** Dinge fertig machen, vorbereiten 2 (48)
real [rɪəl] echt, wirklich 4 (70)
really ['rɪəli] wirklich 1 (24)
reason ['riːzn] Grund, Begründung 4 (71) • **for lots of reasons** aus vielen Gründen 6 (105)
red [red] rot Welc (13/150)
°**reflection** [rɪ'flekʃn] Spiegelung

rehearsal [rɪ'hɜ:sl] Probe *(am Theater)* 5 (84/85)
rehearse [rɪ'hɜ:s] proben *(am Theater)* 5 (84/85/170)
remember [rɪ'membə] **1.** sich erinnern (an) 2 (45); **2.** sich *etwas* merken 1 (22) • **Can you remember that?** Kannst du dir das merken? 1 (22)
report [rɪ'pɔ:t]: **1. report (on)** Bericht, Reportage (über) 5 (92) **°2. Report to the class.** Berichte der Klasse.
°rest [rest] Rest
result [rɪ'zʌlt] Ergebnis, Resultat 5 (84/85)
revision [rɪ'vɪʒn] Wiederholung *(des Lernstoffs)* (3)
°rhythm ['rɪðəm] Rhythmus
ride [raɪd] reiten 3 (53/162) • **go riding** ['raɪdɪŋ] reiten gehen 3 (53) **ride a bike** Rad fahren 3 (53/162)
right [raɪt] **1.** richtig Welc (11) • **be right** Recht haben 6 (102) • **That's right.** Das ist richtig. / Das stimmt. Welc (11) • **You need a school bag, right?** Du brauchst eine Schultasche, stimmt's? / nicht wahr? Welc (12)
2. on the right rechts, auf der rechten Seite 5 (89)
3. right after lunch direkt/gleich nach dem Mittagessen 3 (57/164)
right now jetzt sofort; jetzt gerade 3 (57)
°river ['rɪvə] Fluss
road [rəʊd] Straße Welc (10) • **Park Road** [,pɑ:k 'rəʊd] Parkstraße Welc (10)
roll [rəʊl] Brötchen 4 (80)
°roll up [,rəʊl_'ʌp] aufrollen
room [ru:m, rʊm] Raum, Zimmer Welc (9/147)
°RSVP [,ɑ:r_es vi: 'pi:] *(Abkürzung auf Einladungen)* um Antwort wird gebeten *(aus dem Französischen: Répondez s'il vous plaît)*
rubber ['rʌbə] Radiergummi Welc (12/149)
ruler ['ru:lə] Lineal Welc (12/149)
run (-nn-) [rʌn] laufen, rennen 3 (65)

S

said [sed] *Vergangenheitsform von „say"* 5 (88/171)
°sail [seɪl] segeln
°sailor ['seɪlə] Seemann, Matrose
salad ['sæləd] Salat *(als Gericht oder Beilage)* 4 (69)
°salami [sə'lɑ:mi] Salami
°salt [sɔ:lt] Salz
same [seɪm]: **the same ...** der-/die-/dasselbe ...; dieselben ... 6 (102/174) **be/look the same** gleich sein/aussehen 6 (102)
sandwich ['sænwɪtʃ, 'sænwɪdʒ] Sandwich, *(zusammengeklapptes)* belegtes Brot 2 (45)
sat [sæt] *Vergangenheitsform von „sit"* 5 (96/172)
Saturday ['sætədeɪ, 'sætədi] Samstag, Sonnabend Welc (14/150)
sausage ['sɒsɪdʒ] (Brat-, Bock-) Würstchen, Wurst 4 (69)
°save [seɪv] retten
saw [sɔ:] *Vergangenheitsform von „see"* 5 (96/172)
say [seɪ] sagen Welc (12) • **say goodbye** sich verabschieden Welc (17) • **Say hi to Dilip for me.** Grüß Dilip von mir. 3 (56)
°scare away [,skeər_ə'weɪ] verscheuchen, verjagen
scared [skeəd]: **be scared (of)** Angst haben (vor) 5 (97)
scary ['skeəri] unheimlich; gruselig 3 (65)
scene [si:n] Szene 4 (81)
school [sku:l] Schule Welc (12/149) **at school** in der Schule Welc (12/149) **school bag** Schultasche Welc (12/149) • **school subject** Schulfach 1 (23/154)
► S.154 School subjects
science ['saɪəns] Naturwissenschaft 1 (23/154)
sea [si:] Meer, *(die)* See 5 (97)
°season ['si:zn] Jahreszeit
second ['sekənd] zweite(r, s) TOP 1 (35)
°secret ['si:krət] Geheimnis
°section ['sekʃn] Abschnitt
see [si:] sehen Welc (9) • **See?** Siehst du? 4 (81) • **See you.** Bis bald. / Tschüs. 1 (33)
► S.158 (to) look – (to) see – (to) watch
sell [sel] verkaufen 3 (54/163)
sentence ['sentəns] Satz 1 (28/155)
September [sep'tembə] September TOP 1 (35/156)
°shadow ['ʃædəʊ] Schatten
°shake [ʃeɪk] schütteln
share (with) [ʃeə] sich *etwas* teilen (mit) 2 (36)
she [ʃi:] sie Welc (8)
shelf [ʃelf], *pl* **shelves** [ʃelvz] Regal(brett) 2 (36/157)
ship [ʃɪp] Schiff 5 (84/85)
shirt [ʃɜ:t] Hemd 3 (54/163)
shoe [ʃu:] Schuh 3 (54/163)
shop [ʃɒp] **1.** Laden, Geschäft Welc (14); **°2. (-pp-)** einkaufen, einkaufen gehen • **shop assistant** ['ʃɒp_ə,sɪstənt] Verkäufer/in 3 (54) **shopping** ['ʃɒpɪŋ] (das) Einkaufen Welc (12) • **go shopping** einkaufen gehen 3 (63) • **shopping list** Einkaufsliste Welc (12)
short [ʃɔ:t] kurz 4 (70/167)
shorts *(pl)* [ʃɔ:ts] Shorts, kurze Hose 3 (54/163)
shoulder ['ʃəʊldə] Schulter 4 (74/169)
shout [ʃaʊt] schreien, rufen 3 (57) **shout at sb.** jn. anschreien 3 (57/164)
show [ʃəʊ] **1.** zeigen 5 (84/85/170); **2.** Show, Vorstellung 5 (84/85)
shower ['ʃaʊə] Dusche 2 (48) • **have a shower** (sich) duschen 2 (48)
°signal ['sɪgnəl] Signal, Zeichen
°silver ['sɪlvə] Silber
sing [sɪŋ] singen Welc (8/146)
single ['sɪŋgl] ledig, alleinstehend 2 (41)
sink [sɪŋk] Spüle, Spülbecken TOP 2 (50)
°Sir [sɜ:] Sir
sister ['sɪstə] Schwester Welc (8/146)
sit (-tt-) [sɪt] sitzen; sich setzen 1 (20) • **Sit with me.** Setz dich zu mir. / Setzt euch zu mir. 1 (20)
size [saɪz] Größe 3 (54)
skate [skeɪt] Inliner/Skateboard fahren 3 (62) • **skates** [skeɪts] Inliner 3 (62/165)
skateboard ['skeɪtbɔ:d] Skateboard Welc (9/147)
sketch [sketʃ] Sketch 5 (86)
skills file ['skɪlz faɪl] *Anhang mit Lern- und Arbeitstechniken* (3/118)
sleep [sli:p] schlafen 2 (38)
°sleepover ['sli:pəʊvə] Schlafparty
°sleet [sli:t] Schneeregen
°small [smɔ:l] klein
smile [smaɪl] lächeln 6 (103)
snake [sneɪk] Schlange 3 (58)
°snow [snəʊ] Schnee
so [səʊ] **1.** also; deshalb, daher 2 (41); **2. so sweet** so süß 4 (81) • **so far** bis jetzt, bis hierher 6 (110) **3. I think so.** Ich glaube (ja). 5 (98/173) • **I don't think so.** Das finde/glaube ich nicht. 5 (98)
soap [səʊp] Seife 4 (71)
sock [sɒk] Socke, Strumpf 3 (54/163)
sofa ['səʊfə] Sofa TOP 2 (50)
some [səm, sʌm] einige, ein paar 3 (56) • **some cheese/juice/money** etwas Käse/Saft/Geld 4 (69)
somebody ['sʌmbədi] jemand 4 (73)
something ['sʌmθɪŋ] etwas 4 (69) **something to eat** etwas zu essen 4 (69)

sometimes ['sʌmtaɪmz] manchmal 2 (40)
son [sʌn] Sohn 2 (41)
song [sɒŋ] Lied, Song Welc (8/146)
soon [su:n] bald 5 (97)
sorry ['sɒri]: **(I'm) sorry.** Entschuldigung. / Tut mir leid. 1 (21)
Sorry, I'm late. Entschuldigung, dass ich zu spät bin/komme. Welc (12) • **Sorry?** Wie bitte? 1 (21/153)
▶ S.151 „Entschuldigung" / S.153 sorry
sound [saʊnd] **1.** klingen, sich *(gut usw.)* anhören 5 (86); **2.** Laut; Klang 5 (86/171)
°**Spanish** ['spænɪʃ] spanisch
°**speak** [spi:k] sprechen
°**speech bubble** ['spi:tʃ bʌbl] Sprechblase
spell [spel] buchstabieren 1 (22)
sport [spɔ:t] Sport; Sportart 3 (52)
do sport Sport treiben 3 (53/162)
▶ S.162 Sports
spring [sprɪŋ] Frühling 5 (84/85)
spy [spaɪ] Spion/in 2 (48)
stage [steɪdʒ] Bühne 5 (89)
stairs *(pl)* [steəz] Treppe; Treppenstufen TOP 2 (50)
stamp [stæmp] Briefmarke 3 (53)
star [stɑ:] (Film-, Pop-)Star 2 (48)
start [stɑ:t] starten, anfangen, beginnen (mit) 3 (66)
°**statement** ['steɪtmənt] Aussage
station ['steɪʃn] Bahnhof 4 (73)
at the station am Bahnhof 4 (73/168)
°**statue** ['stætʃu:] Statue
°**stay** [steɪ] bleiben • °**stay with** wohnen bei
step [step] Schritt 6 (102) • °**take a step** einen Schritt tun
still [stɪl] (immer) noch 4 (71)
stop (-pp-) [stɒp] **1.** aufhören Welc (14) • **Stop that!** Hör auf damit! / Lass das! Welc (14)
2. anhalten 1 (31)
story ['stɔ:ri] Geschichte, Erzählung 2 (48)
street [stri:t] Straße Welc (12) • **at 7 Hamilton Street** in der Hamiltonstraße 7 Welc (12)
°**stretch** [stretʃ] strecken, dehnen
student ['stju:dənt] Schüler/in; Student/in 1 (20)
studio ['stju:diəʊ] Studio 5 (84/85)
study skills *(pl)* ['stʌdi skɪlz] Lern- und Arbeitstechniken (3)
subject ['sʌbdʒɪkt] Schulfach 1 (23/154)
▶ S.154 School subjects
suddenly ['sʌdnli] plötzlich, auf einmal 3 (65)

summer ['sʌmə] Sommer Welc (12)
Sunday ['sʌndeɪ, 'sʌndi] Sonntag Welc (14/150)
sunglasses *(pl)* ['sʌnglɑ:sɪz] (eine) Sonnenbrille 2 (48)
sure [ʃʊə, ʃɔ:] sicher 5 (88)
°**survey (on)** ['sɜ:veɪ] Umfrage (über, zu)
°**swap (-pp-)** [swɒp] tauschen
sweatshirt ['swetʃɜ:t] Sweatshirt 3 (54/163)
sweet [swi:t] süß 4 (69/167)
sweets *(pl)* Süßigkeiten 4 (69)
swim (-mm-) [swɪm] schwimmen 3 (52/162) • **go swimming** schwimmen gehen 3 (52/162) • **swimming pool** ['swɪmɪŋ pu:l] Schwimmbad, Schwimmbecken TOP 2 (51)
°**sword** [sɔ:d] Schwert
°**swordfish** ['sɔ:dfɪʃ] Schwertfisch
syllable ['sɪləbl] Silbe 5 (92)
°**synchronize watches** ['sɪŋkrənaɪz] Uhren gleichstellen

T

table ['teɪbl] Tisch 1 (18/152) • **table tennis** ['teɪbl tenɪs] Tischtennis 3 (53/162)
take [teɪk] **1.** nehmen Welc (11); **2.** (weg-, hin)bringen 4 (72) • **take 10c off** 10 Cent abziehen TOP 3 (67)
take notes sich Notizen machen 4 (82/170) • **take out** herausnehmen 1 (23) • **take photos** Fotos machen, fotografieren 6 (103)
°**take a step** einen Schritt tun
I'll take it. [aɪl 'teɪk‿ɪt] *(beim Einkaufen)* Ich werde es (ihn, sie) nehmen. / Ich nehme es (ihn, sie). TOP 3 (67)
talk [tɔ:k]: **talk (about)** reden (über), sich unterhalten (über) Welc (8)
talk (to) reden (mit), sich unterhalten (mit) Welc (8)
°**tavern** ['tævən] Schenke, Kneipe
tea [ti:] Tee; *(auch:) leichte Nachmittags- oder Abendmahlzeit* 1 (32)
teach [ti:tʃ] unterrichten, lehren 3 (57) • **teacher** ['ti:tʃə] Lehrer/in 1 (21)
team [ti:m] Team, Mannschaft 3 (60)
teeth [ti:θ] *Plural von „tooth"* 2 (38)
telephone ['telɪfəʊn] Telefon Welc (15) • **telephone number** Telefonnummer Welc (15)
television (TV) ['telɪvɪʒn] Fernsehen 2 (39/158)
tell (about) [tel] erzählen (von), berichten (über) 1 (22/154) • **Tell me your names.** Sagt mir eure Namen. 1 (22)
tennis ['tenɪs] Tennis 1 (22)
terrible ['terəbl] schrecklich, furchtbar 5 (87)
text [tekst] Text (3)
Thank you. ['θæŋk ju:] Danke (schön). Welc (12/149) • **Thanks.** [θæŋks] Danke. 2 (40) • **Thanks a lot!** Vielen Dank! 3 (56)
that [ðət, ðæt] **1.** das (dort) Welc (11); **2.** jene(r, s) 1 (24) • **That's me.** Das bin ich. Welc (10) • **That's right.** Das ist richtig. / Das stimmt. Welc (11) • **that's why** deshalb, darum 6 (103)
3. dass 5 (97)
▶ S.174 this, that – these, those
the [ðə, ði] der, die, das; die Welc (9/147)
°**theatre** ['θɪətə] Theater
their [ðeə] ihr, ihre *(Plural)* Welc (12)
them [ðəm, ðem] sie; ihnen 3 (54)
then [ðen] dann, danach Welc (10)
there [ðeə] **1.** da, dort Welc (11); **2.** dahin, dorthin 2 (42/160) • **in there** dort drinnen 5 (87) • **over there** da drüben, dort drüben 6 (103)
there are es sind (vorhanden); es gibt 1 (18) • **there's** es ist (vorhanden); es gibt 1 (18) • **there isn't a ...** es ist kein/e ...; es gibt kein/e ... 1 (18/152)
▶ S.152 There's ... / There are ...
these [ði:z] diese, die (hier) 3 (54)
▶ S.174 this, that – these, those
they [ðeɪ] sie *(Plural)* Welc (8)
thing [θɪŋ] Ding, Sache Welc (10)
think [θɪŋk] glauben, meinen, denken Welc (11) • **I think so.** Ich glaube (ja). 5 (98/173) • **I don't think so.** Das finde/glaube ich nicht. 5 (98) • °**think of** sich ausdenken
third [θɜ:d] dritte(r, s) TOP 1 (35)
thirsty ['θɜ:sti] durstig 4 (69) • **be thirsty** Durst haben, durstig sein 4 (69)
this [ðɪs] **1.** dies (hier) Welc (8); **2.** diese(r, s) 1 (34) • **this morning/afternoon/evening** heute Morgen/Nachmittag/Abend 5 (88) • °**This is the way ...** So ... / Auf diese Weise ...
▶ S.174 this, that – these, those
those [ðəʊz] die (da), jene (dort) 6 (103)
▶ S.174 this, that – these, those
thousand ['θaʊznd] tausend TOP 1 (35)
throw [θrəʊ] werfen 1 (22)
°**Thud!** [θʌd] Rums!

Thursday ['θɜ:zdeɪ, 'θɜ:zdi] Donnerstag Welc (14/150)
°**tick** [tɪk] Häkchen
ticket ['tɪkɪt] Eintrittskarte 5 (86)
°ticket inspector ['tɪkɪt_ɪn,spektə] Fahrkartenkontrolleur/in
tidy ['taɪdi] aufräumen 4 (72)
°**tie** [taɪ] zusammenbinden
till [tɪl] bis *(zeitlich)* 2 (40)
time [taɪm] Zeit; Uhrzeit Welc (16/151) • **What's the time?** Wie spät ist es? Welc (16/151) • **°The Times** *britische Tageszeitung*
timetable ['taɪmteɪbl] Stundenplan 1 (23)
tired ['taɪəd] müde 5 (88)
°**'Tis** [tɪz] = *It is*
title ['taɪtl] Titel, Überschrift 4 (82)
to [tə, tu] **1.** zu, nach Welc (14) • **to Jenny's** zu Jenny 4 (72) • **to the front** nach vorn 6 (105)
2. an e-mail to eine E-Mail an 3 (56) • **write to** schreiben an 3 (56)
3. quarter to 12 Viertel vor 12 (11.45 / 23.45) Welc (16/151)
4. something to eat etwas zu essen 4 (69) • **try to do** versuchen, zu tun 2 (39)
5. um zu 5 (88)
toast [təʊst] Toast(brot) 2 (38)
today [tə'deɪ] heute Welc (12)
toe [təʊ] Zeh 4 (74/169)
together [tə'geðə] zusammen 1 (21)
toilet ['tɔɪlət] Toilette 1 (28/155)
told [təʊld] *Vergangenheitsform von „tell“* 5 (96/172)
°**tomato** [tə'mɑ:təʊ], *pl* **tomatoes** Tomate
tomorrow [tə'mɒrəʊ] morgen Welc (14)
°**tongue-twister** ['tʌŋtwɪstə] Zungenbrecher
tonight [tə'naɪt] heute Nacht, heute Abend 5 (96)
too [tu:]: **1. from Bristol too** auch aus Bristol Welc (8) • **Me too.** Ich auch. Welc (12)
2. too much/big/expensive zu viel/groß/teuer TOP 3 (67)
took [tʊk] *Vergangenheitsform von „take“* 5 (96/172)
tooth [tu:θ], *pl* **teeth** [ti:θ] Zahn 2 (38)
top [tɒp] **1.** Spitze, oberes Ende 2 (41) • **at the top (of)** oben, am oberen Ende, an der Spitze (von) 2 (41)
2. Top, Oberteil 3 (54)
topic ['tɒpɪk] Thema, Themenbereich (3)
°**tornado** [tɔ:'neɪdəʊ] Tornado, Wirbelsturm

tortoise ['tɔ:təs] Schildkröte 2 (37)
tour (of the house) [tʊə] Rundgang, Tour (durch das Haus) TOP 2 (51)
tower ['taʊə] Turm 6 (100)
town [taʊn] Stadt 5 (89)
°**toy** [tɔɪ] Spielzeug
train [treɪn] Zug 4 (73) • **on the train** im Zug 4 (73/168)
°**train** [treɪn] trainieren • °**trainer** ['treɪnə] Trainer/in
°**translate (into)** [træns'leɪt] übersetzen (in)
tree [tri:] Baum Welc (9/147)
trick [trɪk] (Zauber-)Kunststück, Trick Welc (15) • **do tricks** (Zauber-) Kunststücke machen Welc (15)
trip [trɪp] Reise; Ausflug Welc (17)
°**true** [tru:] wahr
try [traɪ] **1.** versuchen 2 (39); **2.** probieren, kosten 4 (76) • **try and do / try to do** versuchen, zu tun 2 (39)
try on anprobieren *(Kleidung)* 3 (54)
T-shirt ['ti:ʃɜ:t] T-Shirt 2 (46)
Tuesday ['tju:zdeɪ, 'tju:zdi] Dienstag Welc (14/150)
turn [tɜ:n]: **°turn around** sich umdrehen • **turn on the computer** den Computer einschalten 6 (111)
turn [tɜ:n]: **(It's) my turn.** Ich bin dran / an der Reihe. 1 (20)
TV [ti:'vi:] Fernsehen 2 (39/158)
on TV im Fernsehen 2 (39/158)
watch TV fernsehen 2 (39/158)
twin [twɪn]: **twin brother** Zwillingsbruder Welc (8) • **twins** *(pl)* Zwillinge Welc (8/147) • **twin town** Partnerstadt 5 (89)

U

°**unchanging** [,ʌn'tʃeɪndʒɪŋ] gleich bleibend
uncle ['ʌŋkl] Onkel 2 (41)
under ['ʌndə] unter 3 (61)
understand [,ʌndə'stænd] verstehen, begreifen 3 (57)
uniform ['ju:nɪfɔ:m] Uniform Welc (14)
unit ['ju:nɪt] Kapitel, Lektion (3)
up [ʌp] hinauf, herauf, nach oben 4 (72)
°**update** [,ʌp'deɪt] aktualisieren, auf den neuesten Stand bringen
upstairs [,ʌp'steəz] oben; nach oben TOP 2 (50/161)
us [əs, ʌs] uns 2 (48)
use [ju:z] benutzen, verwenden 5 (84/85) • °**used** [ju:zd] gebraucht

usually ['ju:ʒuəli] meistens, gewöhnlich, normalerweise 3 (56)

V

°**veg** [vedʒ] Gemüse
very ['veri] sehr Welc (11)
village ['vɪlɪdʒ] Dorf 6 (100)
virus ['vaɪrəs] Virus 3 (63)
°**visit** ['vɪzɪt] besuchen; besichtigen
visitor ['vɪzɪtə] Besucher/in, Gast TOP 2 (51)
vocabulary [və'kæbjələri] Vokabelverzeichnis, Wörterverzeichnis (3)
voice [vɔɪs] Stimme 5 (87)
volleyball ['vɒlibɔ:l] Volleyball 3 (53/162)

W

wait (for) ['weɪt fɔ:] warten (auf) 4 (73) • **I can't wait to see ...** ich kann es kaum erwarten, ... zu sehen 5 (87)
walk [wɔ:k] (zu Fuß) gehen 3 (56)
°**Wallop!** ['wɒləp] Schepper!
want [wɒnt] (haben) wollen 3 (54)
want to do tun wollen 4 (70)
°wanted ['wɒntɪd] *(polizeilich)* gesucht
wardrobe ['wɔ:drəʊb] Kleiderschrank 2 (36/157)
was [wəz, wɒz]: **(I/he/she/it) was** *Vergangenheitsform von „be“* 1 (33)
How was ...? Wie war ...? 1 (33)
wash [wɒʃ] waschen 2 (38) • **I wash my face.** Ich wasche mir das Gesicht. 2 (38)
watch [wɒtʃ] beobachten, sich *etwas* ansehen; zusehen 2 (39)
watch TV fernsehen 2 (39/158)
► S.158 (to) look – (to) see – (to) watch
watch [wɒtʃ] Armbanduhr 3 (66)
water ['wɔ:tə] Wasser Welc (9/147)
°**way** [weɪ]: **This is the way ...** So ... / Auf diese Weise ...
we [wi:] wir Welc (8/146)
wear [weə] tragen, anhaben *(Kleidung)* 2 (48)
Wednesday ['wenzdeɪ, 'wenzdi] Mittwoch Welc (14/150)
week [wi:k] Woche Welc (14)
days of the week Wochentage Welc (14/150)
weekend [,wi:k'end] Wochenende 2 (36) • **at the weekend** am Wochenende 2 (38/158)
welcome ['welkəm]: **1. welcome sb. (to)** jn. begrüßen, willkommen heißen (in) Welc (16) • **They**

welcome you to ... Sie heißen dich in ... willkommen Welc (16)
2. Welcome (to Bristol). Willkommen (in Bristol). Welc (8);
3. You're welcome. Gern geschehen. / Nichts zu danken. Welc (17)
► S.152 welcome

well [wel]: **Well, ...** Nun, ... / Also, ... Welc (14) • **Oh well ...** Na ja ... / Na gut ... Welc (13)

went [went] *Vergangenheitsform von „go"* 5 (88/171)

were [wə, wɜː]: **(we/you/they) were** *Vergangenheitsform von „be"* 5 (86)

°**wet** [wet] nass

what [wɒt] **1.** was Welc (8/146); **2.** welche(r, s) Welc (13) • **What about ...?** **1.** Was ist mit ...? / Und ...? Welc (6); **2.** Wie wär's mit ...? TOP 3 (67) • **What are you talking about?** Wovon redest du? 4 (82) **What colour is ...?** Welche Farbe hat ...? Welc (13) • **What have we got next?** Was haben wir als Nächstes? 1 (24) • **What page are we on?** Auf welcher Seite sind wir? 1 (28/155) • **What's for homework?** Was haben wir als Hausaufgabe auf? 1 (28/155) • **What's the time?** Wie spät ist es? Welc (16/151) **What's your name?** Wie heißt du? Welc (8/146)

wheelchair ['wiːltʃeə] Rollstuhl Welc (16)

when [wen] **1.** wann TOP 1 (35) **When's your birthday?** Wann hast du Geburtstag? TOP 1 (35/156) **2.** wenn Welc (10); **3.** als 5 (97)

where [weə] **1.** wo Welc (8/146); **2.** wohin 2 (42/160) • **Where are you from?** Wo kommst du her? Welc (8/146)

which [wɪtʃ]: **Which picture ...?** Welches Bild ...? 4 (74)

whisper ['wɪspə] flüstern 6 (103)

white [waɪt] weiß Welc (13/150)

who [huː] wer Welc (11) • **Who are you?** Wer bist du? Welc (11)

why [waɪ] warum Welc (14) • **Why me?** Warum ich? Welc (14) • **that's why** deshalb, darum 6 (103)

win (-nn-) [wɪn] gewinnen 3 (55)

wind [wɪnd] Wind 5 (96/172)

window ['wɪndəʊ] Fenster 1 (28/155)

windy ['wɪndi] windig 5 (96)

winter ['wɪntə] Winter 5 (84/85/170)

with [wɪð] **1.** mit Welc (8); **2.** bei 1 (23) • **Sit with me.** Setz dich zu mir. / Setzt euch zu mir. 1 (20)

without [wɪ'ðaʊt] ohne 2 (41)

woman ['wʊmən], *pl* **women** ['wɪmɪn] Frau 3 (65/165)

°**wonder** ['wʌndə] sich fragen

°**wonderful** ['wʌndəfəl] wunderbar

word [wɜːd] Wort 1 (19) • °**word order** Wortstellung

work [wɜːk] **1.** arbeiten 1 (28/155) **work on sth.** an etwas arbeiten 5 (92) **2.** Arbeit Welc (16) • **at work** bei der Arbeit / am Arbeitsplatz Welc (16)

worksheet ['wɜːkʃiːt] Arbeitsblatt 1 (28/155)

world [wɜːld] Welt 1 (33)

worry (about) ['wʌri] sich Sorgen machen (wegen, um) 4 (81) **Don't worry.** Mach dir keine Sorgen. 4 (81)

would [wəd, wʊd]: **I'd like ... (= I would like ...)** Ich hätte gern ... / Ich möchte gern ... 4 (69) • **Would you like ...?** Möchtest du ...? / Möchten Sie ...? 4 (69) • **I'd like to go (= I would like to go)** ich würde gern gehen / ich möchte gehen 6 (101) **I wouldn't like to go** ich würde nicht gern gehen / ich möchte nicht gehen 6 (101)

write [raɪt] schreiben 1 (22) **write down** aufschreiben 1 (23) **write to** schreiben an 3 (56)

wrong [rɒŋ] falsch, verkehrt 1 (20)

Y

year [jɪə] **1.** Jahr Welc (8/146); **2.** Jahrgangsstufe 5 (84/85)

yellow ['jeləʊ] gelb Welc (13/150)

yes [jes] ja Welc (8/146)

yesterday ['jestədeɪ, 'jestədi] gestern 5 (86) • **yesterday morning/afternoon/evening** gestern Morgen/Nachmittag/Abend 5 (87)

yoga ['jəʊgə] Yoga 3 (57)

you [juː] **1.** du; Sie Welc (8/146) **You're welcome.** Gern geschehen. / Nichts zu danken. Welc (17) **2.** ihr Welc (10) • **you two** ihr zwei Welc (12) **3.** dir; dich; euch Welc (10)
► S.148 you – I/me

young [jʌŋ] jung 5 (96)

your [jɔː] **1.** dein/e Welc (8/146) **What's your name?** Wie heißt du? Welc (8/146) **2.** Ihr Welc (17); **3.** euer/eure 1 (21)

°**yourself** [jə'self, jɔː'self]: **about yourself** über dich selbst

°**youth** [juːθ] Jugend, Jugend-

Z

zero ['zɪərəʊ] null Welc (15)

Das **German – English Dictionary** enthält den **Lernwortschatz** dieses Bandes. Es kann dir eine erste Hilfe sein, wenn du vergessen hast, wie etwas auf Englisch heißt.
Wenn du wissen möchtest, wo das englische Wort zum ersten Mal in *English G 21* vorkommt, dann kannst du im **English – German Dictionary** (S. 176–188) nachschlagen.

▸ Der Pfeil verweist auf Kästchen im Vocabulary (S. 146–175), in denen du weitere Informationen findest.

A

Abend evening ['i:vnɪŋ]; *(später Abend)* night [naɪt] • **am Abend, abends** in the evening
Abendbrot, -essen dinner ['dɪnə]
Abendbrot essen have dinner
zum Abendbrot for dinner
aber but [bət, bʌt]
abziehen: 10 Cent abziehen take 10c off [ˌteɪk‿'ɒf]
addieren (zu) add (to) [æd]
Aktivität activity [æk'tɪvəti]
alle *(die ganze Gruppe)* all [ɔ:l]
allein alone [ə'ləʊn]
alleinstehend single ['sɪŋgl]
alles everything ['evriθɪŋ]; all [ɔ:l]
Alphabet alphabet ['ælfəbet]
als *(zeitlich)* when [wen]
also *(daher, deshalb)* so [səʊ]
Also, ... Well, ... [wel]
alt old [əʊld]
am 1. am Bahnhof at the station
am oberen Ende / an der Spitze (von) at the top (of) • **am Telefon** on the phone
2. *(zeitlich)* **am 13. Juni** on 13th June
am Morgen/Nachmittag/Abend in the morning/afternoon/evening
am Ende (von) at the end (of)
am Freitag on Friday • **am Freitagmorgen** on Friday morning
am nächsten Morgen/Tag the next morning/day • **am Wochenende** at the weekend
amüsieren: sich amüsieren have fun [hæv 'fʌn]
an: an dem/den Tisch (dort) at that table • **an der Spitze** at the top (of) • **an der/die Tafel** on the board • **schreiben an** write to
andere(r, s) other ['ʌðə] • **die anderen** the others • **ein(e) andere(r, s) ...** another ... [ə'nʌðə]
anders (als) different (from) ['dɪfrənt]
anfangen (mit) start [stɑ:t]
Angst haben (vor) be afraid (of) [ə'freɪd]; be scared (of) [skeəd]
anhaben *(Kleidung)* wear [weə]
anhalten stop [stɒp]
anhören 1. sich etwas anhören listen to sth. ['lɪsn]; **2. sich gut anhören** sound good [saʊnd]
anklopfen (an) knock (on) [nɒk]
anmalen paint [peɪnt]
anprobieren *(Kleidung)* try on [ˌtraɪ‿'ɒn]
Anruf call [kɔ:l]; phone call ['fəʊn kɔ:l]
anrufen call [kɔ:l]; phone [fəʊn]
anschauen look at [lʊk]
anschreien shout at [ʃaʊt]
ansehen: sich etwas ansehen look at sth. [lʊk]; watch sth. [wɒtʃ]
Antwort (auf) answer (to) ['ɑ:nsə]
antworten answer ['ɑ:nsə]
anziehen: sich anziehen get dressed [get 'drest]
Apfel apple ['æpl]
Apfelsine orange ['ɒrɪndʒ]
April April ['eɪprəl]
Arbeit work [wɜ:k] • **bei der Arbeit/am Arbeitsplatz** at work
arbeiten (an) work (on) [wɜ:k]
Arbeitsblatt worksheet ['wɜ:kʃi:t]
Arbeits- und Lerntechniken study skills ['stʌdi skɪlz]
arm poor [pɔ:, pʊə]
Arm arm [ɑ:m]
Armbanduhr watch [wɒtʃ]
Artikel article ['ɑ:tɪkl]
auch: auch aus Bristol from Bristol too [tu:] • **Ich auch.** Me too.
auf on [ɒn] • **auf dem Bild/Foto** in the picture/photo • **auf einmal** suddenly ['sʌdnli] • **auf Englisch** in English • **Auf geht's!** Let's go.
Auf Wiedersehen. Goodbye. [ˌgʊd'baɪ]
aufführen *(Szene, Dialog)* act [ækt]
Aufgabe *(im Schulbuch)* exercise ['eksəsaɪz]; *(Job)* job [dʒɒb]
aufgeregt *(nervös)* nervous ['nɜ:vəs]
aufhören stop [stɒp]
aufmachen open ['əʊpən]
aufräumen tidy ['taɪdi]
Aufsatz essay ['eseɪ]
aufschreiben write down [ˌraɪt 'daʊn]
aufstehen get up [ˌget‿'ʌp]
Auge eye [aɪ]
August August ['ɔ:gəst]
aus: Ich komme/bin aus ... I'm from ... [frəm, frɒm] • **aus ... (heraus/hinaus)** out of ... ['aʊt‿əv] • **aus dem Zug/Bus aussteigen** get off the train/bus • **aus vielen Gründen** for lots of reasons
Ausdruck *((Rede-)Wendung)* phrase [freɪz]
Ausflug trip [trɪp]
ausgehen *(weg-, rausgehen)* go out
aussehen: anders/toll/alt aussehen look different/great/old [lʊk]
gleich aussehen look the same
außerhalb seines Zimmers outside his room [ˌaʊt'saɪd]
Aussprache pronunciation [prəˌnʌnsi'eɪʃn]
aussteigen (aus dem Zug/Bus) get off (the train/bus) [ˌget‿'ɒf]
aussuchen: (sich) etwas aussuchen choose sth. [tʃu:z]
auswählen choose [tʃu:z]
Auto car [kɑ:]
Autsch! Ouch! [aʊtʃ]

B

Baby baby ['beɪbi]
Badewanne bath [bɑ:θ]
Badezimmer bathroom ['bɑ:θru:m]
Badminton badminton ['bædmɪntən]
Bahnhof station ['steɪʃn] • **am Bahnhof** at the station
bald soon [su:n]
Ball ball [bɔ:l]
Banane banana [bə'nɑ:nə]
Band *(Musikgruppe)* band [bænd]
Bank *(Sparkasse)* bank [bæŋk]
Bankräuber/in bank robber ['rɒbə]
Baseball baseball ['beɪsbɔ:l]
Basketball basketball ['bɑ:skɪtbɔ:l]
Baum tree [tri:]
beantworten answer ['ɑ:nsə]
beeilen: sich beeilen hurry up [ˌhʌri‿'ʌp]
beenden finish ['fɪnɪʃ]
beginnen (mit) start [stɑ:t]
begreifen understand [ˌʌndə'stænd]
Begründung reason ['ri:zn]
bei: bei den Shaws zu Hause at the Shaws' house • **bei der Arbeit** at work • **Englisch bei Mr Kingsley** English with Mr Kingsley
beide both [bəʊθ]
Bein leg [leg]
Beispiel example [ɪg'zɑ:mpl] • **zum Beispiel** for example
benötigen need [ni:d]
benutzen use [ju:z]
beobachten watch [wɒtʃ]
bereit ready ['redi]
Bericht (über) report (on) [rɪ'pɔ:t]
berichten (über) tell (about) [tel]
besser better ['betə]

beste: der/die/das beste ...; die besten ... the best ... [best]
Besucher/in visitor ['vɪzɪtə]
Bett bed [bed]
Beutel bag [bæg]
Bibliothek library ['laɪbrəri]
Bild picture ['pɪktʃə] • **auf dem Bild** in the picture
Biologie biology [baɪ'ɒlədʒi]
bis *(zeitlich)* till [tɪl] • **Bis bald.** See you. ['si: ju:] • **bis jetzt / bis hierher** so far
bitte 1. *(in Fragen und Aufforderungen)* please [pli:z]; **2. Bitte sehr. / Hier bitte.** Here you are.; **3. Bitte, gern geschehen.** You're welcome. ['welkəm]; **4. Wie bitte?** Sorry? ['sɒri] ► S.159 „bitte"
blau blue [blu:]
Bleistift pencil ['pensl]
Bleistiftanspitzer pencil sharpener ['pensl ʃɑ:pnə]
bloß just [dʒʌst]; only ['əʊnli]
Boot boat [bəʊt]
brauchen need [ni:d]
braun brown [braʊn]
Brieffreund/in *(im Internet)* e-friend ['i:frend]
Briefmarke stamp [stæmp]
Brille: (eine) Brille glasses *(pl)* ['glɑ:sɪz]
bringen: (mit-, her)bringen bring [brɪŋ] • **(weg-, hin)bringen** take [teɪk]
Brot bread *(no pl)* [bred]
Brötchen roll [rəʊl]
Brücke bridge [brɪdʒ]
Bruder brother ['brʌðə]
Buch book [bʊk]
Bücherei library ['laɪbrəri]
Buchstabe letter ['letə]
buchstabieren spell [spel]
Bühne stage [steɪdʒ]
Bus bus [bʌs]

C

Café café ['kæfeɪ]
CD CD [,si:'di:] • **CD-Spieler** CD player [,si:'di: ,pleɪə]
Cent cent (c) [sent]
Champion champion ['tʃæmpiən]
Chor choir ['kwaɪə]
Cola cola ['kəʊlə]
Comic-Heft comic ['kɒmɪk]
Computer computer [kəm'pju:tə]
cool cool [ku:l]
Cornflakes cornflakes ['kɔ:nfleɪks]
Cousin, Cousine cousin ['kʌzn]

D

da, dahin *(dort, dorthin)* there [ðeə] **da drüben** over there [,əʊvə 'ðeə]
daheim at home [ət 'həʊm]
daher so [səʊ]
danach *(zeitlich)* after that [,ɑ:ftə 'ðæt]
Danke. Thank you. ['θæŋk ju:]; Thanks. **Vielen Dank!** Thanks a lot!
dann then [ðen]
darstellende Kunst drama ['drɑ:mə]
darum that's why ['ðæts ,waɪ]
das *(Artikel)* the [ðə, ði]
das (dort) *(Singular)* that [ðət, ðæt]; *(Plural)* those [ðəʊz] • **Das bin ich.** That's me.
dass that [ðət, ðæt]
dasselbe the same [seɪm]
Datum date [deɪt]
decken: den Tisch decken lay the table [,leɪ ðə 'teɪbl]
dein(e) your [jɔ:]
denken think [θɪŋk]
der *(Artikel)* the [ðə, ði]
derselbe the same [seɪm]
deshalb so [səʊ]; that's why ['ðæts ,waɪ]
Detektiv/in detective [dɪ'tektɪv]
deutlich clear [klɪə]
Deutsch; deutsch; Deutsche(r) German ['dʒɜ:mən]
Deutschland Germany ['dʒɜ:məni]
Dezember December [dɪ'sembə]
dich you [ju:]
die *(Artikel)* the [ðə, ði]
die (dort) *(Singular)* that [ðət, ðæt]; *(Plural)* those [ðəʊz] • **die (hier)** *(Singular)* this [ðɪs]; *(Plural)* these [ði:z] ► S.174 this, that – these, those
Diele hall [hɔ:l]
Dienstag Tuesday ['tju:zdeɪ, 'tju:zdi] *(siehe auch unter „Freitag")*
dies (hier); diese(r, s) *(Singular)* this [ðɪs]; *(Plural)* these [ði:z]
dieselbe(n) the same [seɪm]
Ding thing [θɪŋ]
dir you [ju:]
Disko disco ['dɪskəʊ]
Donnerstag Thursday ['θɜ:zdeɪ, 'θɜ:zdi] *(siehe auch unter „Freitag")*
doppelt, Doppel- double ['dʌbl]
Dorf village ['vɪlɪdʒ]
dort, dorthin there [ðeə] • **dort drinnen** in there [,ɪn 'ðeə] • **dort drüben** over there [,əʊvə 'ðeə]
Dossier dossier ['dɒsieɪ]
Drachen kite [kaɪt]
dran: Ich bin dran. It's my turn. [tɜ:n]
draußen outside [,aʊt'saɪd]
drinnen inside [,ɪn'saɪd] • **dort drinnen** in there [,ɪn 'ðeə] • **hier drinnen** in here [,ɪn 'hɪə]
dritte(r, s) third [θɜ:d]
drüben: da/dort drüben over there [,əʊvə 'ðeə]
drücken push [pʊʃ]
du you [ju:]
dunkel dark [dɑ:k]
durcheinander: alles durcheinanderbringen make a mess [,meɪk_ə 'mes]
dürfen can [kən, kæn]; may [meɪ]
Durst haben, durstig sein be thirsty ['θɜ:sti]
Dusche shower ['ʃaʊə]
duschen; sich duschen have a shower ['ʃaʊə]
DVD DVD [,di: vi:' di:]

E

echt real [rɪəl]
Ecke corner ['kɔ:nə]
Eile: in Eile sein, es eilig haben be in a hurry ['hʌri]
ein(e) a, an [ə, ən]; one ['wʌn] **ein(e) andere(r, s) ...** another ... [ə'nʌðə] • **ein paar** some [səm, sʌm] **eines Tages** one day
einfach *(nicht schwierig)* easy ['i:zi] **einfach nur** just [dʒʌst]
Einfall *(Idee)* idea [aɪ'dɪə]
einige some [səm, sʌm]
einigen: sich einigen (auf) agree (on) [ə'gri:]
einkaufen: einkaufen gehen go shopping [,gəʊ 'ʃɒpɪŋ] • **(das) Einkaufen** shopping
einladen (zu) invite (to) [ɪn'vaɪt]
Einladung (zu) invitation (to) [,ɪnvɪ'teɪʃn]
einmal: auf einmal suddenly ['sʌdnli]
eins, ein, eine one ['wʌn]
einschalten *(Computer usw.)* turn on [,tɜ:n_'ɒn]
einsteigen (in den Zug/Bus) get on (the train/bus) [,get_'ɒn]
Eintrittskarte ticket ['tɪkɪt]
einzig: der einzige Gast the only guest ['əʊnli]
Eis *(Speiseeis)* ice cream [,aɪs 'kri:m]
Elefant elephant ['elɪfənt]
Eltern parents ['peərənts]
E-Mail (an) e-mail (to) ['i:meɪl]
Ende 1. end [end] • **am Ende (von)** at the end (of) • **zu Ende machen** finish ['fɪnɪʃ] • **zu Ende sein** be over ['əʊvə]
2. oberes Ende *(Spitze)* top [tɒp] **am oberen Ende** at the top
enden finish ['fɪnɪʃ]
endlich at last [ət 'lɑ:st]
Englisch; englisch English ['ɪŋglɪʃ]
Enkel/in grandchild ['græntʃaɪld], *pl* grandchildren ['græntʃɪldrən]

Entschuldigung **1.** *(Tut mir leid)* I'm sorry. ['sɒri] • **Entschuldigung, dass ich zu spät komme.** Sorry, I'm late. **2. Entschuldigung, …** *(Darf ich mal stören?)* Excuse me, … [ɪk'skju:z mi:]
► S.151 „Entschuldigung"

er **1.** *(männliche Person)* he [hi:]; **2.** *(Ding, Tier)* it [ɪt]

Erdkunde geography [dʒi'ɒgrəfi]

erforschen explore [ɪk'splɔ:]

ergänzen add (to) [æd]

Ergebnis result [rɪ'zʌlt]

erinnern: sich erinnern (an) remember [rɪ'membə]

erkunden explore [ɪk'splɔ:]

erste(r, s) first [fɜ:st] • **als Erstes** first • **der erste Tag** the first day **der/die Erste sein** be first

erwarten: ich kann es kaum erwarten, … zu sehen I can't wait to see … [weɪt]

erzählen (von) tell (about) [tel]

Erzählung story ['stɔ:ri]

es it [ɪt] • **es gibt** *(es ist vorhanden)* there's; *(es sind vorhanden)* there are ► S.152 There's … / There are …

Essen food [fu:d]

essen eat [i:t] • **Abendbrot essen** have dinner • **Toast zum Frühstück essen** have toast for breakfast

Esszimmer dining room ['daɪnɪŋ ru:m]

etwas **1.** something ['sʌmθɪŋ]; **2.** *(ein bisschen)* **etwas Käse/Saft** some cheese/juice [səm, sʌm]

euch you [ju:]

euer, eure your [jɔ:]

Euro euro ['jʊərəʊ]

F

fahren: Inliner/Skateboard fahren skate [skeɪt] • **Rad fahren** ride a bike [,raɪd ə 'baɪk]

Fahrrad bike [baɪk]

fallen; fallen lassen drop [drɒp]

falsch wrong [rɒŋ]

Familie family ['fæməli]

Fan fan [fæn]

fantastisch fantastic [fæn'tæstɪk]

Farbe colour ['kʌlə] • **Welche Farbe hat …?** What colour is …?

Februar February ['februəri]

Federball badminton ['bædmɪntən]

Federmäppchen pencil case ['pensl keɪs]

Fehler mistake [mɪ'steɪk]

Fenster window ['wɪndəʊ]

Ferien holidays ['hɒlədeɪz]

Fernsehen television ['telɪvɪʒn]; TV [ti:'vi:] • **im Fernsehen** on TV

fernsehen watch TV [,wɒtʃ ti:'vi:]

fertig *(bereit)* ready ['redi] • **sich fertig machen (für)** *(sich vorbereiten)* get ready (for) • **Dinge fertig machen (für)** get things ready (for)

Film film [fɪlm]

Filmstar film star ['fɪlm stɑ:]

Filzstift felt tip ['felt tɪp]

finden *(entdecken)* find [faɪnd]

Finger finger ['fɪŋgə]

Fisch fish, *pl* fish [fɪʃ]

Flasche bottle ['bɒtl] • **eine Flasche Milch** a bottle of milk

Fleisch meat [mi:t]

Flur hall [hɔ:l]

Flussdiagramm flow chart ['fləʊ tʃɑ:t]

flüstern whisper ['wɪspə]

folgen follow ['fɒləʊ]

Football American football [ə,merɪkən 'fʊtbɔ:l]

fort away [ə'weɪ]

Foto photo ['fəʊtəʊ] • **auf dem Foto** in the photo • **Fotos machen** take photos

Fotoapparat camera ['kæmərə]

fotografieren take photos [teɪk 'fəʊtəʊz]

Frage question ['kwestʃn] • **Fragen stellen** ask questions

fragen ask [ɑ:sk] • **nach etwas fragen** ask about sth.

Französisch French [frentʃ]

Frau woman ['wʊmən], *pl* women ['wɪmɪn] • **Frau Brown** Mrs Brown ['mɪsɪz] • **Frau White** *(unverheiratet)* Miss White [mɪs]

frei [fri:] free • **freie Zeit** free time

Freitag Friday ['fraɪdeɪ, 'fraɪdi] **freitagabends, am Freitagabend** on Friday evening • **freitagnachts, Freitagnacht** on Friday night

Freizeit free time [,fri: 'taɪm]

Freund/in friend [frend]

frieren be cold [kəʊld]

froh happy ['hæpi]

Frucht, Früchte fruit [fru:t]

früh early ['ɜ:li]

Frühling spring [sprɪŋ]

Frühstück breakfast ['brekfəst] **zum Frühstück** for breakfast

frühstücken have breakfast

Frühstückspension Bed and Breakfast (B&B) [,bed_ən 'brekfəst]

Füller pen [pen]

für for [fə, fɔ:]

furchtbar terrible ['terəbl]

Fuß foot [fʊt], *pl* feet [fi:t]

Fußball football ['fʊtbɔ:l]

Fußballschuhe, -stiefel football boots ['fʊtbɔ:l bu:ts]

Fußboden floor [flɔ:]

Futter food [fu:d]

füttern feed [fi:d]

G

ganz: den ganzen Tag (lang) all day **die ganze Zeit** all the time • **Das ist ganz falsch.** This is all wrong.

Garten garden ['gɑ:dn]

Gast guest [gest]; *(Besucher/in)* visitor ['vɪzɪtə]

geben give [gɪv] • **es gibt** *(es ist vorhanden)* there's; *(es sind vorhanden)* there are
► S.152 There's … / There are …

Geburtstag birthday ['bɜ:θdeɪ] **Ich habe im Mai / am 13. Juni Geburtstag.** My birthday is in May / on 13th June. • **Wann hast du Geburtstag?** When's your birthday?

Gedicht poem ['pəʊɪm]

Gefahr danger ['deɪndʒə]

gegen against [ə'genst]

Gegenteil opposite ['ɒpəzɪt]

Gegenwart present ['preznt]

gehen **1. gehen (nach, zu)** go (to) [gəʊ] • **(zu Fuß) gehen** walk [wɔ:k] **Auf geht's!** Let's go. • **einkaufen/reiten/schwimmen gehen** go shopping/riding/swimming • **ins Bett gehen** go to bed • **nach Hause gehen** go home **2. Es geht um Mr Green.** This is about Mr Green.

gelangen *(hinkommen)* get [get]

gelb yellow ['jeləʊ]

Geld money ['mʌni]

genug enough [ɪ'nʌf]

Geografie geography [dʒi'ɒgrəfi]

gerade: jetzt gerade right now [raɪt 'naʊ]

Geräusch noise [nɔɪz]

gern: Ich hätte gern … / Ich möchte gern … I'd like … (= I would like …) **Ich schwimme/tanze/… gern.** I like swimming/dancing/… • **Ich würde gern gehen** I'd like to go **Ich würde nicht gern gehen** I wouldn't like to go • **Gern geschehen.** You're welcome. ['welkəm]

gernhaben like [laɪk]

Geschäft shop [ʃɒp]

geschehen (mit) happen (to) ['hæpən]

Geschenk present ['preznt]

Geschichte **1.** story ['stɔ:ri]; **2.** *(vergangene Zeiten)* history ['hɪstri]

geschieden divorced [dɪ'vɔ:st]

Geschirrspülmaschine dishwasher ['dɪʃwɒʃə]

Gesicht face [feɪs]

gestern yesterday ['jestədeɪ, 'jestədi] **gestern Morgen/Nachmittag/Abend** yesterday morning/afternoon/evening

Getränk drink [drɪŋk]

Gewinn prize [praɪz]
gewinnen win [wɪn]
gewöhnlich usually ['ju:ʒuəli]
Gitarre guitar [gɪ'tɑ:] • **Gitarre spielen** play the guitar
Glas glass [glɑ:s] • **ein Glas Wasser** a glass of water
glauben think [θɪŋk] • **Das glaube ich nicht. / Ich glaube nicht.** I don't think so. • **Ich glaube (ja).** I think so.
gleich **1. gleich sein/aussehen** be/look the same [seɪm] **2. gleich nach dem Mittagessen** right after lunch [raɪt]
Glocke bell [bel]
Glück: Viel Glück (bei/mit ...)! Good luck (with ...)! [gʊd 'lʌk]
glücklich happy ['hæpi]
Grammatik grammar ['græmə]
groß big [bɪg]
großartig great [greɪt]
Größe *(Schuhgröße usw.)* size [saɪz]
Großeltern grandparents ['grænpeərənts]
Großmutter grandmother ['grænmʌðə]
Großstadt city ['sɪti]
Großvater grandfather ['grænfɑ:ðə]
grün green [gri:n]
Grund reason ['ri:zn] • **aus vielen Gründen** for lots of reasons
Gruppe group [gru:p]; *(Musikgruppe)* band [bænd]
gruselig scary ['skeəri]
Gruß: Liebe Grüße, ... *(Briefschluss)* Love ... [lʌv]
Grüß Dilip von mir. Say hi to Dilip for me.
gucken look [lʊk]
gut good [gʊd]; *(okay)* OK [əʊ'keɪ] **Guten Morgen.** Good morning. **Guten Tag.** Hello.; *(nachmittags)* Good afternoon.

H

Haar, Haare hair *(no pl)* [heə]
haben have got ['hæv gɒt] • **Ich habe keinen Stuhl.** I haven't got a chair. • **Ich habe am 13. Juni/im Mai Geburtstag.** My birthday is on 13th June/in May. • **Wann hast du Geburtstag?** When's your birthday? • **haben wollen** want [wɒnt] **Was haben wir als Hausaufgabe auf?** What's for homework?
Hähnchen chicken ['tʃɪkɪn]
halb zwölf half past 11 [hɑ:f]
Hallo! Hi! [haɪ]; Hello. [hə'ləʊ]
Hamburger hamburger ['hæmbɜ:gə]
Hamster hamster ['hæmstə]
Hand hand [hænd]
Handy mobile (phone) ['məʊbaɪl]
hassen hate [heɪt]
häufig often ['ɒfn]
Haus house [haʊs] • **im Haus der Shaws / bei den Shaws zu Hause** at the Shaws' house • **nach Hause gehen** go home [həʊm] • **nach Hause kommen** come home; get home • **zu Hause** at home
Hausaufgabe(n) homework *(no pl)* ['həʊmwɜ:k] • **die Hausaufgabe(n) machen** do homework • **Was haben wir als Hausaufgabe auf?** What's for homework?
Haustier pet [pet]
Haustür front door [,frʌnt 'dɔ:]
Heim home [həʊm]
heiß hot [hɒt]
heißen **1. Ich heiße ...** My name is ... **Wie heißt du?** What's your name? **2. Sie heißen dich in ... willkommen** They welcome you to ... ['welkəm]
helfen help [help]
Hemd shirt [ʃɜ:t]
herauf up [ʌp]
heraus: aus ... heraus out of ... ['aʊt_əv]
herausfinden find out [,faɪnd_'aʊt]
herausnehmen take out [,teɪk_'aʊt]
herbringen bring [brɪŋ]
Herbst autumn ['ɔ:təm]
Herd cooker ['kʊkə]
hereinkommen come in [,kʌm_'ɪn]
Herr Brown Mr Brown ['mɪstə]
herumgeben pass round [,pɑ:s 'raʊnd]
herunter down [daʊn]
Herzlichen Glückwunsch zum Geburtstag. Happy birthday. [,hæpi 'bɜ:θdeɪ]
heute today [tə'deɪ] • **heute Morgen/Nachmittag/Abend** this morning/afternoon/evening **heute Nacht** tonight [tə'naɪt]
hier here [hɪə] • **Hier bitte.** *(Bitte sehr.)* Here you are. • **hier drinnen** in here [,ɪn 'hɪə]
hierher here [hɪə]
Hilfe help [help]
hinauf up [ʌp]
hinaufklettern (auf) climb [klaɪm] **Klettere auf einen Baum.** Climb a tree.
hinaus: aus ... hinaus out of ... ['aʊt_əv]
hinein: in ... hinein into ... ['ɪntə, 'ɪntʊ]
hinkommen *(gelangen)* get [get]
hinunter down [daʊn]
hinzufügen (zu) add (to) [æd]
Hobby hobby ['hɒbi], *pl* hobbies
Hockey hockey ['hɒki]
Hockeyschuhe hockey shoes [ʃu:z]
hören hear [hɪə]
hübsch pretty ['prɪti]
Huhn chicken ['tʃɪkɪn]
Hülle cover ['kʌvə]
Hund dog [dɒg]
hundert hundred ['hʌndrəd]
Hunger haben, hungrig sein be hungry ['hʌŋgri]

I

ich I [aɪ] • **Ich auch.** Me too. [,mi: 'tu:] • **Das bin ich.** That's me. **Warum ich?** Why me?
Idee idea [aɪ'dɪə]
ihm him; *(bei Dingen, Tieren)* it
ihn him; *(bei Dingen, Tieren)* it
ihnen them [ðəm, ðem]
Ihnen *(höfliche Anrede)* you [ju:]
ihr *(Plural von „du")* you [ju:]
ihr: Hilf ihr. Help her. [hə, hɜ:]
ihr(e) *(besitzanzeigend)* *(zu „she")* her [hə, hɜ:]; *(zu „they")* their [ðeə]
Ihr(e) your [jɔ:]
im: im Fernsehen on TV • **im Haus der Shaws** at the Shaws' house **im Mai** in May • **im Radio** on the radio • **im Zug** on the train
immer always ['ɔ:lweɪz] • **immer noch** still [stɪl]
in in • **in ... (hinein)** into ... ['ɪntə, 'ɪntʊ] • **in der ...straße** in ... Street **in der Hamiltonstraße 7** at 7 Hamilton Street • **in der Nacht** at night • **in der Nähe von** near **in der Schule** at school • **in Eile sein** be in a hurry • **in den Zug/ Bus einsteigen** get on the train/ bus • **ins Bett gehen** go to bed
Infinitiv infinitive [ɪn'fɪnətɪv]
Information(en) (über) information (about/on) *(no pl)* [,ɪnfə'meɪʃn]
Inliner skates [skeɪts] • **Inliner fahren** skate
innen (drin) inside [,ɪn'saɪd]
Innenstadt city centre [,sɪti 'sentə]
interessant interesting ['ɪntrəstɪŋ]
Internet internet ['ɪntənet]
irgendwelche any ['eni]

J

ja yes [jes]
Jahr year [jɪə]
Jahrgangsstufe year [jɪə]
Januar January ['dʒænjuəri]
Jazz jazz [dʒæz]
Jeans jeans *(pl)* [dʒi:nz]

jede(r, s) ... *(Begleiter)* **1.** every ... ['evri] **2.** *(jeder einzelne)* each ... [i:tʃ]
jemand somebody ['sʌmbədi]
jene(r, s) *(Singular)* that [ðət, ðæt]; *(Plural)* those [ðəʊz]
jetzt now [naʊ] • **jetzt gerade, jetzt sofort** right now
Job job [dʒɒb]
Judo judo ['dʒu:dəʊ] • **Judo machen** do judo
Jugend- junior ['dʒu:niə]
Jugendliche(r) kid [kɪd]
Juli July [dʒu'laɪ]
jung young [jʌŋ]
Junge boy [bɔɪ]
Juni June [dʒu:n]
Junioren- junior ['dʒu:niə]

K

Käfig cage [keɪdʒ]
Kalender calendar ['kælɪndə]
kalt cold [kəʊld]
Kamera camera ['kæmərə]
Kaninchen rabbit ['ræbɪt]
Karotte carrot ['kærət]
Karte *(Post-, Spielkarte)* card [kɑ:d]
Kartoffel potato [pə'teɪtəʊ], *pl* potatoes
Kartoffelchips crisps *(pl)* [krɪsps]
Käse cheese [tʃi:z]
Kästchen, Kasten box [bɒks]
Katze cat [kæt]
kaufen buy [baɪ]
kein(e) no; not a; not (...) any • **Ich habe keinen Stuhl.** I haven't got a chair. • **Ich mag kein(e) ...** I don't like ... • **keine Musik mehr** no more music
Keks biscuit ['bɪskɪt]
kennen know [nəʊ]
kennenlernen meet [mi:t]
Kind child [tʃaɪld], *pl* children ['tʃɪldrən]; kid [kɪd]
Kirche church [tʃɜ:tʃ]
Kiste box [bɒks]
Klang sound [saʊnd]
klar clear [klɪə]
Klasse class [klɑ:s]; form [fɔ:m] **Klassenkamerad/in** classmate ['klɑ:smeɪt] • **Klassenlehrer/in** class teacher; form teacher • **Klassenzimmer** classroom ['klɑ:sru:m]
Klavier piano [pi'ænəʊ] • **Klavier spielen** play the piano
Klebestift glue stick ['glu: stɪk]
Klebstoff glue [glu:]
Kleid dress [dres]
Kleiderschrank wardrobe ['wɔ:drəʊb]
klein little ['lɪtl]
Kleinstadt town [taʊn]

klettern climb [klaɪm] • **Klettere auf einen Baum.** Climb a tree.
Klingel bell [bel]
klingen sound [saʊnd]
klopfen (an) knock (on) [nɒk]
Klub club [klʌb]
klug clever ['klevə]
Knie knee [ni:]
komisch *(witzig)* funny ['fʌni]
kommen come [kʌm]; *(hinkommen)* get [get] • **Ich komme aus ...** I'm from ... • **nach Hause kommen** come home; get home • **zu spät kommen** be late
König king [kɪŋ]
können can [kən, kæn] • **ich kann nicht ...** I can't ... [kɑ:nt]
kontrollieren *(prüfen)* check [tʃek]
Kopf head [hed]
Korb basket ['bɑ:skɪt] • **ein Korb Äpfel** a basket of apples
Körper body ['bɒdi]
kosten *(Essen probieren)* try [traɪ]
kosten: Er/Sie/Es kostet 1 Pfund. It's £1. • **Sie kosten 35 Pence.** They are 35p. • **Wie viel kostet/kosten ...?** How much is/are ...?
kostenlos free [fri:]
Krug jug [dʒʌg] • **ein Krug Orangensaft** a jug of orange juice
Küche kitchen ['kɪtʃɪn]
Kuchen cake [keɪk]
Küchenschrank cupboard ['kʌbəd]
Kugelschreiber pen [pen]
Kühlschrank fridge [frɪdʒ]
Kunst art [ɑ:t]
kurz short [ʃɔ:t] • **kurze Hose** shorts *(pl)* [ʃɔ:ts]

L

lächeln smile [smaɪl]
lachen laugh [lɑ:f]
Laden *(Geschäft)* shop [ʃɒp]
Lampe lamp [læmp]
Land country ['kʌntri]
lang long [lɒŋ] • **drei Tage lang** for three days
langweilig boring ['bɔ:rɪŋ]
Lärm noise [nɔɪz]
Lasagne lasagne [lə'zænjə]
lassen: Lass das! Stop that! • **Lass uns ... / Lasst uns ...** Let's ... [lets]
laufen run [rʌn]
laut loud [laʊd]
Laut sound [saʊnd]
leben live [lɪv]
Leben life [laɪf], *pl* lives [laɪvz]
Lebensmittel food [fu:d]
ledig single ['sɪŋgl]
leer empty ['empti]

legen *(hin-, ablegen)* put [pʊt]
lehren teach [ti:tʃ]
Lehrer/in teacher ['ti:tʃə]
leicht *(nicht schwierig)* easy ['i:zi]
leid: Tut mir leid. I'm sorry. ['sɒri]
leise quiet ['kwaɪət]
Lektion *(im Schulbuch)* unit ['ju:nɪt]
lernen learn [lɜ:n]
Lern- und Arbeitstechniken study skills ['stʌdi skɪlz]
lesen read [ri:d]
letzte(r, s) last [lɑ:st]
Leute people ['pi:pl]
Liebe Grüße, ... *(Briefschluss)* Love ... [lʌv]
Lieber Jay, ... Dear Jay ... [dɪə]
Liebling dear [dɪə]
Lieblings-: meine Lieblingsfarbe my favourite colour ['feɪvərɪt]
Lied song [sɒŋ]
lila purple ['pɜ:pl]
Limonade lemonade [ˌlemə'neɪd]
Lineal ruler ['ru:lə]
links, auf der linken Seite on the left [left]
Liste list [lɪst]
Loch hole [həʊl]

M

machen do [du:]; make [meɪk] • **die Hausaufgabe(n) machen** do homework • **Fotos machen** take photos • **Judo machen** do judo **sich Notizen machen** take notes **sich Sorgen machen (wegen, um)** worry (about) ['wʌri] • **(Zauber-) Kunststücke machen** do tricks **Reiten macht Spaß.** Riding is fun.
Mädchen girl [gɜ:l]
Magazin *(Zeitschrift)* magazine [ˌmægə'zi:n]
Magst du ...? Do you like ...?
Mai May [meɪ]
malen paint [peɪnt]
Mama mum [mʌm]
manchmal sometimes ['sʌmtaɪmz]
Mann man [mæn], *pl* men [men]
Mannschaft team [ti:m]
Mappe *(des Sprachenportfolios)* dossier ['dɒsieɪ]
Marmelade *(Orangenmarmelade)* marmalade ['mɑ:məleɪd]
März March [mɑ:tʃ]
Mathematik maths [mæθs]
Maus mouse [maʊs], *pl* mice [maɪs]
Meer sea [si:]
Meerschweinchen guinea pig ['gɪni pɪg]
mehr more [mɔ:] • **keine Musik mehr** no more music

mein(e) my [maɪ]
meinen *(glauben)* think [θɪŋk]
meist: die meisten Leute most people [məʊst]
meistens usually ['ju:ʒuəli]
Meister/in *(Champion)* champion ['tʃæmpiən]
Menschen people ['pi:pl]
merken: sich etwas merken remember sth. [rɪ'membə]
mich me [mi:]
Milch milk [mɪlk]
Mindmap mind map ['maɪnd mæp]
Minute minute ['mɪnɪt]
mir me [mi:]
mit with [wɪð]
mitbringen bring [brɪŋ]
Mitschüler/in classmate ['klɑ:smeɪt]
Mittagessen lunch [lʌntʃ] • **zum Mittagessen** for lunch
Mittagspause lunch break ['lʌntʃ breɪk]
Mitte centre ['sentə]; middle ['mɪdl]
Mitteilung *(Notiz)* note [nəʊt]
Mittwoch Wednesday ['wenzdeɪ, 'wenzdi] *(siehe auch unter „Freitag")*
Mobiltelefon mobile phone [,məʊbaɪl 'fəʊn]; mobile ['məʊbaɪl]
möchte: Ich möchte gern ... (haben) I'd like ... (= I would like ...) [laɪk] **Ich möchte gehen** I'd like to go **Ich möchte nicht gehen** I wouldn't like to go • **Möchtest du / Möchten Sie ...?** Would you like ...?
Modell*(-auto, -schiff)* model ['mɒdl]
mögen like [laɪk]
Möhre carrot ['kærət]
Monat month [mʌnθ]
Montag Monday ['mʌndeɪ, 'mʌndi] *(siehe auch unter „Freitag")*
morgen tomorrow [tə'mɒrəʊ]
Morgen morning ['mɔ:nɪŋ] • **am Morgen, morgens** in the morning
MP3-Spieler MP3 player [,empi:'θri: ,pleɪə]
müde tired ['taɪəd]
Mund mouth [maʊθ]
murren grumble ['grʌmbl]
Museum museum [mju'zi:əm]
Musical musical ['mju:zɪkl]
Musik music ['mju:zɪk]
müssen have to; must [mʌst]
Mutter mother ['mʌðə]
Mutti mum [mʌm]

N

Na ja ... / Na gut ... Oh well ... [əʊ 'wel]
nach 1. *(örtlich)* to [tə, tu] • **nach Hause gehen** go home • **nach Hause kommen** come home; get home • **nach oben** up; *(im Haus)* upstairs [,ʌp'steəz] • **nach unten** down; *(im Haus)* downstairs [,daʊn'steəz] • **nach vorn** to the front [frʌnt]
2. *(zeitlich)* after • **Viertel nach 11** quarter past 11 [pɑ:st]
3. nach etwas fragen ask about sth. [ə'baʊt]
Nachbar/in neighbour ['neɪbə]
Nachmittag afternoon [,ɑ:ftə'nu:n] **am Nachmittag, nachmittags** in the afternoon
nächste(r, s): am nächsten Tag the next day [nekst] • **der Nächste sein** be next • **Was haben wir als Nächstes?** What have we got next?
Nacht night [naɪt] • **heute Nacht** tonight [tə'naɪt] • **in der Nacht, nachts** at night
nahe (bei) near [nɪə]
Nähe: in der Nähe von near [nɪə]
Name name [neɪm]
Nase nose [nəʊz]
natürlich of course [əv 'kɔ:s]
Naturwissenschaft science ['saɪəns]
neben next to [nekst]
nehmen take [teɪk] • **Ich nehme es.** *(beim Einkaufen)* I'll take it.
nein no [nəʊ]
nennen call [kɔ:l]
nervös nervous ['nɜ:vəs]
nett nice [naɪs]
neu new [nju:]
nicht not [nɒt] • **Das glaube ich nicht. / Ich glaube nicht.** I don't think so. • **..., nicht wahr?** ..., right?
Nichts zu danken. You're welcome. ['welkəm]
nie, niemals never ['nevə]
noch: noch ein(e) ... another ... [ə'nʌðə]; one more ... [mɔ:] • **noch einmal** again [ə'gen] • **(immer) noch** still [stɪl]
nörgeln grumble ['grʌmbl]
normalerweise usually ['ju:ʒuəli]
Notiz note [nəʊt] • **sich Notizen machen** take notes
November November [nəʊ'vembə]
null 0 [əʊ]; zero ['zɪərəʊ]
Nummer number ['nʌmbə]
nun now [naʊ] • **Nun, ...** Well, ... [wel]
nur only ['əʊnli]; just [dʒʌst] • **nur zum Spaß** just for fun

O

oben *(an der Spitze)* at the top (of) [tɒp]; *(im Haus)* upstairs [,ʌp'steəz] **nach oben** up; *(im Haus)* upstairs
oberhalb von over ['əʊvə]
Oberteil top [tɒp]
Obst fruit [fru:t]
Obstsalat fruit salad ['fru:t ,sæləd]
oder or [ɔ:]
öffnen; sich öffnen open ['əʊpən]
oft often ['ɒfn]
ohne without [wɪ'ðaʊt]
Ohr ear [ɪə]
Ohrring earring ['ɪərɪŋ]
okay OK [əʊ'keɪ]
Oktober October [ɒk'təʊbə]
Oma grandma ['grænmɑ:]
Onkel uncle ['ʌŋkl]
Opa grandpa ['grænpɑ:]
Orange orange ['ɒrɪndʒ] • **Orangenmarmelade** marmalade ['mɑ:məleɪd] • **Orangensaft** orange juice ['ɒrɪndʒ dʒu:s]
orange(farben) orange ['ɒrɪndʒ]
Ort place [pleɪs]

P

paar: ein paar some [səm, sʌm]
Päckchen, Packung packet ['pækɪt] **ein Päckchen Pfefferminzbonbons** a packet of mints
Paket parcel ['pɑ:sl]
Papa dad [dæd]
Papagei parrot ['pærət]
Papier paper ['peɪpə]
Park park [pɑ:k]
Partner/in partner ['pɑ:tnə]
Partnerstadt twin town [,twɪn 'taʊn]
Party party ['pɑ:ti]
passen fit [fɪt]
passieren (mit) happen (to) ['hæpən]
Pause break [breɪk]
Pence pence (p) [pens]
Pfefferminzbonbons mints [mɪnts]
Pferd horse [hɔ:s]
Pfund *(britische Währung)* pound (£) [paʊnd] • **Es kostet 1 Pfund.** It's £1.
Piano piano [pi'ænəʊ]
pink(farben) pink [pɪŋk]
Pirat/in pirate ['paɪrət]
Pizza pizza ['pi:tsə]
Plan plan [plæn]
Platz *(Ort, Stelle)* place [pleɪs]
Plätzchen biscuit ['bɪskɪt]
plötzlich suddenly ['sʌdnli]
Polizei police *(pl)* [pə'li:s]
Poltergeist poltergeist ['pəʊltəgaɪst]
Pommes frites chips *(pl)* [tʃɪps]
Poster poster ['pəʊstə]
Präsentation presentation [,prezn'teɪʃn]
präsentieren: (jm.) etwas präsentieren present sth. (to sb.) [prɪ'zent]
Preis *(Kaufpreis)* price [praɪs]; *(Gewinn)* prize [praɪz]

Probe *(am Theater)* rehearsal [rɪ'hɜ:sl]
proben *(am Theater)* rehearse [rɪ'hɜ:s]
probieren try [traɪ]
Programm programme ['prəʊgræm]
Projekt (über, zu) project (on, about) ['prɒdʒekt]
prüfen *(überprüfen)* check [tʃek]
putzen clean [kli:n] • **Ich putze mir die Zähne.** I clean my teeth.

Q

Quiz quiz [kwɪz], *pl* quizzes ['kwɪzɪz]

R

Rad fahren ride a bike [ˌraɪd_ə 'baɪk]
Radiergummi rubber ['rʌbə]
Radio radio ['reɪdiəʊ] • **im Radio** on the radio
Rap rap [ræp]
Ratespiel quiz [kwɪz], *pl* quizzes ['kwɪzɪz]
Raum room [ru:m]
Recht haben be right [raɪt]
rechts, auf der rechten Seite on the right [raɪt]
reden (mit, über) talk (to, about) [tɔ:k]
Regal(brett) shelf [ʃelf], *pl* shelves [ʃelvz]
reichen *(weitergeben)* pass [pɑ:s]
Reihe: Du bist an der Reihe. It's your turn. [tɜ:n]
Reise trip [trɪp]
reiten ride [raɪd] • **reiten gehen** go riding
Religion *(Religionsunterricht)* RE [ˌɑ:r_'i:], Religious Education [rɪˌlɪdʒəs_edʒu'keɪʃn]
rennen run [rʌn]
Reportage (über) report (on) [rɪ'pɔ:t]
Resultat result [rɪ'zʌlt]
richtig right [raɪt]
Rollstuhl wheelchair ['wi:ltʃeə]
rosa pink [pɪŋk]
rot red [red]
rufen call [kɔ:l]; shout [ʃaʊt] • **die Polizei rufen** call the police
ruhig quiet ['kwaɪət]
Rundgang (durch das Haus) tour (of the house) [tʊə]

S

Sache thing [θɪŋ]
Saft juice [dʒu:s]
sagen say [seɪ] • **Sagt mir eure Namen.** Tell me your names. [tel]
Salat *(Gericht, Beilage)* salad ['sæləd]
sammeln collect [kə'lekt]
Samstag Saturday ['sætədeɪ, 'sætədi] *(siehe auch unter „Freitag")*
Sandwich sandwich ['sænwɪtʃ]
Satz sentence ['sentəns]
sauber clean [kli:n]
Schachtel packet ['pækɪt]
Schale bowl [bəʊl] • **eine Schale Cornflakes** a bowl of cornflakes
Schatz dear [dɪə]
schauen look [lʊk]
Schauspiel drama ['drɑ:mə]
schicken *(Post, E-Mail)* mail [meɪl]
schieben push [pʊʃ]
Schiff boat [bəʊt]; ship [ʃɪp]
Schildkröte tortoise ['tɔ:təs]
schlafen sleep [sli:p]; *(nicht wach sein)* be asleep [ə'sli:p]
Schlafzimmer bedroom ['bedru:m]
schlagen hit [hɪt]
Schlange snake [sneɪk]
schlau clever ['klevə]
schlecht bad [bæd]
schließen *(zumachen)* close [kləʊz]
schließlich at last [ət 'lɑ:st]
schlimm bad [bæd]
Schlüssel key [ki:]
Schlüsselwort key word ['ki: wɜ:d]
schnell quick [kwɪk]
Schokolade chocolate ['tʃɒklət]
schön beautiful ['bju:tɪfl]; *(nett)* nice [naɪs]
Schrank cupboard ['kʌbəd]; *(Kleiderschrank)* wardrobe ['wɔ:drəʊb]
schrecklich terrible ['terəbl]
schreiben (an) write (to) [raɪt]
Schreibtisch desk [desk]
schreien shout [ʃaʊt]
Schritt step [step]
Schuh shoe [ʃu:]
Schule school [sku:l] • **in der Schule** at school
Schüler/in student ['stju:dənt]
Schulfach (school) subject ['sʌbdʒɪkt]
Schulheft exercise book ['eksəsaɪz bʊk]
Schulklasse class [klɑ:s]; form [fɔ:m]
Schultasche school bag ['sku:l bæg]
Schulter shoulder ['ʃəʊldə]
Schüssel bowl [bəʊl]
schwarz black [blæk]
schwer *(schwierig)* difficult ['dɪfɪkəlt]
Schwester sister ['sɪstə]
schwierig difficult ['dɪfɪkəlt]
Schwimmbad, -becken swimming pool ['swɪmɪŋ pu:l]
schwimmen swim [swɪm]
schwimmen gehen go swimming
See *(die See, das Meer)* sea [si:]
sehen see [si:] • **Siehst du?** See?
sehr very ['veri] • **Er mag sie sehr.** He likes her a lot. [ə 'lɒt]
Seife soap [səʊp]
sein *(Verb)* be [bi:]
sein(e) *(besitzanzeigend)* *(zu „he")* his; *(zu „it")* its
Seite *(Buch-, Heftseite)* page [peɪdʒ]
Auf welcher Seite sind wir? What page are we on?
selbstverständlich of course [əv 'kɔ:s]
senden *(Post, E-Mail)* mail [meɪl]
September September [sep'tembə]
Sessel armchair ['ɑ:mtʃeə]
setzen: sich setzen sit [sɪt] • **Setz dich / Setzt euch zu mir.** Sit with me.
Shorts shorts *(pl)* [ʃɔ:ts]
Show show [ʃəʊ]
sicher sein *(keine Zweifel haben)* be sure [ʃʊə, ʃɔ:]
sie **1.** *(weibliche Person)* she [ʃi:]
Frag sie. Ask her. [hə, hɜ:]
2. *(Ding, Tier)* it [ɪt]
3. *(Plural)* they [ðeɪ] • **Frag sie.** Ask them. [ðəm, ðem]
4. Sie *(höfliche Anrede)* you [ju:]
Silbe syllable ['sɪləbl]
singen sing [sɪŋ]
sitzen sit [sɪt]
Skateboard skateboard ['skeɪtbɔ:d]
Skateboard fahren skate [skeɪt]
Sketch sketch [sketʃ]
so süß so sweet [səʊ]
Socke sock [sɒk]
Sofa sofa ['səʊfə]
Sohn son [sʌn]
Sommer summer ['sʌmə]
Song song [sɒŋ]
Sonnabend Saturday ['sætədeɪ, 'sætədi] *(siehe auch unter „Freitag")*
Sonnenbrille: (eine) Sonnenbrille sunglasses *(pl)* ['sʌnglɑ:sɪz]
Sonntag Sunday ['sʌndeɪ, 'sʌndi] *(siehe auch unter „Freitag")*
Sorgen: sich Sorgen machen (wegen, um) worry (about) ['wʌri] • **Mach dir keine Sorgen.** Don't worry.
sowieso anyway ['eniweɪ]
Spaß fun [fʌn] • **Spaß haben** have fun • **nur zum Spaß** just for fun
Reiten macht Spaß. Riding is fun.
Viel Spaß! Have fun! ► S.174 fun
spät late [leɪt] • **Wie spät ist es?** What's the time? • **zu spät sein/kommen** be late
später later ['leɪtə]
Spiel game [geɪm]; *(Wettkampf)* match [mætʃ]
spielen play [pleɪ]; *(Szene, Dialog)* act [ækt] • **Fußball spielen** play football • **Gitarre/Klavier spielen** play the guitar/the piano
Spieler/in player ['pleɪə]
Spion/in spy [spaɪ]

Spitze *(oberes Ende)* top [tɒp] • **an der Spitze (von)** at the top (of)
Sport; Sportart sport [spɔ:t] • **Sport treiben** do sport ► S.162 Sports
Sportunterricht PE [ˌpi:‿'i:], Physical Education [ˌfɪzɪkəl‿edʒu'keɪʃn]
Sprache language ['læŋgwɪdʒ]
Spülbecken, Spüle sink [sɪŋk]
Stadt *(Großstadt)* city ['sɪti]; *(Kleinstadt)* town [taʊn]
Stadtzentrum city centre [ˌsɪti 'sentə]
Stall *(für Kaninchen)* hutch [hʌtʃ]
Stammbaum family tree ['fæməli tri:]
Star *(Film-, Popstar)* star [stɑ:]
starten start [stɑ:t]
stellen *(hin-, abstellen)* put [pʊt]
Fragen stellen ask questions
Stichwort *(Schlüsselwort)* key word ['ki: wɜ:d]
Stiefel boot [bu:t]
still quiet ['kwaɪət]
Stimme voice [vɔɪs]
stimmen: Das stimmt. That's right. [raɪt] • **..., stimmt's?** ..., right?
stoßen push [pʊʃ]
Straße road [rəʊd]; street [stri:t]
streiten: sich streiten argue ['ɑ:gju:]
Strumpf sock [sɒk]
Stück piece [pi:s] • **ein Stück Papier** a piece of paper
Student/in student ['stju:dənt]
Studio studio ['stju:diəʊ]
Stuhl chair [tʃeə]
Stunde *(Schulstunde)* lesson ['lesn]
Stundenplan timetable ['taɪmteɪbl]
süß sweet [swi:t]
Süßigkeiten sweets *(pl)* [swi:ts]
Sweatshirt sweatshirt ['swetʃɜ:t]
Szene scene [si:n]

T

Tafel *(Wandtafel)* board [bɔ:d] • **an der/die Tafel** on the board
Tag day [deɪ] • **drei Tage (lang)** for three days • **eines Tages** one day
Guten Tag. Hello.; *(nachmittags)* Good afternoon. [gʊd‿ɑ:ftə'nu:n]
Tagebuch diary ['daɪəri]
Tante aunt [ɑ:nt]
Tanz dance [dɑ:ns]
tanzen dance [dɑ:ns]
Tanzen dancing ['dɑ:nsɪŋ]
Tanzstunden, Tanzunterricht dancing lessons ['dɑ:nsɪŋ ˌlesnz]
Tasche *(Tragetasche, Beutel)* bag [bæg]
Tätigkeit activity [æk'tɪvəti]
tausend thousand ['θaʊznd]
Team team [ti:m]
Tee tea [ti:]
Teil part [pɑ:t]
teilen: sich etwas teilen (mit jm.) share sth. (with sb.) [ʃeə]
Telefon (tele)phone ['telɪfəʊn] • **am Telefon** on the phone
Telefonnummer (tele)phone number ['telɪfəʊn ˌnʌmbə]
Teller plate [pleɪt] • **ein Teller Pommes frites** a plate of chips
Tennis tennis ['tenɪs]
Termin appointment [ə'pɔɪntmənt]
Terminkalender diary ['daɪəri]
teuer expensive [ɪk'spensɪv]
Text text [tekst]
Theaterstück play [pleɪ]
Thema, Themenbereich topic ['tɒpɪk]
Tier *(Haustier)* pet [pet]
Tierhandlung pet shop ['pet ʃɒp]
Tisch table ['teɪbl]
Tischtennis table tennis ['teɪbl tenɪs]
Titel title ['taɪtl]
Toast(brot) toast [təʊst]
Tochter daughter ['dɔ:tə]
Toilette toilet ['tɔɪlət]
toll fantastic [fæn'tæstɪk]; great [greɪt]
Top *(Oberteil)* top [tɒp]
Torte cake [keɪk]
tot dead [ded]
töten kill [kɪl]
Tour (durch das Haus) tour (of the house) [tʊə]
tragen *(Kleidung)* wear [weə]
trainieren practise ['præktɪs]
Traum dream [dri:m] • **Traumhaus** dream house
treffen; sich treffen meet [mi:t]
Treppe(nstufen) stairs *(pl)* [steəz]
Trick *(Zauberkunststück)* trick [trɪk]
trinken drink [drɪŋk] • **Milch zum Frühstück trinken** have milk for breakfast
Tschüs. Bye. [baɪ]; See you. ['si: ju:]
T-Shirt T-shirt ['ti:ʃɜ:t]
tun do [du:] • **Tue, was ich tue.** Do what I do. • **tun müssen** have to do • **tun wollen** want to do [wɒnt]
Tut mir leid. I'm sorry. ['sɒri]
Tür door [dɔ:]
Türklingel doorbell ['dɔ:bel]
Turm tower ['taʊə]
Turnen *(Sportunterricht)* PE [ˌpi:‿'i:], Physical Education [ˌfɪzɪkəl‿edʒu'keɪʃn]
Tut mir leid. I'm sorry. ['sɒri]
Tüte bag [bæg]

U

üben practise ['præktɪs]
über about [ə'baʊt]; *(räumlich)* over ['əʊvə]
überall everywhere ['evriweə]
überprüfen check [tʃek]
Überschrift title ['taɪtl]
Übung *(Schulbuch)* exercise ['eksəsaɪz]
Übungsheft exercise book ['eksəsaɪz bʊk]
Uhr 1. *(Armbanduhr)* watch [wɒtʃ]; *(Wand-, Stand-, Turmuhr)* clock [klɒk]
2. elf Uhr eleven o'clock • **7 Uhr morgens/vormittags** 7 am [ˌeɪ‿'em]
7 Uhr nachmittags/abends 7 pm [ˌpi:‿'em] • **um 8 Uhr 45** at 8.45
Uhrzeit time [taɪm]
um 1. um 8.45 at 8.45; **2. Es geht um Mr Green.** This is about Mr Green.; **3. um zu** to
umsehen: sich umsehen look round [ˌlʊk 'raʊnd]
und and [ənd, ænd]
unheimlich scary ['skeəri]
Uniform uniform ['ju:nɪfɔ:m]
Unordnung: alles in Unordnung bringen make a mess [ˌmeɪk‿ə 'mes]
uns us [əs, ʌs]
unser(e) our ['aʊə]
unten *(im Haus)* downstairs [ˌdaʊn'steəz] • **nach unten** down [daʊn]; *(im Haus)* downstairs
unter under ['ʌndə]
unterhalten: sich unterhalten (mit, über) talk (to, about) [tɔ:k]
Unterricht lessons *(pl)* ['lesnz]
unterrichten teach [ti:tʃ]
unterschiedlich different ['dɪfrənt]

V

Vater father ['fɑ:ðə]
Vati dad [dæd]
Verabredung appointment [ə'pɔɪntmənt]
verabschieden: sich verabschieden say goodbye [ˌseɪ gʊd'baɪ]
verbinden *(einander zuordnen)* link [lɪŋk]
Verein club [klʌb]
verfolgen follow ['fɒləʊ]
verheiratet (mit) married (to) ['mærɪd]
verkaufen sell [sel]
Verkäufer/in shop assistant ['ʃɒp‿əˌsɪstənt]
verkehrt *(falsch)* wrong [rɒŋ]
verknüpfen *(einander zuordnen)* link [lɪŋk]
verletzen hurt [hɜ:t]
verrückt mad [mæd]
verschieden different ['dɪfrənt]
verstecken; sich verstecken hide [haɪd]

verstehen understand [ˌʌndə'stænd]
versuchen try [traɪ]
verwenden use [juːz]
viel a lot [ə 'lɒt]; lots of; much [mʌtʃ] **viele** lots of; many ['meni] • **Viel Glück!** Good luck! • **viel mehr** lots more • **Viel Spaß!** Have fun! **wie viel?** how much? • **wie viele?** how many? **Vielen Dank!** Thanks a lot! ► S.172 „viel", „viele"
vielleicht maybe ['meɪbi]
Viertel: Viertel nach 11 quarter past 11 ['kwɔːtə] • **Viertel vor 12** quarter to 12
violett purple ['pɜːpl]
Virus virus ['vaɪrəs]
Vogel bird [bɜːd]
Vokabelverzeichnis vocabulary [və'kæbjələri]
voll full [fʊl]
Volleyball volleyball ['vɒlibɔːl]
von of [əv, ɒv]; from [frəm, frɒm] • **ein Aufsatz von ...** an essay by ... [baɪ]
vor 1. *(räumlich)* in front of [ɪn 'frʌnt‿əv]; 2. *(zeitlich)* **vor dem Abendessen** before dinner [bɪ'fɔː] • **vor einer Minute** a minute ago [ə'gəʊ] **Viertel vor 12** quarter to 12
vorbei sein be over ['əʊvə]
vorbereiten: Dinge vorbereiten get things ready ['redi] • **sich vorbereiten (auf)** get ready (for)
Vormittag morning ['mɔːnɪŋ]
vorstellen: (jm.) etwas vorstellen *(präsentieren)* present sth. (to sb.) [prɪ'zent]
Vorstellung *(Präsentation)* presentation [ˌprezn'teɪʃn]; *(Show)* show [ʃəʊ]

W

wählen *(auswählen)* choose [tʃuːz]
wann when [wen]
warten (auf) wait (for) [weɪt]
warum why [waɪ]
was what [wɒt] • **Was haben wir als Hausaufgabe auf?** What's for homework? • **Was ist mit ...?** What about ...? • **Was kostet/kosten ...?** How much is/are ...?
waschen wash [wɒʃ] • **Ich wasche mir das Gesicht.** I wash my face.
Wasser water ['wɔːtə]
Wechselgeld change [tʃeɪndʒ]
weg away [ə'weɪ] • **weg sein** *(nicht zu Hause sein)* be out [aʊt]
weggehen *(raus-, ausgehen)* go out
wehtun hurt [hɜːt]
weil because [bɪ'kɒz]
weiß white [waɪt]
weit (entfernt) far [fɑː]
weitere(r, s): ein(e) weitere(r, s) one more [mɔː]
weitergeben pass [pɑːs]
weitermachen go on [ˌgəʊ‿'ɒn]
welche(r, s) which [wɪtʃ] • **Auf welcher Seite sind wir?** What page are we on? [wɒt] • **Welche Farbe hat ...?** What colour is ...?
Wellensittich budgie ['bʌdʒi]
Welt world [wɜːld]
wenigstens at least [ət 'liːst]
wenn *(zeitlich)* when [wen]
wer who [huː]
werfen throw [θrəʊ]
wie 1. *(Fragewort)* how [haʊ] • **Wie bitte?** Sorry? ['sɒri] • **Wie heißt du?** What's your name? • **Wie spät ist es?** What's the time? **wie viel?** how much? • **wie viele?** how many? • **Wie war ...?** How was ...? • **Wie wär's mit ...?** What about ...? **2. wie ein Filmstar** like a film star [laɪk]
wieder again [ə'gen]
Wiederholung *(des Lernstoffs)* revision [rɪ'vɪʒn]
Wiedersehen: Auf Wiedersehen. Goodbye. [ˌgʊd'baɪ]
willkommen: Willkommen (in ...). Welcome (to ...). ['welkəm] • **Sie heißen dich in ... willkommen** They welcome you to ...
Wind wind [wɪnd]
windig windy ['wɪndi]
Winter winter ['wɪntə]
wir we [wiː]
wirklich 1. *(Adverb: tatsächlich)* really ['rɪəli]; 2. *(Adjektiv: echt)* real [rɪəl]
wissen know [nəʊ] • **..., wissen Sie./..., weißt du.** ..., you know. • **Weißt du was, Sophie?** You know what, Sophie? • **Woher weißt du ...?** How do you know ...?
Witz joke [dʒəʊk]
witzig funny ['fʌni]
wo where [weə] • **Wo kommst du her?** Where are you from?
Woche week [wiːk]
Wochenende weekend [ˌwiːk'end] **am Wochenende** at the weekend
Wochentage days of the week
Woher weißt du ...? How do you know ...? [nəʊ]
wohin where [weə]
Wohltätigkeitsbasar jumble sale ['dʒʌmbl seɪl]
wohnen live [lɪv]
Wohnung flat [flæt]
Wohnungstür front door [ˌfrʌnt 'dɔː]
Wohnzimmer living room ['lɪvɪŋ ruːm]
wollen *(haben wollen)* want [wɒnt] **tun wollen** want to do
Wort word [wɜːd]
Wörterbuch dictionary ['dɪkʃənri]
Wörterverzeichnis vocabulary [və'kæbjələri]; *(alphabetisches)* dictionary ['dɪkʃənri]
Wovon redest du? What are you talking about?
Wurst, Würstchen sausage ['sɒsɪdʒ]

Y

Yoga yoga ['jəʊgə]

Z

Zahl number ['nʌmbə]
Zahn tooth [tuːθ], *pl* teeth [tiːθ] • **Ich putze mir die Zähne.** I clean my teeth.
zanken: sich zanken argue ['ɑːgjuː]
Zauberkunststück trick [trɪk] • **Zauberkunststücke machen** do tricks
Zeh toe [təʊ]
zeigen show [ʃəʊ]
Zeit time [taɪm]
Zeitschrift magazine [ˌmægə'ziːn]
Zeitung newspaper ['njuːspeɪpə]
Zentrum centre ['sentə]
ziehen pull [pʊl]
Ziffer number ['nʌmbə]
Zimmer room [ruːm]
zu 1. *(örtlich)* to [tə, tu] • **zu Jenny** to Jenny's • **zu Hause** at home **Setz dich zu mir.** Sit with me. **2. zum Beispiel** for example [ɪg'zɑːmpl] • **zum Frühstück/Mittagessen/Abendbrot** for breakfast/lunch/dinner **3. zu viel** too much [tuː] • **zu spät sein/kommen** be late **4. versuchen zu tun** try and do / try to do **5. um zu** to
zuerst first [fɜːst]
Zug train [treɪn] • **im Zug** on the train
Zuhause home [həʊm]
zuhören listen (to) ['lɪsn]
zumachen close [kləʊz]
zumindest at least [ət 'liːst]
zurück (nach) back (to) [bæk]
zusammen together [tə'geðə]
zusätzlich extra ['ekstrə]
zusehen watch [wɒtʃ]
zweite(r, s) second ['sekənd]
Zwillinge twins *(pl)* [twɪnz]
Zwillingsbruder twin brother ['twɪn ˌbrʌðə]

Classroom English

Zu Beginn und am Ende des Unterrichts

Guten Morgen, Frau ...	**Good morning, Mrs/Miss ...**	*(bis 12 Uhr)*
Guten Tag, Herr ...	**Good afternoon, Mr ...**	*(ab 12 Uhr)*
Entschuldigung, dass ich zu spät komme.	**Sorry, I'm late.**	
Auf Wiedersehen! / Bis morgen.	**Goodbye. / See you tomorrow.**	

Du brauchst Hilfe

Können Sie mir bitte helfen?	**Can you help me, please?**
Auf welcher Seite sind wir, bitte?	**What page are we on, please?**
Was heißt ... auf Englisch/Deutsch?	**What's ... in English/German?**
Können Sie bitte ... buchstabieren?	**Can you spell ..., please?**
Können Sie es bitte an die Tafel schreiben?	**Can you write it on the board, please?**

Hausaufgaben und Übungen

Tut mir leid, ich habe mein Schulheft nicht dabei.	**Sorry, I haven't got my exercise book.**
Ich verstehe diese Übung nicht.	**I don't understand this exercise.**
Ich kann Nummer 3 nicht lösen.	**I can't do number 3.**
Entschuldigung, ich bin noch nicht fertig.	**Sorry, I haven't finished.**
Ich habe ... Ist das auch richtig?	**I've got ... Is that right too?**
Tut mir leid, das weiß ich nicht.	**Sorry, I don't know.**
Was haben wir (als Hausaufgabe) auf?	**What's for homework?**

Wenn es Probleme gibt

Kann ich es auf Deutsch sagen?	**Can I say it in German?**
Können Sie/Kannst du bitte lauter sprechen?	**Can you speak louder, please?**
Können Sie/Kannst du das bitte noch mal sagen?	**Can you say that again, please?**
Kann ich bitte das Fenster öffnen/zumachen?	**Can I open/close the window, please?**
Kann ich bitte zur Toilette gehen?	**Can I go to the toilet, please?**

Partnerarbeit

Kann ich mit Julian arbeiten?	**Can I work with Julian?**
Kann ich bitte dein Lineal/deinen Filzstift/... haben?	**Can I have your ruler/felt tip/..., please?**
Danke. / Vielen Dank.	**Thank you. / Thanks a lot.**
Du bist dran.	**It's your turn.**

Diese Arbeitsanweisungen findest du häufig im Schülerbuch

Act out your dialogue for the class.	Spielt der Klasse euren Dialog vor.
Ask questions (about the pictures).	Stelle Fragen (zu den Bildern).
Answer the questions.	Beantworte die Fragen.
Check your answers.	Überprüfe deine Antworten.
Choose the right word.	Wähle das richtige Wort aus.
Compare with your partner.	Vergleiche mit deinem Partner/deiner Partnerin.
Complete the sentences.	Vervollständige die Sätze.
Copy the chart.	Schreib die Tabelle ab.
Correct the sentences.	Verbessere die Sätze.
Fill in the correct form.	Setze die richtige Form ein.
Find the missing words.	Finde die fehlenden Wörter.
Listen. / Listen again.	Hör zu. / Hör noch einmal zu.
Make a chart/a mind map/a page for your dossier.	Fertige eine Tabelle/Mindmap/Seite für dein Dossier an.
Match the numbers and the letters.	Ordne die Nummern den Buchstaben zu.
Practise the dialogue.	Übt den Dialog.
Prepare a dialogue.	Bereitet einen Dialog vor.
Put the pictures in the right order.	Bring die Bilder in die richtige Reihenfolge.
Read the sentences.	Lies die Sätze.
Right or wrong?	Richtig oder falsch?
Swap charts.	Tauscht die Tabellen.
Take notes.	Mach dir Notizen.
Take turns.	Wechselt euch ab.
Talk to your partner about your picture.	Sprich mit deinem Partner/deiner Partnerin über dein Bild.
Tell your partner about your picture.	Erzähle deinem Partner/deiner Partnerin etwas über dein Bild.
Tick the right box.	Mach einen Haken in das richtige Kästchen.
Use the words from the box.	Verwende die Wörter aus dem Kasten.
What is the odd word out?	Welches Wort passt nicht dazu?
What's different?	Was ist anders?
Work with a partner.	Arbeite mit einem Partner/einer Partnerin zusammen.
Write the sentences.	Schreib die Sätze auf.

First names (Vornamen)

Ananda [ə'nændə]
Ann [æn]
Anna ['ænə]
Anne [æn]
Barnabas ['bɑ:nəbəs]
Becky ['beki]
Catherine ['kæθrɪn]
Dan [dæn]
Daniel ['dænjəl]
Dilip ['dɪlɪp]
Elizabeth [ɪ'lɪzəbəθ]
Emily ['eməli]
Gyles [dʒaɪlz]
Hannah ['hænə]
Harry ['hæri]
Henry ['henri]
Howard ['haʊəd]
Indira [ɪn'dɪərə]
Isabel ['ɪzəbel]
Jack [dʒæk]
James [dʒeɪmz]
Jane [dʒeɪn]
Jay [dʒeɪ]
Jennifer ['dʒenɪfə]
Jenny ['dʒeni]
Jim [dʒɪm]
Jo [dʒəʊ]
John [dʒɒn]
Jonah ['dʒəʊnə]
Larry ['læri]
Laura ['lɔ:rə]
Lee [li:]
Les [lez]
Lisa ['li:sə, 'li:zə]
Liz [lɪz]
Mark [mɑ:k]
Mary ['meəri]
Mervyn ['mɜ:vɪn]
Michael ['maɪkl]
Michelle [mɪ'ʃel]
Millie ['mɪli]
Myra ['maɪrə]
Nicole [nɪ'kəʊl]
Nora ['nɔ:rə]
Pat [pæt]
Patrick ['pætrɪk]
Paul [pɔ:l]
Peter ['pi:tə]
Polly ['pɒli]
Prunella [pru'nelə]
Roger ['rɒdʒə]
Sally ['sæli]
Sam [sæm]
Sanjay ['sændʒeɪ]
Sheeba ['ʃi:bə]
Sheila ['ʃi:lə]
Shirley ['ʃɜ:li]
Simon ['saɪmən]
Sophie ['səʊfi]
Toby ['təʊbi]
Wanda ['wɒndə]
Winston ['wɪnstən]

Family names (Familiennamen)

Barker ['bɑ:kə]
Baxter ['bækstə]
Baynton ['beɪntən]
Bonny ['bɒni]
Brandreth ['brændrɪθ]
Carter-Brown [ˌkɑ:tə 'braʊn]
Cohn Livingstone [ˌkəʊn 'lɪvɪŋstən]
Gupta ['gʊptə]
Hanson ['hænsn]
Hitchcock ['hɪtʃkɒk]
Kapoor [kə'pɔ:, kə'pʊə]
King [kɪŋ]
Kingsley ['kɪŋzli]
McGough [mə'gɒf]
Parker ['pɑ:kə]
Rackham ['rækəm]
Scott [skɒt]
Shaw [ʃɔ:]
Smith [smɪθ]
Thompson ['tɒmpsən]

Place names (Ortsnamen)

Australia [ɒ'streɪliə]
Bath [bɑ:θ]
Bristol ['brɪstl]
Cabot Tower [ˌkæbət 'taʊə]

Clifton Suspension Bridge
[ˌklɪftən sə'spenʃn brɪdʒ]

Clifton Village [ˌklɪftən 'vɪlɪdʒ]
Cooper Street ['ku:pə stri:t]
Cotham ['kɒtəm]

Cotham Park Road
[ˌkɒtəm pɑ:k 'rəʊd]

Delhi ['deli]
The Downs [daʊnz]
England ['ɪŋglənd]
Frogmore Street ['frɒgmɔ: stri:t]
Germany ['dʒɜ:məni]
Hamilton Street ['hæməltən stri:t]
Hanover ['hænəʊvə]

The Hippodrome Theatre
[ˌhɪpədrəʊm 'θɪətə]

India ['ɪndiə]

The Industrial Museum
[ɪnˌdʌstriəl mju'zi:əm]

London ['lʌndən]
New York [ˌnju: 'jɔ:k]
New Zealand [nju: 'zi:lənd]
Paris ['pærɪs]
Portway ['pɔ:tweɪ]
Uganda [ju'gændə]

Other names (Andere Namen)

Halloween [ˌhæləʊ'i:n]
Hokey Cokey [ˌhəʊki 'kəʊki]
IMAX ['aɪmæks]
Oxfam ['ɒksfæm]

Illustrationen

Graham-Cameron Illustration, UK: Fliss Cary, Grafikerin (wenn nicht anders angegeben); **Roland Beier**, Berlin (Vignetten vordere Umschlaginnenseite; S.6/7; S.17 unten; 28; 38 oben; 39; 45 oben; 58 Mitte; 59 Mitte; 62 oben li.; 88; 94 oben; 95; 99; 103 Mitte; 106; 107; 109 Mitte u. unten; 112/113 unten; 118–175); **Carlos Borrell**, Berlin (Karten vordere und hintere Umschlaginnenseite); **Johann Brandstetter**, Winhöring/Kronberg (S. 96–98; 124); **Julie Colthorpe**, Berlin (S. 17 oben; 48 oben; 52 Bild 5; 53 Bild 6).

Fotos

Rob Cousins, Bristol (wenn im Bildquellenverzeichnis nicht anders angegeben)

Bildquellen

Alamy, Abingdon (S. 41 Grandma Shaw: Eliane Farray-Sulle; S. 64 unten: Comstock Images; S. 100 Bild 2: Rolf Richardson); **Artquest**, London (S. 67 oben re.); **Bank of England**, London (S. 67 banknotes, reproduced with kind permission); **Britain on View**, London (S. 101 Bild 4); **British Heart Foundation**, London (S. 113 Mitte); **BTZ** Bremer Touristik-Zentrale Gesellschaft für Marketing & Service mbH (S. 125); **Corbis**, Düsseldorf (S. 9 Bild 3: Ariel Skelley; S. 52 Bild 4: LWA-Dann Tardif; S. 56 Mitte; S. 76 re.: Jutta Klee); **Corel Library** (S. 86; S. 89); **Gareth Evans**, Berlin (S. 30; S. 60; S. 64 oben; S. 70; S. 80 Bild 1 u. 3; S. 84/85 pinboard); **Brian Harris Photographer**, Saffron Walden (S. 101 Bild 6); **Bernhard Hunger**, Dettingen (S. 35 unten; S. 51); **Image Point**, Zürich (S. 47: mm-images); **Ingram Publishing**, UK (S. 80 Bild 2); **Juniors Bildarchiv**, Ruhpolding (S. 37 Bild E); **Keystone**, Hamburg (S. 9 Bild 4: TopFoto.co.uk); **Ling Design Ltd.**, Kent (S. 112 oben re.); Courtesy of **The Medici Society Limited**, London (S. 112 oben li.); **Picture-Alliance**, Frankfurt/Main (S. 62 hockey: dpa; basketball, tennis, judo, volleyball: dpa/dpaweb; football: PA_WIRE); **Tobias Schumacher**, Kleinfischlingen (S. 21); **Statics Ltd.**, London: David Wojtowycz (S. 113 re.); **Hartmut Tschepe**, Berlin (S. 17 unten); **Andrea Ulrich**, Bonn (S. 28); **Carita Watts**, Sweden (S. 123).

Titelbild

Rob Cousins, Bristol; **IFA-Bilderteam**, Ottobrunn (Hintergrund Union Jack: Jon Arnold Images); **mpixel/Achim Meissner**, Krefeld (Himmel).

Textquellen

S. 99: "Ode to a Goldfish" by Gyles Brandreth from: *Discovering Poetry. A Poetry Course for Key Stage 3* by Denise Scott. © Rigby Heinemann 1991. Adaptations © Sue Stewart 1993, Heinemann Educational Publishers, Oxford 1993; "The Poetry United Chant" by Les Baynton from: *The Works.* Poems chosen by Paul Cookson. © Paul Cookson 2000, Macmillan Children's Books, London 2000; "Reflection" by Myra Cohn Livingstone from the anthology: *My Hundred Favourite Rhymes*, Bell & Hyman Ltd., London, 1983; "The Cabbage is a Funny Veg" by Roger McGough from the collection: *Another day on your foot and I would have died*, Macmillan Children's Books, London, 1996.
